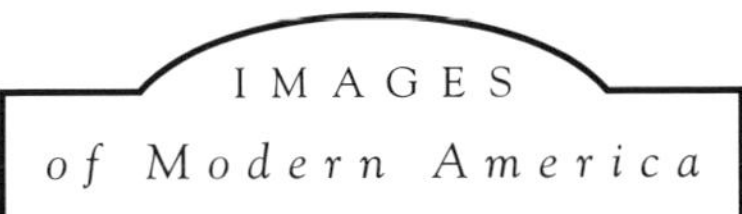

GREENSBORO

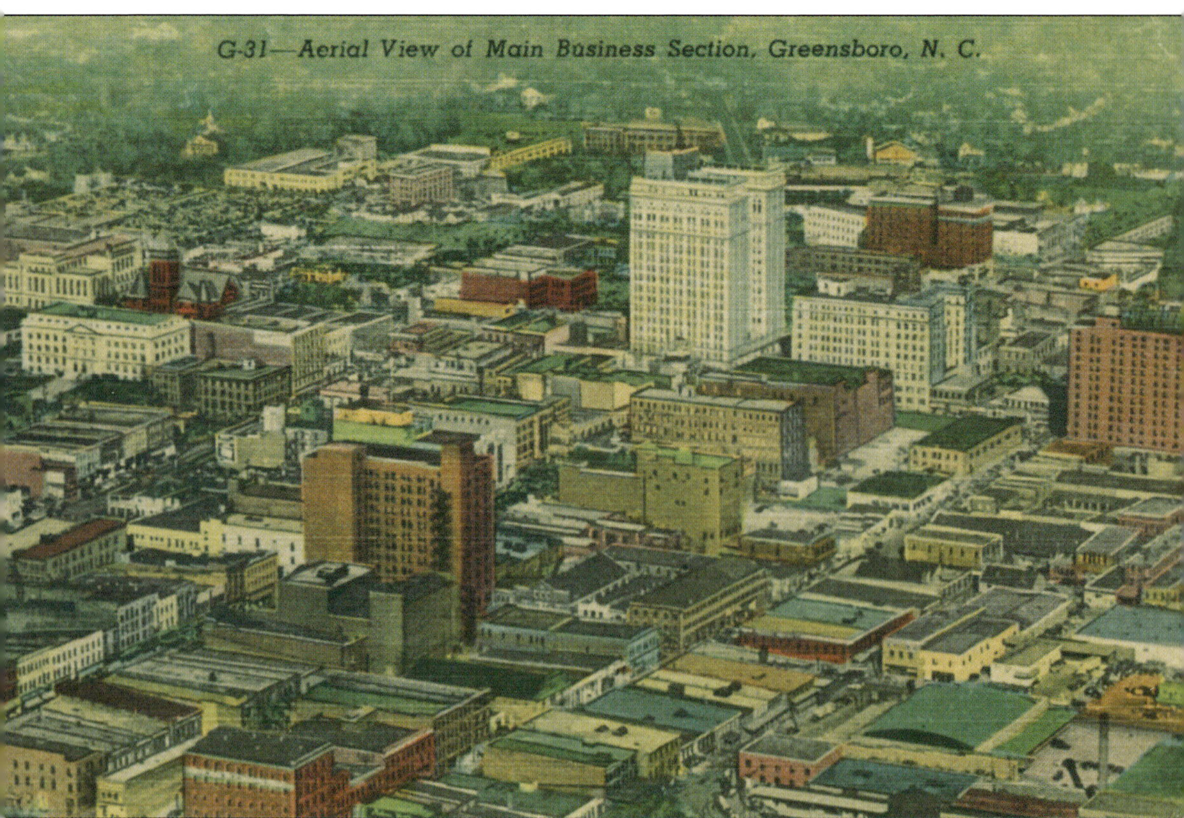

This postcard shows an aerial view of center-city Greensboro in the late 1950s. Downtown Greensboro had more pigeons and fewer skyscrapers at that time. More people shopped for clothing downtown, at department stores as well as boutiques and haberdasheries. Restaurants and bars existed downtown but, as a whole, they were not as upscale as the ones in the center city today. (Courtesy of Ben Matthews.)

ON THE FRONT COVER: Clockwise from top left:
Downtown Greensboro and fountain at Center City Park (courtesy of Lynn Donovan; see page 67), train on Greensboro railroad track (courtesy of Lynn Donovan; see page 94), Derek Jeter of the Greensboro Hornets (courtesy of Ann Cook; see page 56), counter stools from former downtown Woolworth store, now the International Civil Rights Center & Museum (courtesy of Lynn Donovan; see page 68), Millennium Gate at Phill G. McDonald Plaza (courtesy of Lynn Donovan; see page 53).

ON THE BACK COVER: From left to right:
Visitors check out the Carolina SciQuarium at Greensboro Science Center (courtesy of Lynn Donovan; see page 55), the International Civil Rights Center & Museum (courtesy of Lynn Donovan; see page 68), a crowd takes in a Grasshoppers game at NewBridge Bank Park (courtesy of Lynn Donovan; see page 47).

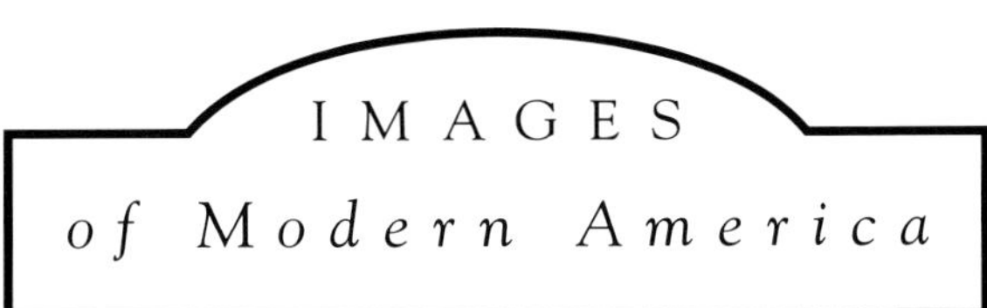

GREENSBORO

Kevin Reid

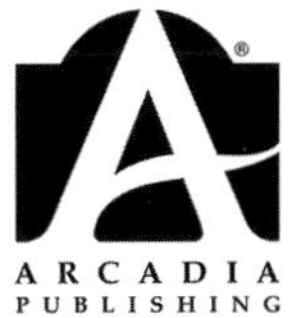

Copyright © 2014 by Kevin Reid
ISBN 978-1-4671-2127-9

Published by Arcadia Publishing
Charleston, South Carolina

Printed in the United States of America

Library of Congress Control Number: 2013946795

For all general information, please contact Arcadia Publishing:
Telephone 843-853-2070
Fax 843-853-0044
E-mail sales@arcadiapublishing.com
For customer service and orders:
Toll-Free 1-888-313-2665

Visit us on the Internet at www.arcadiapublishing.com

To Judy Hudson. Wish you were here.

CONTENTS

ACKNOWLEDGMENTS

As a writer, not a high-tech guy, I have to thank first and foremost Armondo Collins, the coordinator of the Digital Media Commons Department at the Walter C. Jackson Library at the University of North Carolina at Greensboro. UNCG, with its nine-floor tower, has the best library in the Triad, and the personnel to match. In addition, I received willing help from Greensboro's Central Library and the library at Guilford College, my alma mater. I have to thank three downtown merchants who went the extra mile, both by lending me postcards and by giving me suggestions and sharing their memories about life in Greensboro. They are, in alphabetical order, Bill Brooks of Coe Grocery, Gregory Haas of Gregory's Jewelry, and Ben Matthews of the Browsery: Used & Rare Books.

I would like to thank Lynn Donovan, an excellent photographer, who gratefully arranged for me to use some of her impressive work.

The archivist at the Greensboro Historical Museum was also helpful, under trying circumstances. Elise Allison was able to get me a variety of photographs, even though she had to spend some time in the hospital with back surgery and, due to renovation at the museum, she could not always get to the photograph collection. Photographs from the Greensboro Historical Museum were taken by the late Carol Martin where noted in the text. Unless otherwise noted, the rest of the images are courtesy of the author.

I would also like to thank my acquisitions editor at Arcadia Publishing, Katie Owens, for her patience as well as her expertise on getting such a project completed.

INTRODUCTION

In 1958, Greensboro celebrated its sesquicentennial. Indeed, there was much to celebrate. The textile industry, which had begun in the 1830s in Greensborough, as it was spelled then, and which was enhanced by the placement of the North Carolina Railroad and the Cone brothers' discovery of the area, was reaching its peak. Cone Mills was the world's top producer of denim and, with its manufacturing operations more concentrated here, the top employer in the city. Burlington Industries was the world's largest textile company, and Blue Bell was the top manufacturer of overalls. Greensboro was also an insurance center, to the point of being referred to as the Hartford of the South. Another feather in the city's cap was Vicks, the producer of Vicks VapoRub and other nationally known health care products. The city had landed a major manufacturing plant for tobacco giant P. Lorillard as well as a major distribution center for Sears, Roebuck and Co. Furthermore, the city was filled with colleges. Women's College, North Carolina A&T, Greensboro College, and Bennett College were within walking distance of downtown. Guilford College was just west, in its namesake town that would eventually become annexed into the city.

Greensboro had recently extended its boundaries. It began in 1957 with 18.4 square miles within its city limits, but on July 1 of that year, it added more than 31 square miles by annexing the town of Hamilton Lakes, the community of Bessemer, and areas to the north and south of the city.

After a failed attempt to build an arena on North Elm Street, the Greensboro Coliseum was dedicated on Lee Street at the fairgrounds site on October 24, 1959. The coliseum has continued to expand over the years. It has played a key role in the city's history and remains the most important building in Greensboro. In the last half century, when outsiders have read a newspaper article or seen a dateline of Greensboro, it has more likely than not touched on something that took place at the coliseum.

The colleges, particularly A&T, played a major role in social change, which arguably was Greensboro's greatest contribution to history in the period since its sesquicentennial. There is no question that the actions of A&T students, and those who joined them in their cause, spurred integration in the South.

The colleges continued to grow. Women's College and A&T became universities. Branches of Guilford Technical Community College came to town, as did the law school of a university not far past the county line to the east. In a changing economy, GTCC has become a key resource for retraining displaced workers and preparing Greensboro natives for what is needed in the new workforce.

At the beginning of the 1960s, downtown Greensboro was still known as the place to shop for clothes. Major department stores Belk, Meyers, and Ellis Stone were in the heart of downtown, and Sears, Roebuck and Co., Montgomery Ward, Kress, and others had a strong retail presence there. Men's clothing stores, such as Hall Putnam, Younts-DeBoe, and Vanstory's, and women's shops, like Montaldo's, Prago Guys, and Brownhills, brought shoppers downtown. After Friendly Shopping Center opened, downtown had competition, but it was still king. The game, however, was starting to change. When the Four Seasons Mall opened in the 1970s, downtown no longer was the place to shop. The haberdasheries, boutiques, and department stores began an exodus.

When it comes to major-league sports, the Professional Golfers' Association of America (PGA) has been a constant presence in Greensboro since the Greater Greensboro Open started here in 1938. After a hiatus because of World War II, PGA golf has presented an annual event in Greensboro. The tournament has changed names, changed courses, and changed the month in which it is played, but it continues to entertain Greensboro golf enthusiasts and draw others to the city each year. The Wyndham Championship continues to attract the superstars of golf.

The Greensboro Coliseum hosted the highest-ranked sports teams to play here. The Carolina Cougars played in the American Basketball Association (ABA), an upstart league set up in 1967 to compete with the established National Basketball Association. The Cougars took over for the old Houston Mavericks franchise in 1969 and stayed until 1974. Based at the coliseum, the Cougars played 30 percent of their home games in Charlotte and 30 percent of their home games in Raleigh, even though they drew much better while in Greensboro. Their best season was 1972–1973, when they made the playoffs and had the ABA Player of the Year (Billy Cunningham) and ABA Coach of the Year (Larry Brown). Upon the disintegration of the ABA, a few teams were able to merge into the NBA, but not the Cougars. After the 1973–1974 season, the Cougars moved to St. Louis.

Greensboro also had a National Hockey League (NHL) team. After the 1996 season, the Hartford Whalers announced they were leaving for North Carolina, where they would be known as the Carolina Hurricanes. The first two years the Hurricanes played in the state, they competed at the Greensboro Coliseum while a new arena in Raleigh was being built. While they played here, the Cougars and the Hurricanes drew national coverage.

An irony concerning the NHL is that Greensboro, as earlier mentioned, was once referred to the Hartford of the South. The city may have temporarily stolen Hartford's NHL team, but it never measured up to Hartford in terms of the insurance industry. Greensboro's Jefferson Standard Life Insurance owned the sole skyscraper in town at one time. The city also boasted Pilot Life Insurance Company, with an impressive campus near Sedgefield, and Southern Life Insurance Company, which later built a downtown skyscraper. In addition, the Dixie Fire Insurance Company and other smaller ones existed in Greensboro. In the end, the city lost those companies, usually because of buyouts by out-of-town firms. Greensboro's tallest structure is the Lincoln Life Insurance building, but its tenants take their orders from Pennsylvania.

A related irony is that Jefferson Standard actually began in Raleigh before moving to Greensboro. The Gate City had a larger population at the time, and it continued to dominate the Capital City until the 1970s.

More damaging for Greensboro's economy has been the domestic crisis in textiles. Textile production continued to remain upbeat throughout the 1960s and beyond, but King Cotton is now as imploded as the hotel that once bore that name. In 1971, Burlington Industries moved into a larger, state-of-the-art world headquarters, but it was not long before that company started suffering from economic adversity. Guilford Mills, while creating new marketing niches, actually grew dramatically during this period, only to ultimately experience the same fate as Burlington and Cone—Chapter 11 bankruptcy followed by a buyout. Today's global economy allows goods to be produced more cheaply in other countries, even when considering the cost of transportation to the United States.

Greensboro is now struggling to find a new identity. This book will explore how that new identity can be found.

One

DEPARTING

Greensboro has been hit hard by the changing world economy. The difference in wages paid in the United States and those paid in many other countries has persuaded entrepreneurs to hire labor abroad, including Mexico. While some of the textile companies initially saved some money with this practice, it eventually allowed for competition to wreak havoc upon these businesses. Changing times led to the elimination of Sears's superior catalog-order system, which had enabled the company to dominate merchandising throughout the world for decades. Sears still exists as a retailer, but it has fallen behind some of the big-box competitors.

Companies not included in the following pages include Texfi, which was a very successful operation before double-knit fabric went out of style. Pomona Terra Cotta was located in the western part of town. It ended with an explosion that killed four people. Another staple of the economy was Western Electric, at the corner of Spring Garden Street and Merritt Drive. When another Western Electric facility opened just east of town, that was the beginning of the end for the one in Greensboro, and the McLeansville plant did not last.

Some companies are still around but are operated by folks outside of Greensboro. And many others are simply gone. Missing from these pages are the Hall Putnams and Montaldos, mentioned earlier. Also gone from Greensboro's illustrious history without further mention in this book are some legendary hangouts of teenagers and others. The Boar & Castle, Hot Shoppes, and Honeys and its famous Sky Castle fall into this category, as do longtime restaurants such as Antons and McClures, cafeterias like S&W and Mayfair, and smaller eateries like Toddle House, Apple House, and Jan's House. These restaurants made their mark on city life. Gone also are famous supper clubs, such as the Plantation Supper Club and Green's Supper Club. Other nightclubs, including the Castaways, the Jokers Three, and the Carlotta, also left their marks.

The following pages offer a closer look at establishments that are no longer here.

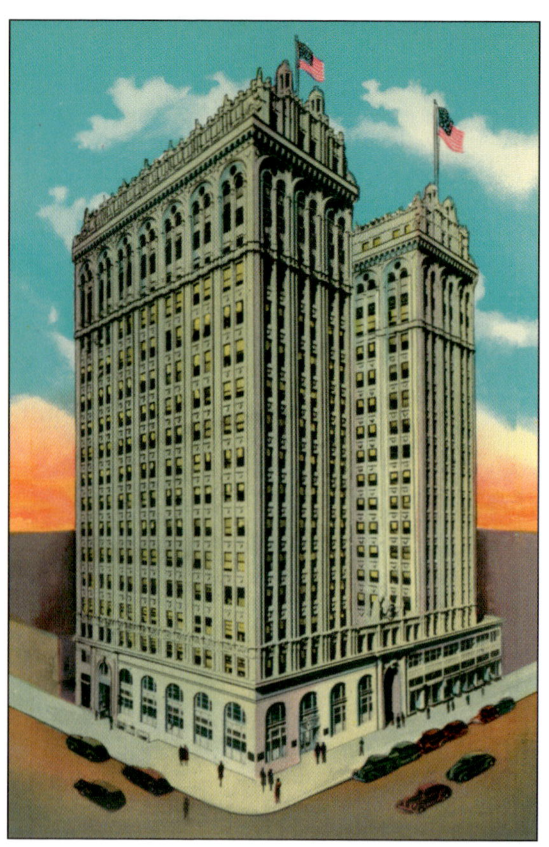

For decades, Jefferson Standard Life stood out in Greensboro. Its headquarters was built in 1923 at 101 North Elm Street. The company's leaders helped shape the city as well as their own firm. It merged with Pilot Life Insurance Company, also a recognizable name in Greensboro. In March 2006, Lincoln Financial Group, a Philadelphia company, acquired Jefferson-Pilot, and that name is now displayed on top of the building. (Courtesy of Ben Matthews.)

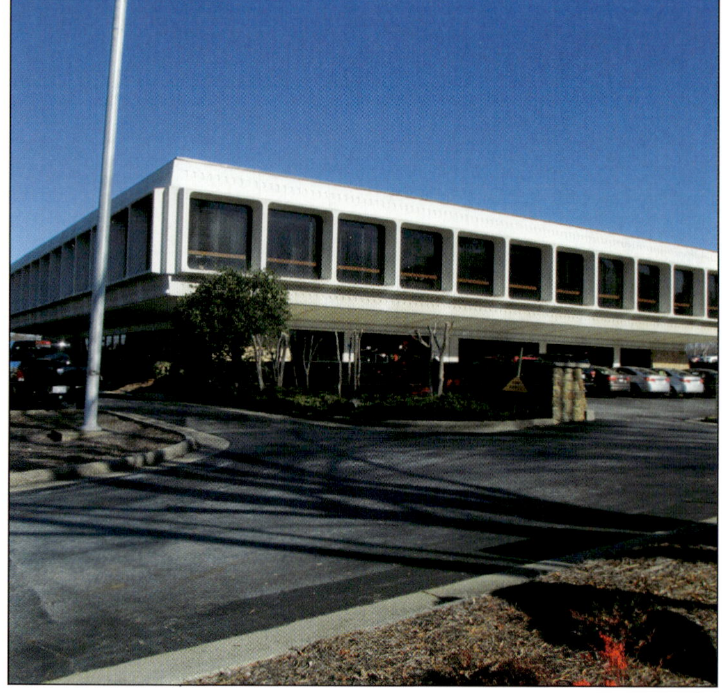

Home Federal Savings & Loan Company, founded in 1913, became the largest savings and loan in North Carolina. Its longtime headquarters was at 113 North Greene Street. Under Greensboro mayor James Melvin, who served as the company's president, the bank moved to 444 North Elm Street (pictured) and changed its name to First Home Federal Savings & Loan Company. In 1998, its assets were purchased by Central Carolina Bank. The building is now owned by VF Corporation.

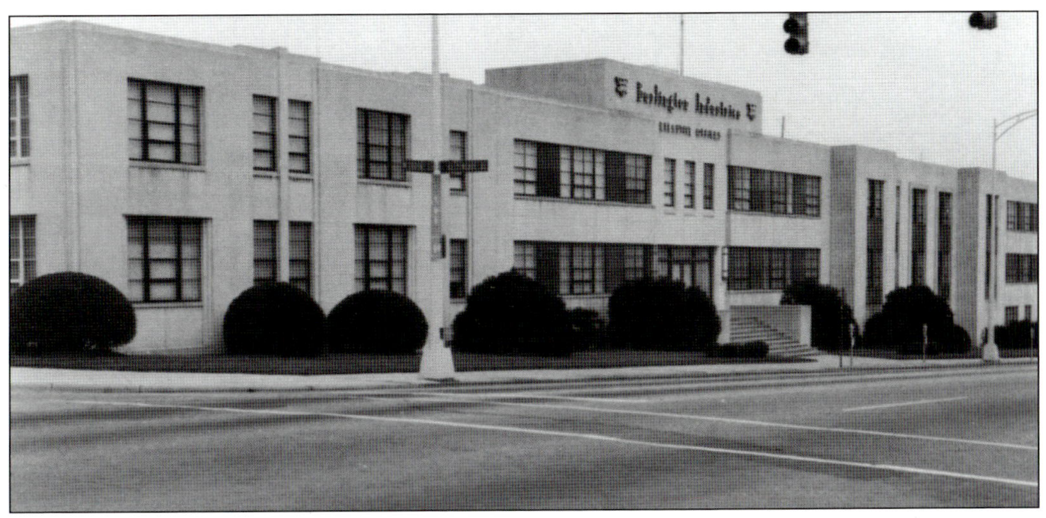

Founded in 1923 by J. Spencer Love, Burlington Mills pioneered a synthetic textile called rayon. In order to obtain easier railway access to New York, it moved its headquarters from Burlington to Greensboro, to an office at 301 North Eugene Street (shown above). In 1962, the year Love died, the company, as Burlington Industries, became the first textile firm to exceed $1 billion in sales. In 1971, Burlington built its headquarters at 3300 West Friendly Avenue (below) and continued to expand. Already strong in women's hosiery, men's socks, and furniture, the company expanded into blankets, sheets, draperies, carpets, and towels. International competition caused Burlington to declare bankruptcy in 2002. (Both, courtesy of ITG Corporation.)

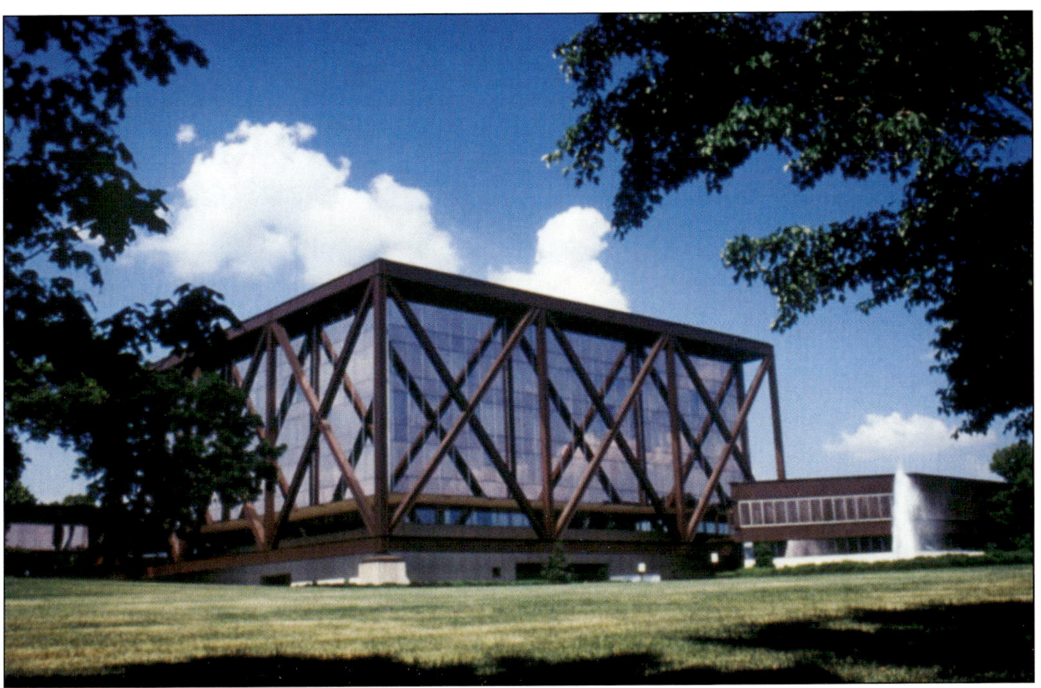

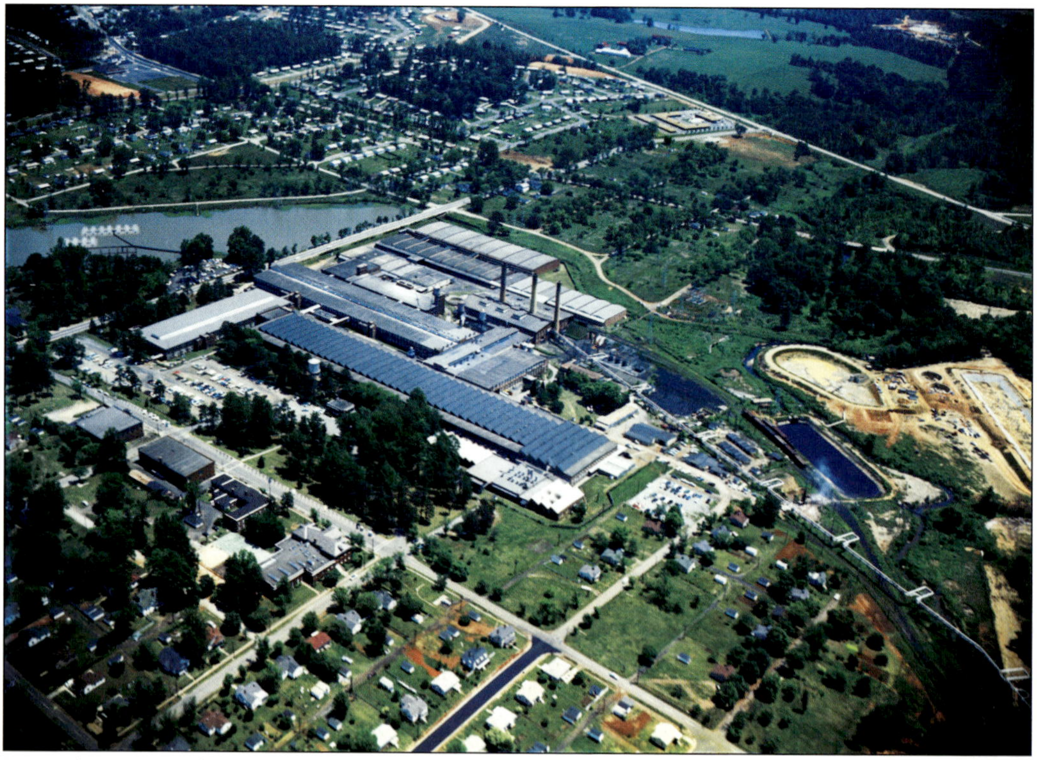

In 1895, Moses and Ceasar Cone established Proximity Manufacturing Mill. In 1899, they started a cotton-flannel factory, Revolution Cotton Mills, as well as the White Oak plant. They built company housing, schools, and churches for employees. The company grew and consolidated its name to Cone Mills, becoming the largest denim producer in the world. Overseas competition forced Cone to declare Chapter 11 bankruptcy in 2004. (Courtesy of Carol Martin/Greensboro Historical Museum Collection.)

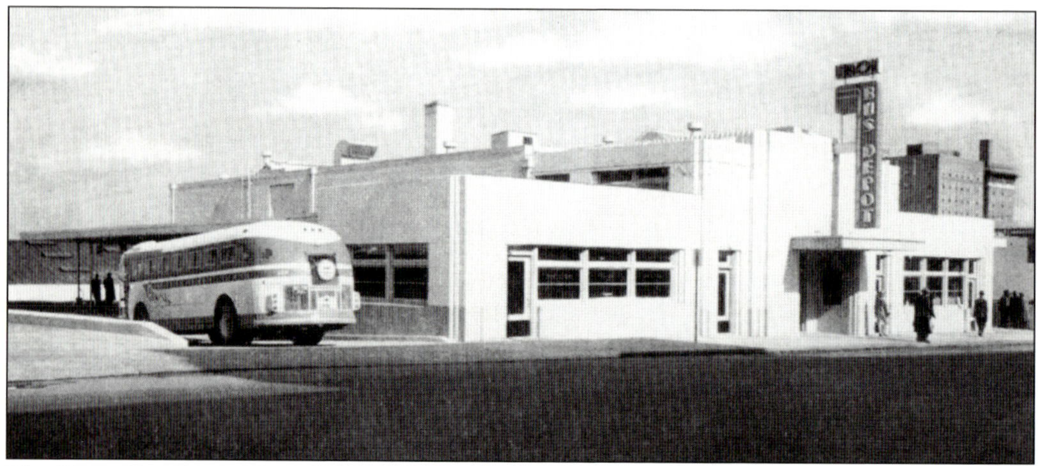

The Union Bus Depot was set up around 1930 at 312 West Gaston Street. It got its name because it served Atlantic Greyhound, Carolina Trailways, and Queen City Trailways lines. Gaston Street eventually became Friendly Avenue. The station moved to West Lee Street when West Market Street United Methodist Church purchased the lot for an early-childhood education center. The facility is now at the J. Douglas Galyon Depot. (Courtesy of Ben Matthews.)

In 1960, Security National
Bank of Greensboro merged
with American Commercial
Bank in Charlotte to form
North Carolina National
Bank. It had two headquarters,
one on the first floor of the
Jefferson Standard Building, at
101 North Elm Street, and the
other in Charlotte. The two
headquarters soon consolidated
in Charlotte. Pictured here
is the opening of its Friendly
Center branch. The firm
eventually became Bank of
America. (Courtesy of Carol
Martin/Greensboro Historical
Museum Collection.)

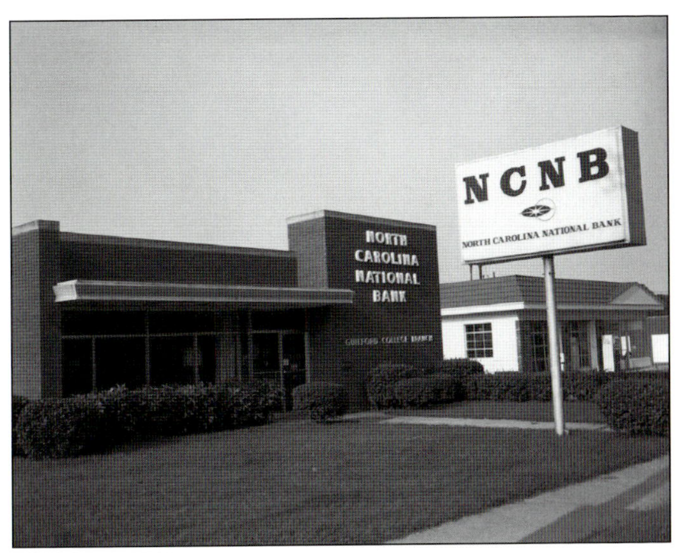

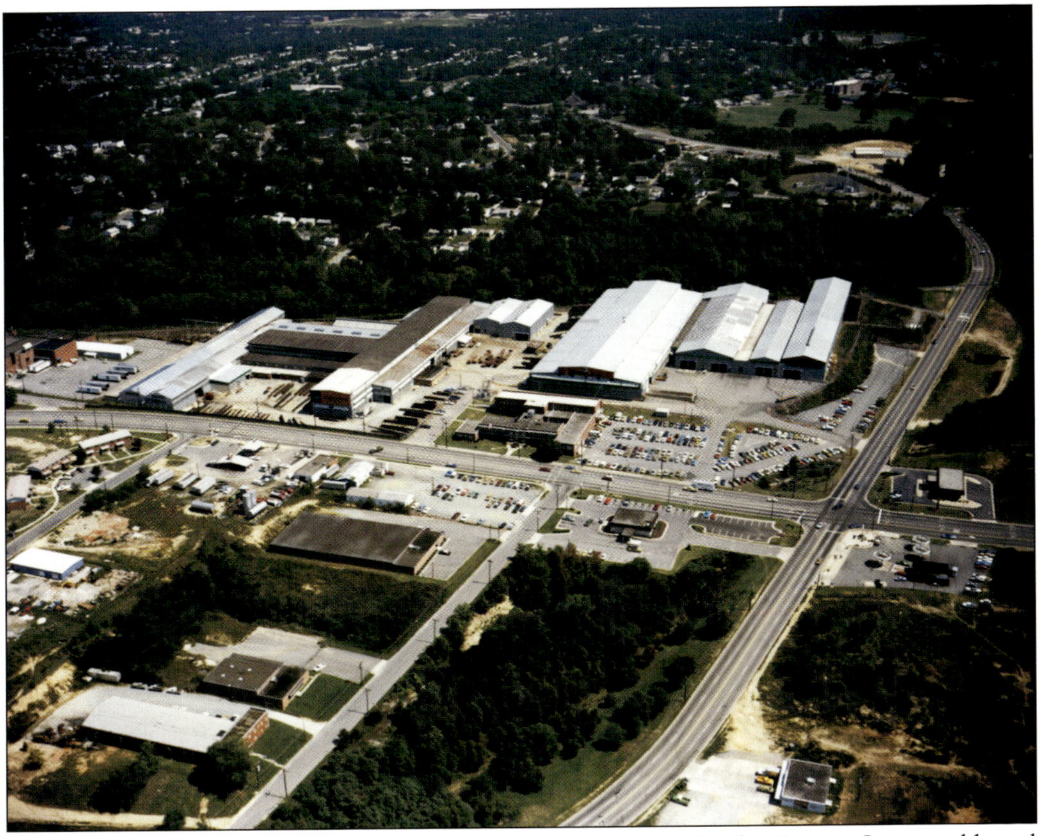

Carolina Steel & Iron Company, founded in 1919 at 1451 South Elm-Eugene Street, sold steel
that it modified for industrial use. In the late 1950s, it began to produce steel girders for highway
and bridge construction. In 1999, the company was purchased by Hirschfeld, Inc., of San Angelo,
Texas. Carolina Steel was absorbed by Hirschfeld in 2008, and the plant closed. (Courtesy of
Carol Martin/Greensboro Historical Museum Collection.)

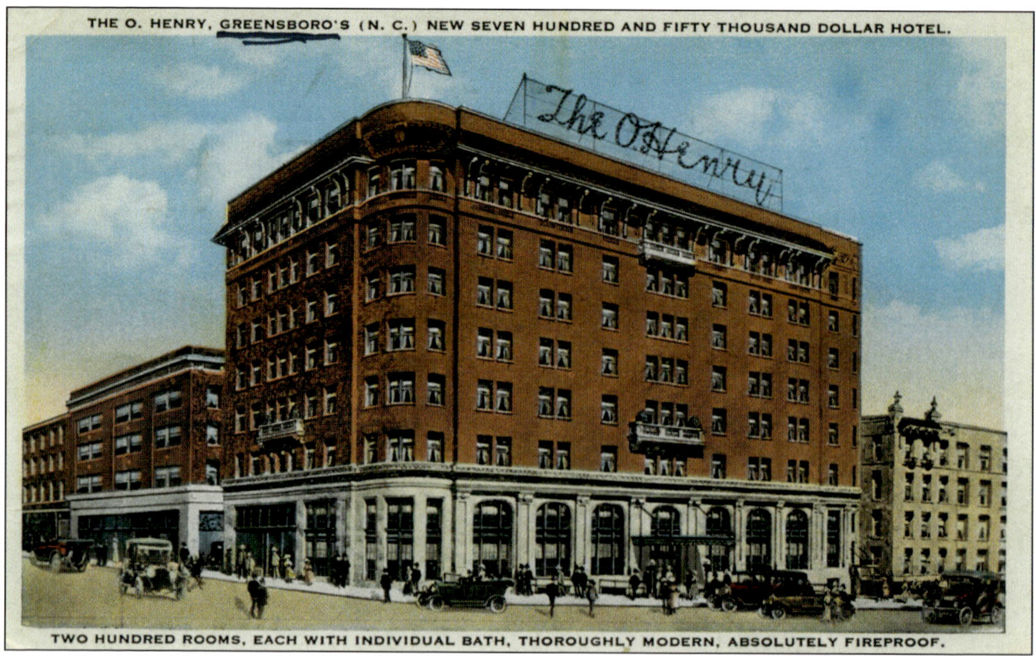

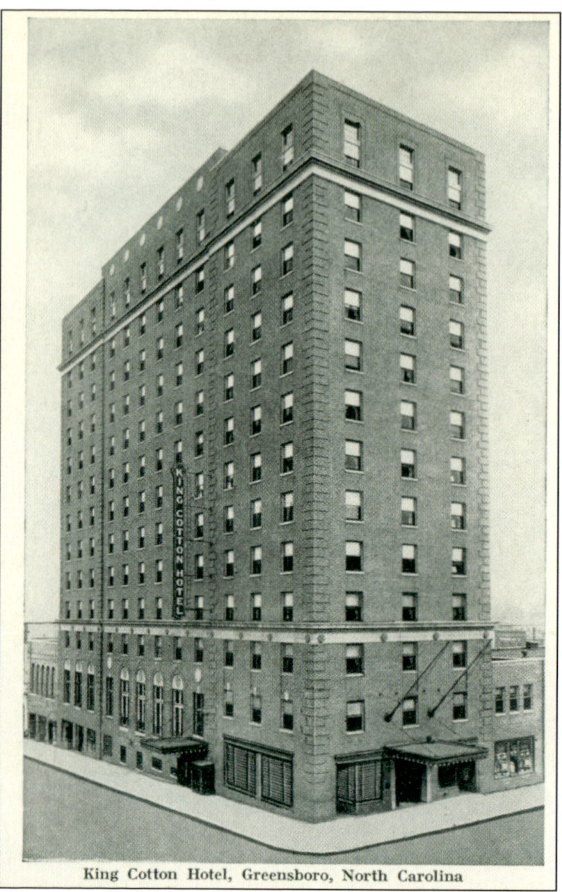

King Cotton Hotel, Greensboro, North Carolina

The O. Henry Hotel (above) opened at the corner of Elm and Bellemeade Streets in 1919. The King Cotton Hotel (left) began in 1927 at the southeast corner of East Market and Davie Streets. They enjoyed decades as prestigious hotels, but in 1961, the occupancy of the King Cotton was only 20 percent. The O. Henry gained some notoriety in 1962, when a social club at Greensboro High School held a party there that got out of hand. The King Cotton closed in 1965 and reopened two years later as a boardinghouse before closing again. It was imploded in 1971 and replaced by a building for the daily newspaper. The O. Henry closed in 1975, when rooms were renting for $7. It was demolished and replaced by a new Southern Life Building. (Both, courtesy of Ben Matthews.)

Founded in 1890, Vicks was built by Smith Richardson, son of founder Lunsford Richardson. By the 1960s, Vicks had several established brands, including Vicks VapoRub and NyQuil. The company had two plants in Greensboro, including this one at 325 West Wendover Avenue. By 1979, it had reached $1 billion in sales. The business was purchased by Procter & Gamble in 1985. (Courtesy of Carol Martin/ Greensboro Historical Museum Collection.)

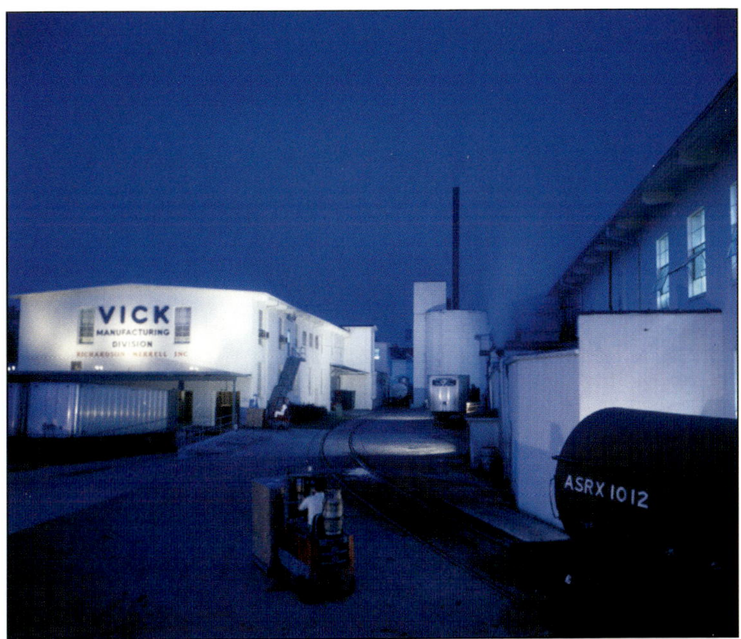

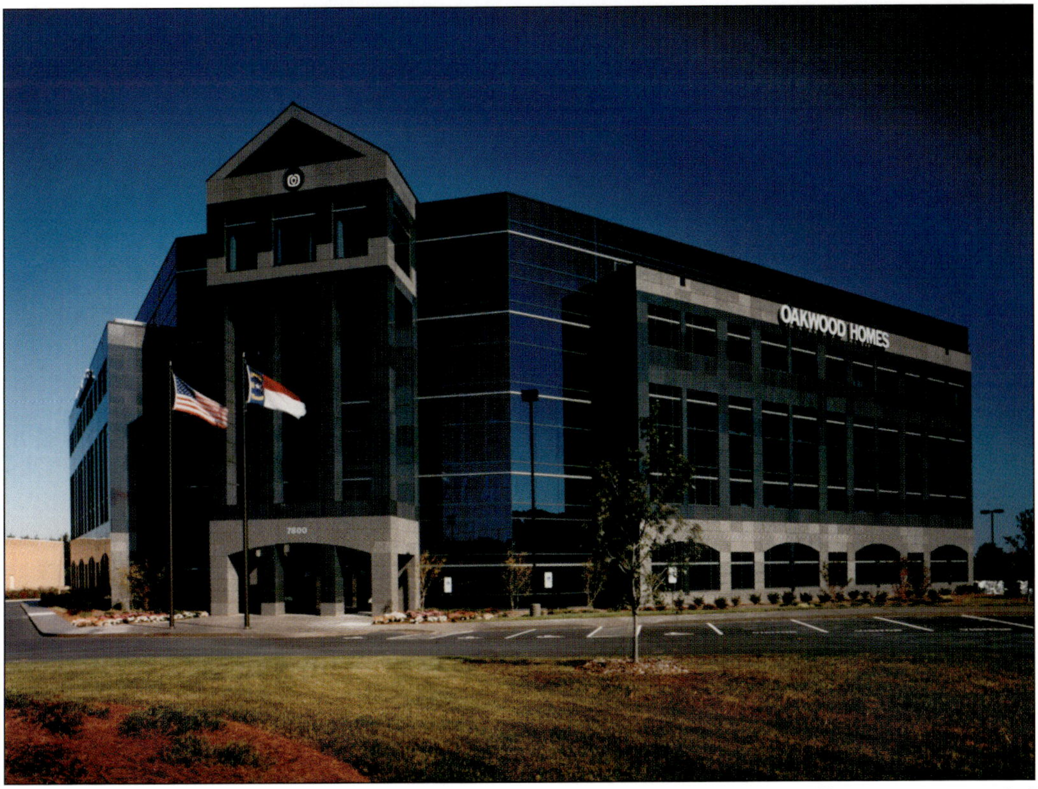

Oakwood Homes was founded in 1946 at 3601 High Point Road. The company's offices were surrounded by mobile homes it had built. Business grew, and in 1996, Oakwood moved to 7800 McCloud Road (pictured). Shortly after, a recession hit the economy, slowing sales. In 2003, the company was purchased by Clayton Homes of Maryville, Tennessee. (Courtesy of Vanderbilt Mortgage and Finance, Inc.)

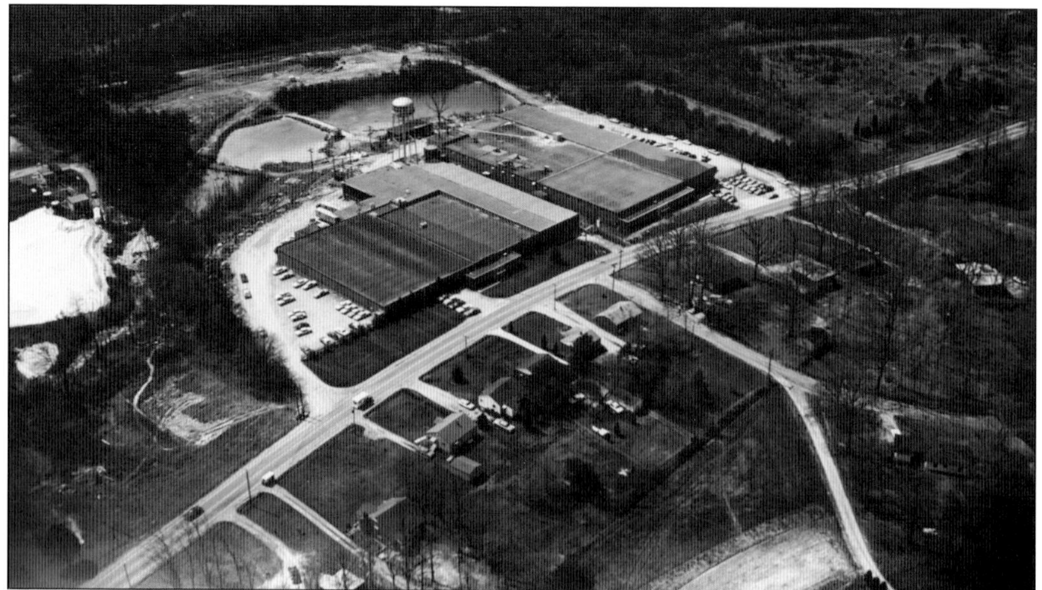

Guilford Mills, founded in 1946, opened its first knitting plant in 1960. In 1961, its first dyeing and finishing plant was established, and Charles "Chuck" Hayes, who became president in 1968, was hired. He built Guilford Mills into a Fortune 500 company, with headquarters at 4951 West Market Street, before stepping down as CEO in November 1999. The following July, the Greensboro plant closed, and in 2002, the company declared bankruptcy. After reorganization, it continued to manufacture textile products for automotive companies and other specialty uses, but it was moved to Wilmington, North Carolina. In 2012, it was sold to Lear Corporation. The company remains the leading US producer of warp, or flat, knit fabric. (Both, courtesy of Carol Martin/Greensboro Historical Museum Collection.)

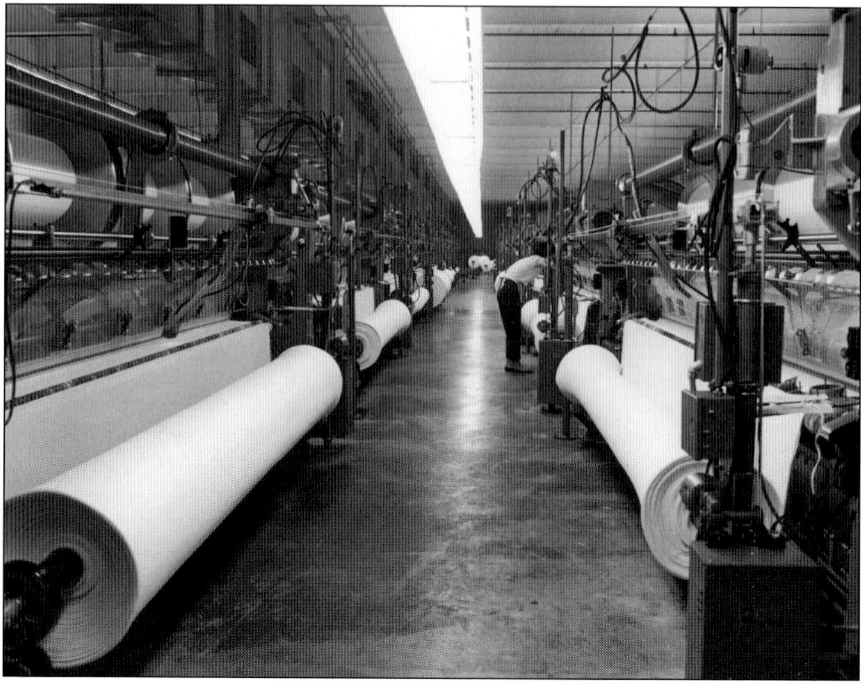

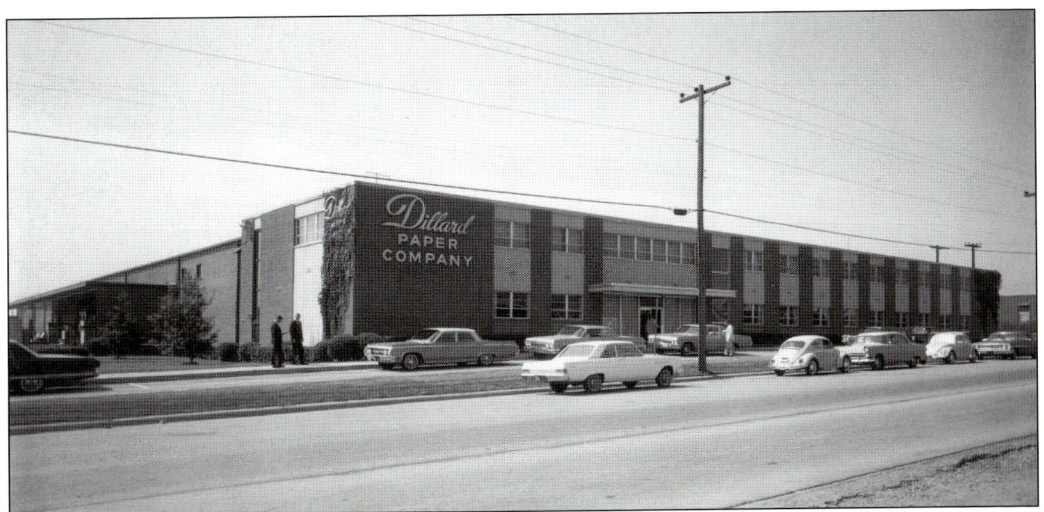

Dillard Paper Company, founded in 1926 by Stark Dillard, was the largest paper distributor in the Southeast by 1960. By 1990, Dillard Paper, then with headquarters at 3900 Spring Garden Street, had annual sales of $500 million and offices or warehouses in 20 cities. In 1991, it was acquired by International Paper Company, which still operates from that address. (Courtesy of Carol Martin/Greensboro Historical Museum Collection.)

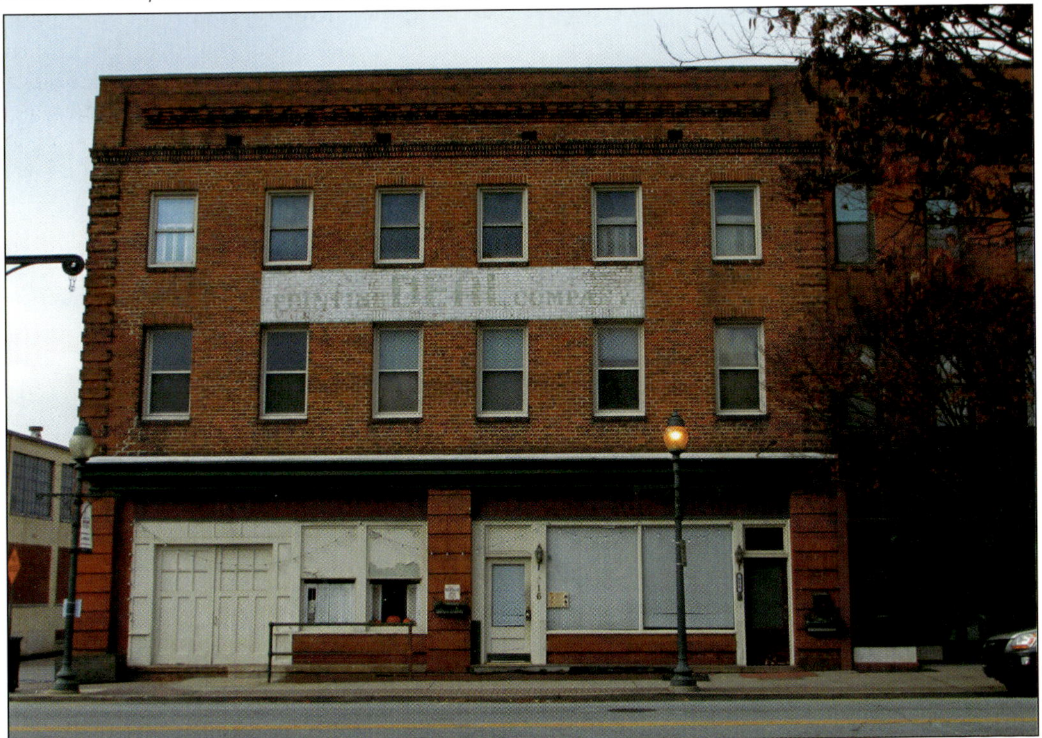

Deal Printing Company was established in the 1940s and lasted until 2011. The company's name still appears faintly on the building at 616 South Elm Street (shown here). Also of historical interest is the fact that NASCAR had offices at this location from the 1940s until 1962, when operations were moved full-time to headquarters in Daytona Beach, Florida. NASCAR official Charlie Tate kept a second-floor office here until 1980.

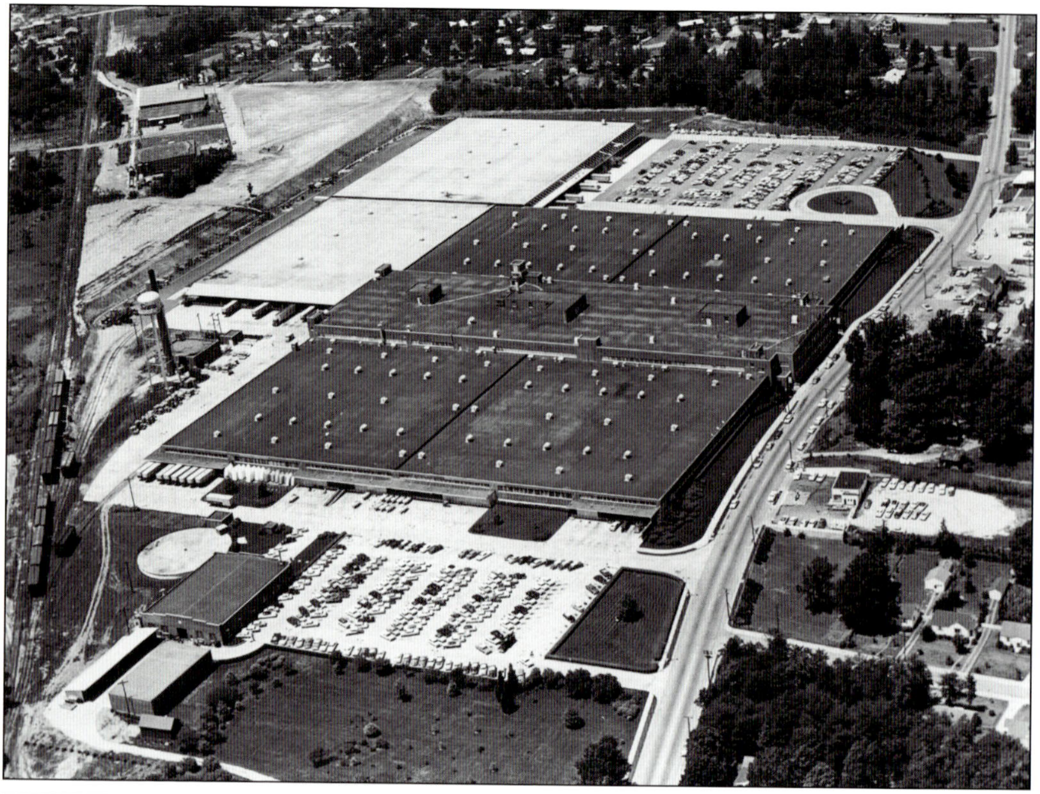

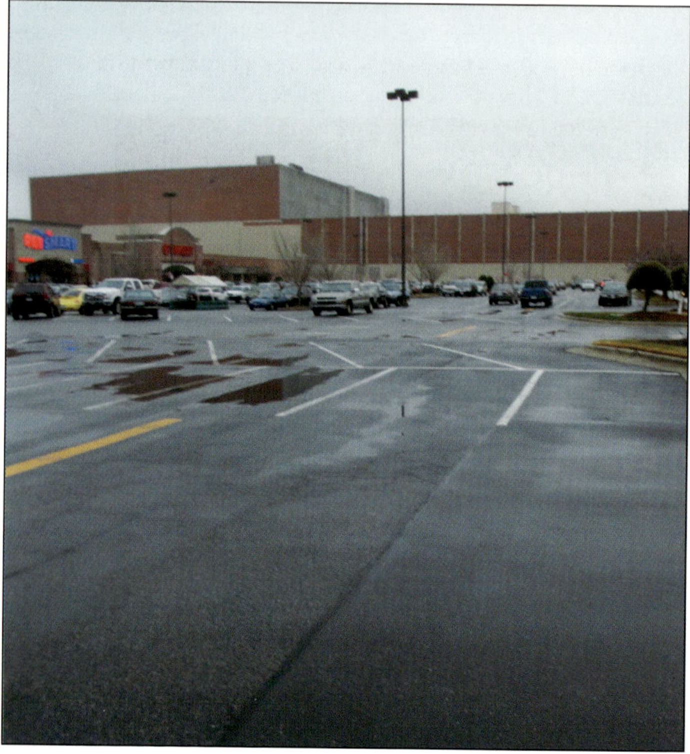

In 1947, Sears, Roebuck and Co. built a mail-order distribution center that supplied catalog merchandise for several states. The building, at 2600 Lawndale Drive, was the largest facility under one roof in Greensboro. The structure is seen in the above photograph in 1961. In 1970, the building shown on the left was added, making the Sears facility the largest under one roof in North Carolina. Sears terminated all of its mail-order activity in 1993. Soon after, the older part of the building went down, replaced by Shops at Kirkwood. The 1970 addition still stands. (Above, courtesy of Carol Martin/ Greensboro Historical Museum Collection.)

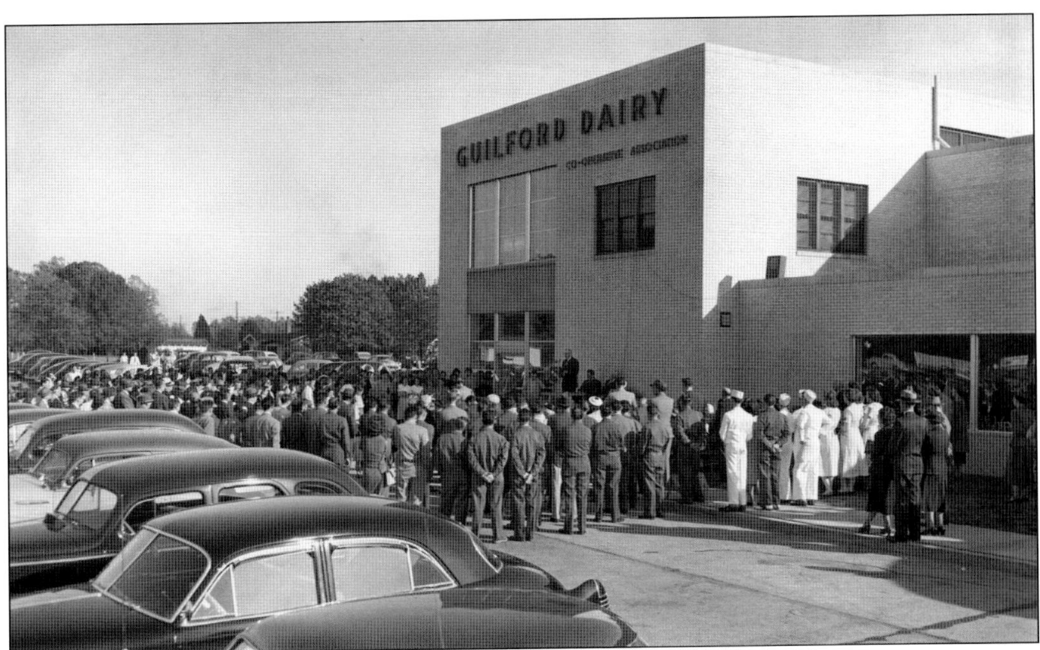

Guilford Dairy, a cooperative of dairy farmers founded in 1930, moved its headquarters from 1704 West Lee Street to 3939 West Market Street in 1947. An ice cream parlor was located next door to its old headquarters, and one was placed in its new headquarters. The dairy went on to place such parlors at Summit, Plaza, and Friendly shopping centers, as well as some in nearby towns. These parlors later became Mayberry Ice Cream Shoppes. Summit has the only Mayberry that remains in Greensboro. In the 1970s, Guilford Dairy bought Farmers Dairy in Winston-Salem and became United Dairies. This was purchased in the late 1970s by Flav-O-Rich, which closed the plant in 2002. The building was eventually demolished. A storage unit and a Sheetz station operate on the site now. (Both, courtesy of Carol Martin/Greensboro Historical Museum Collection.)

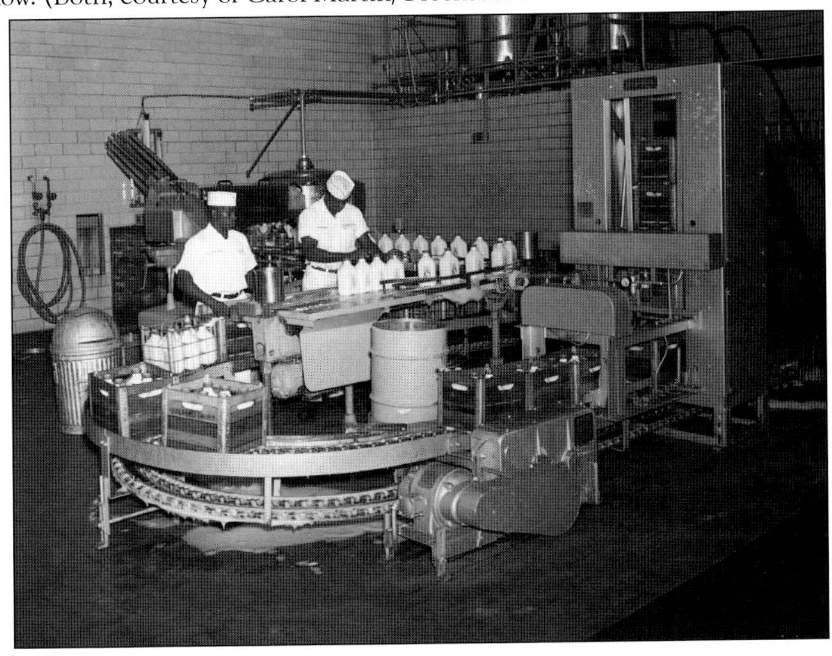

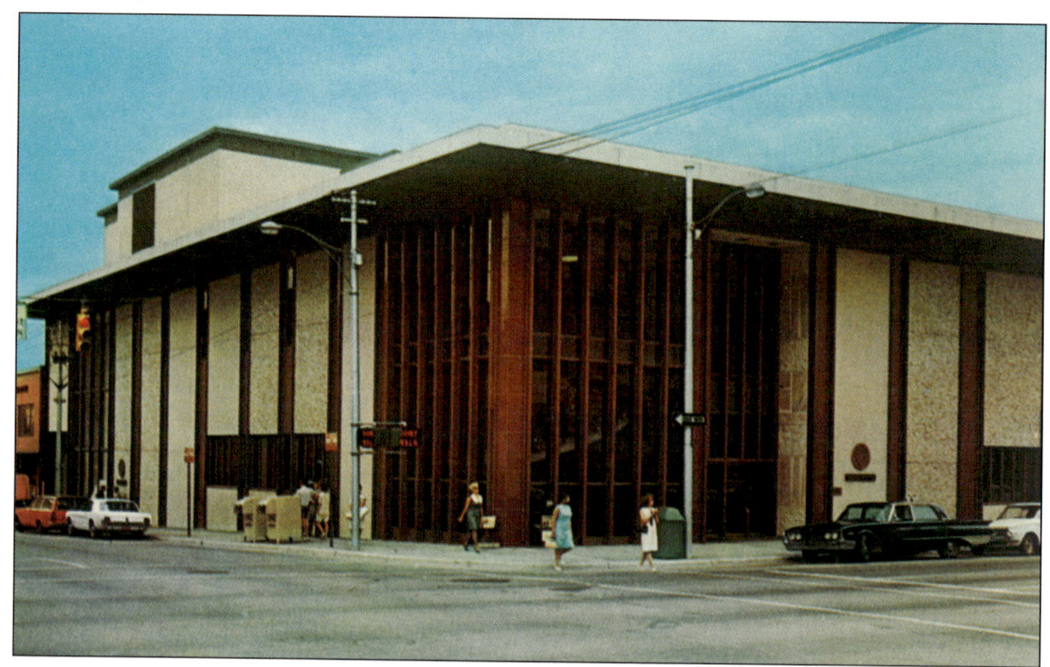

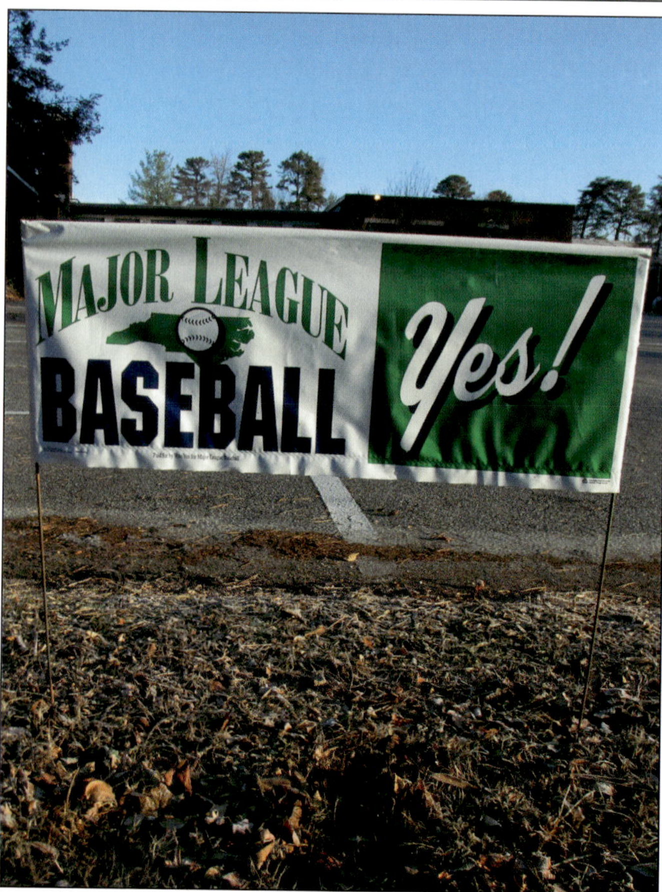

The Greensboro Public Library had outgrown the 10,124 square feet of space it was allocated at the Richardson Center, which it shared with the Greensboro Historical Museum and other community organizations since 1939. A 1961 bond issue for a new library passed, and officials decided to build it at 201 North Greene Street. This 1964 building (above) served Greensboro as its central library for 34 years. In 1995, a group announced an effort to bring a Major League Baseball team to the Triad. Donald Beaver, who owned nursing homes as well as minor-league baseball teams, was in line to be the principal owner. A referendum took place in 1998 to impose a one percent tax on all prepared food in Guilford and Forsyth Counties to raise money for most of the stadium. The referendum failed, ending the effort. (Above, courtesy of Bill Brooks.)

Two

REMAINING

Some institutions manage to survive, although it is often not easy. It is a credit to the people of Greensboro that much has been saved. Some structures, such as the Blandwood Mansion, were headed in the direction of Bellemeade, the historic home of Greensboro's original textile entrepreneur that went down to make way for a short-lived grocery store.

The arrival of the Greensboro Coliseum to the fairgrounds did not mean the end of the Central Carolina Fair, a part of Greensboro for 112 years and counting. It did, however, put an end to the NASCAR races on the track around the fair, which was demolished to provide a site for the coliseum. Fortunately, the airport remains. Now called Piedmont Triad International Airport, it could be a major contributor to Greensboro's future. Moses Cone Hospital is also still around. It has grown to the point that it is Greensboro's largest employer outside of the government.

The portion of the area where the Battle of Guilford Courthouse took place is another example of the will of the people to save a piece of history. The battle site might very well have become part of the large commercial district in that part of town today. Instead, it is a federal park where the battle is reenacted each year on its anniversary.

Greensboro had lost Blue Bell as a headquarters, but VF Corporation, which had acquired Blue Bell, decided that the Gate City was a better place for its headquarters than the suburb of Reading, Pennsylvania, where it had been. In a similar vein, P. Lorillard, the tobacco giant, had a plant here, and eventually decided on moving its headquarters to Greensboro, from New York.

The Southeastern Building has been in the city since 1919, and it greatest days may be ahead. The same could even be true for the Carolina Theatre, endangered more than once, but standing since 1927.

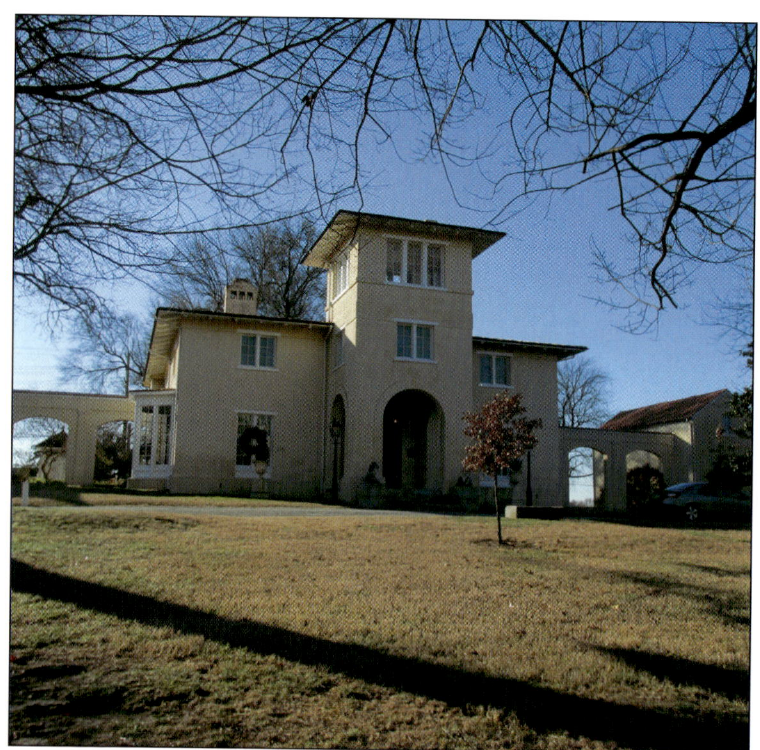

Blandwood was built as a farmhouse in 1795 by Charles Bland. Gov. John Morehead bought the property and completed its expansion in 1845. The Greensboro Preservation Society wanted to buy Blandwood, considered to be the nation's oldest standing example of Italianate architecture. The site was purchased in July 1968 and deeded to Greensboro. Dedicated in 1976, it now serves as the headquarters of the Greensboro Preservation Society.

Whitestone, a Masonic and Eastern Star community, was founded in 1912 as the Masonic and Eastern Star Home. It was located west of Greensboro in an area that has since become part of the city. It was taken over by Whitestone in 2011. Greensboro has many retirement communities, including Friends Homes, WellSpring, and Fountain Manor.

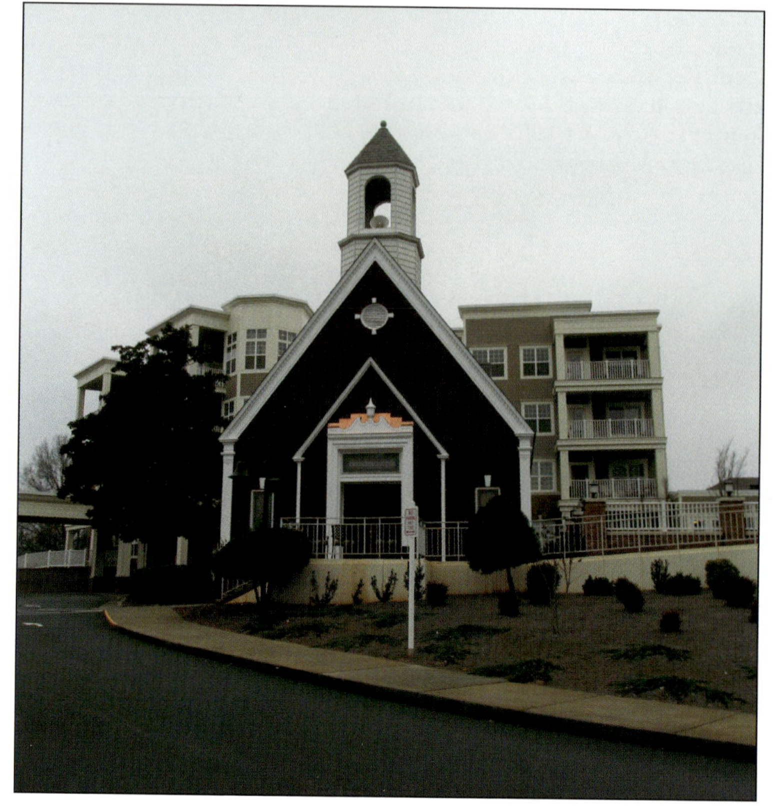

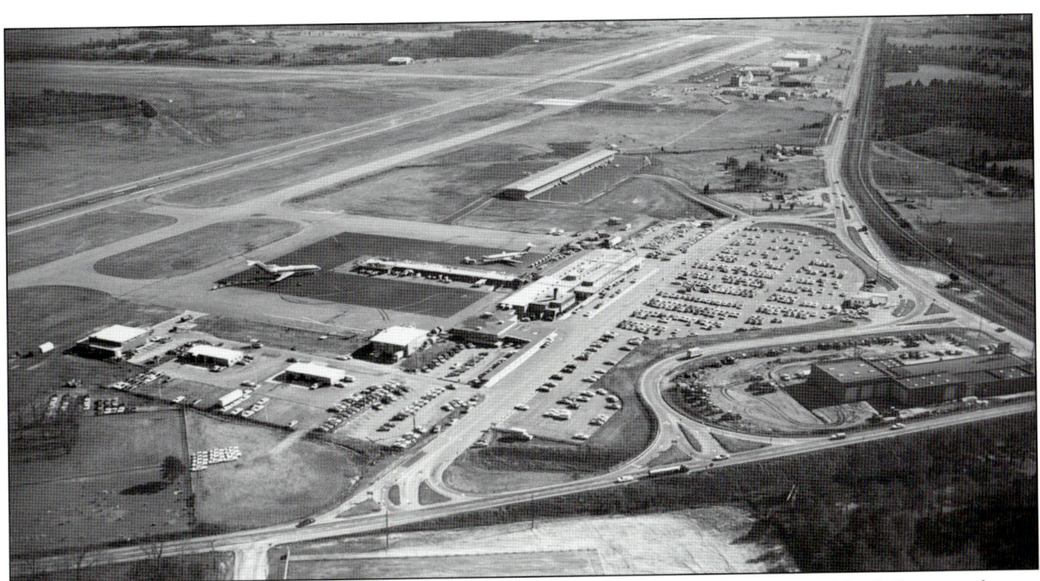

In 1927, the Tri-City Airport Commission selected 112 acres in western Guilford County for an airfield. Because the commission selected property in the community of Friendship (now in the city limits of Greensboro) rather than in Winston-Salem, then North Carolina's largest city, the Twin City refused further support of the project. Greensboro and Guilford County jointly purchased the property from Paul and Helen Lindley and named it Lindley Field. In 1942, the Greensboro–High Point Airport Authority was given responsibility to run the airport. The authority had representatives from Greensboro, High Point, and Sedgefield. In 1958, a 34,000-square-foot terminal replaced nearby Lindley Field as Greensboro's airport and became known as Greensboro–High Point Regional Airport (above). By 1975, airport officials were planning for a new terminal. It was completed in 1982 and named Piedmont Triad International Airport in 1987. A model of the airport (below) is on display inside the terminal. (Above, courtesy of Carol Martin/Greensboro Historical Museum Collection.)

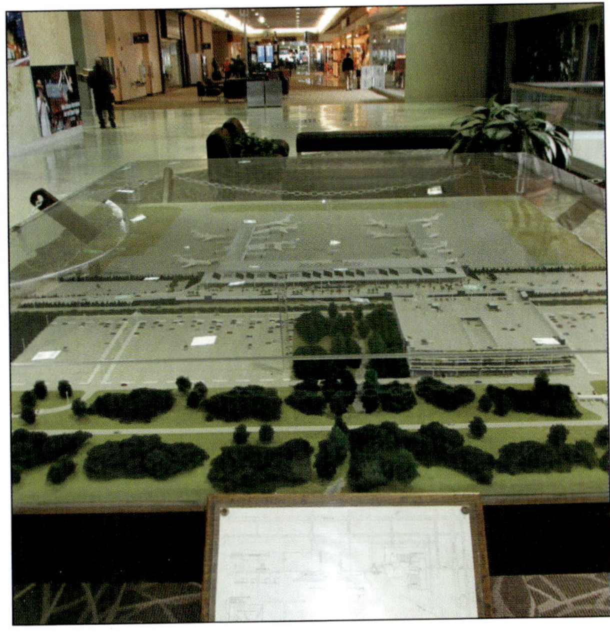

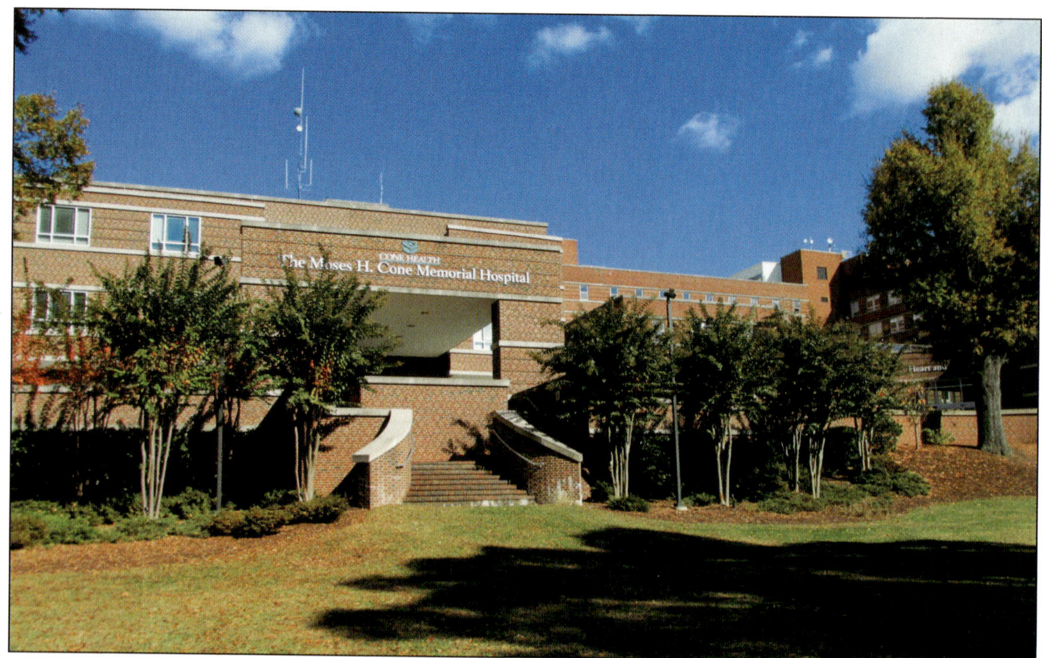

Bertha Cone set up a trust fund to memorialize her late husband, Moses H. Cone, after his death in 1908. Upon Bertha's death in 1947, her share of the family's inheritance was directed toward the founding of the Moses H. Cone Memorial Hospital (above). In 1953, it opened at 1200 North Elm Street with 310 beds and rates as low as $8 per room. Not only has it expanded significantly, but it has added other institutions around town, including, in the 1970s, Charter Hills, at 700 Walter Reed Drive. It treated mental illness as well as drug and alcohol dependency, and it now operates as the Behavioral Health Hospital for Cone Health (below).

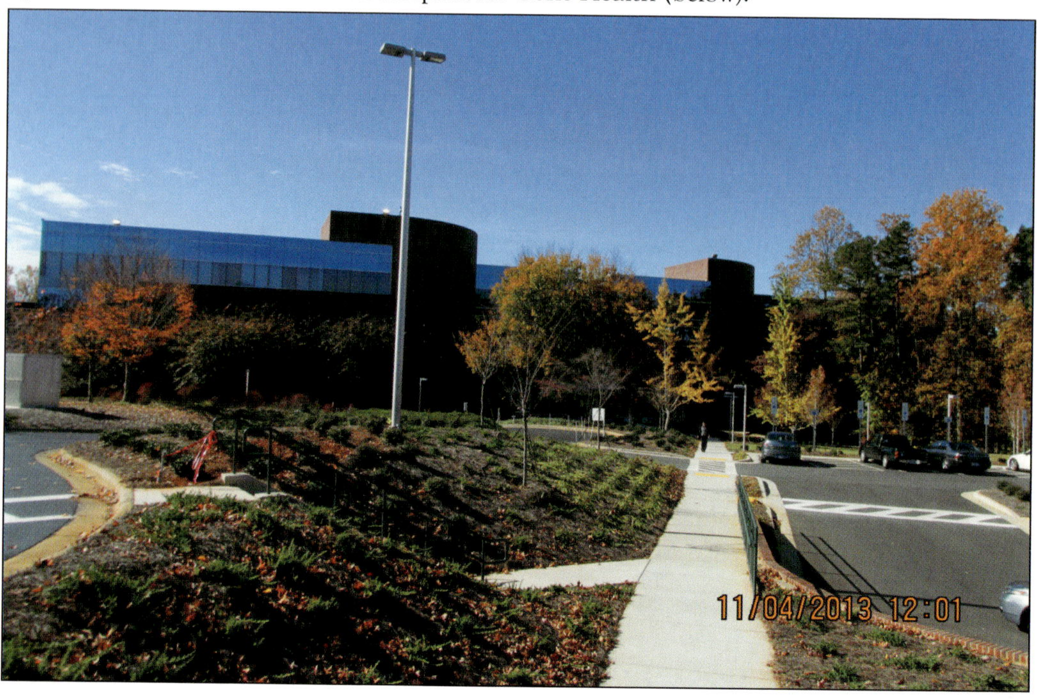

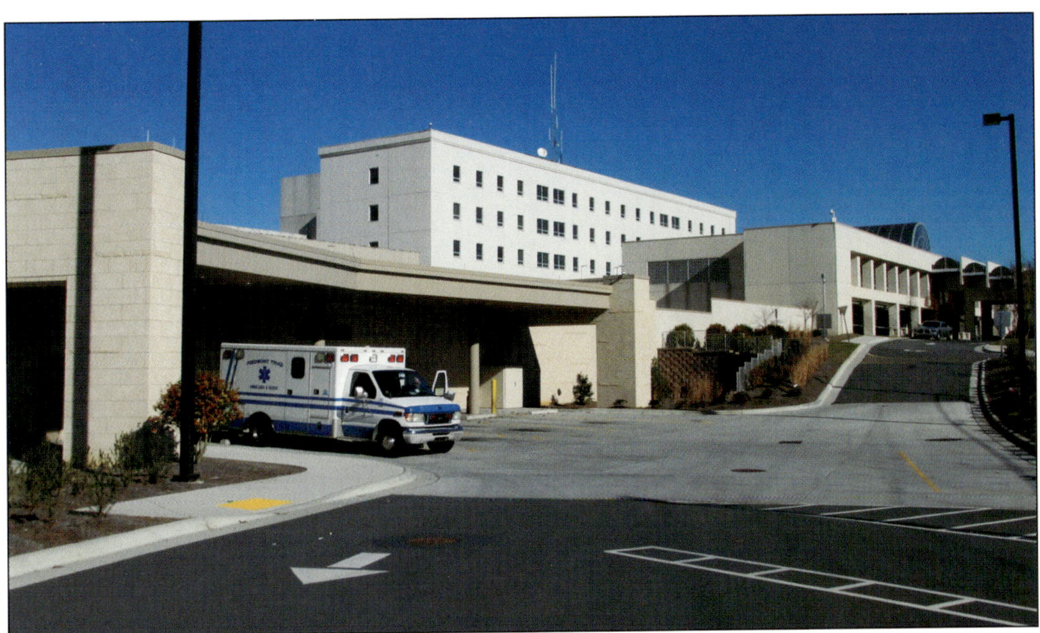

Wesley Long Hospital is older than Cone. Founded at 338 North Elm Street in 1917, it was Greensboro's largest hospital until Cone opened in 1953. L. Richardson Hospital, which served African Americans during the Jim Crow era, is no longer a hospital. Wesley Long moved to 501 North Elam Avenue (above) in 1961. After Cone Health took it over, it expanded to 175 beds. It recently added a 29,000-square-foot emergency department. Also on that site is the Cone Health Cancer Center, which used to be part of Wesley Long. Women's Hospital opened in 1990 at 801 Green Valley Road (below). It is a maternity hospital that also addresses other issues of female health. In addition to these hospitals, Cone Health operates others in nearby communities.

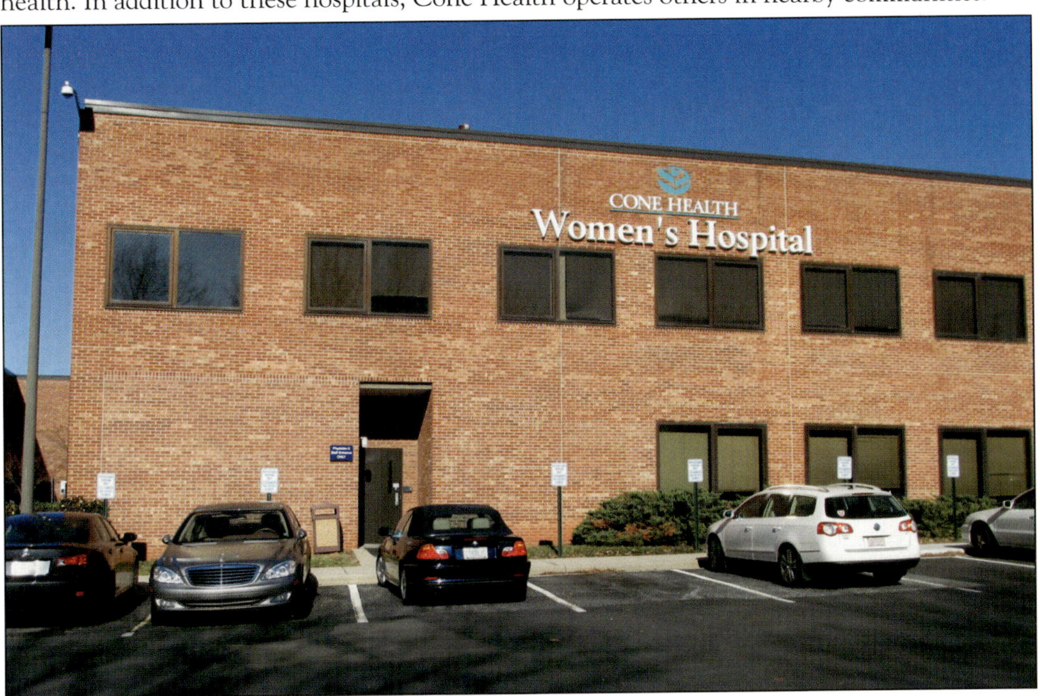

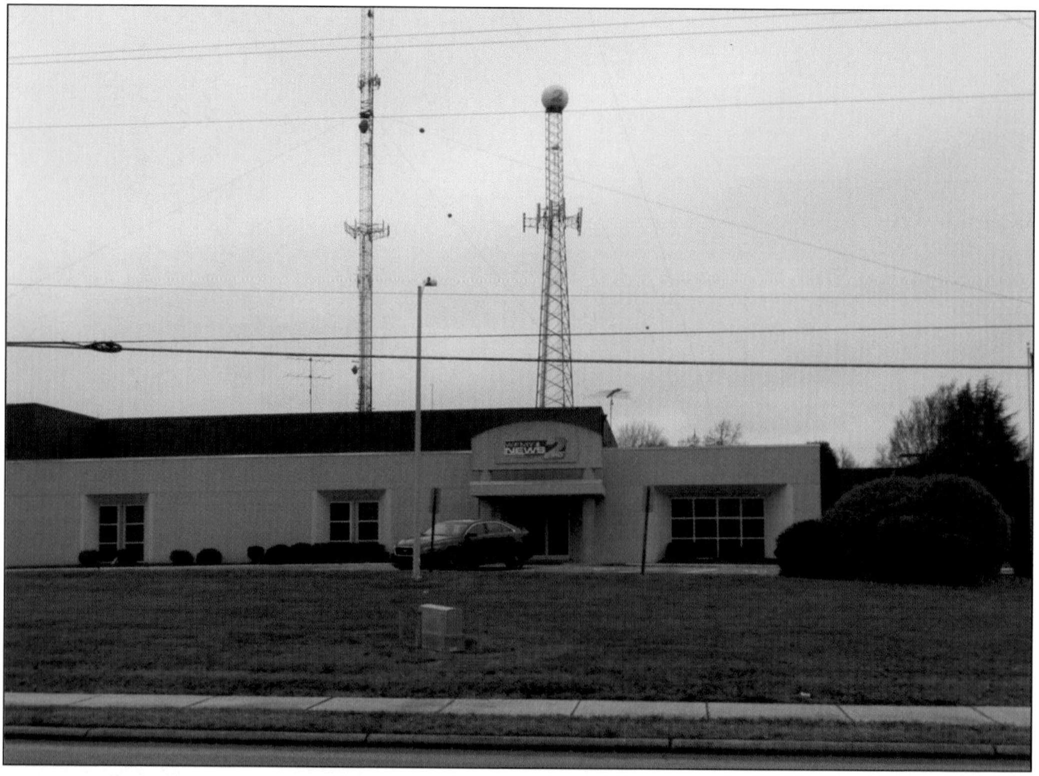

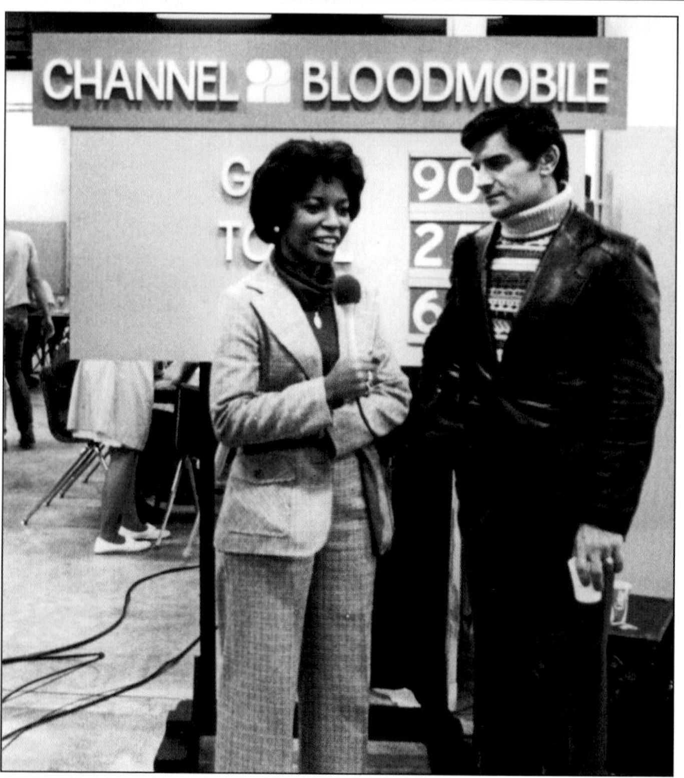

WFMY, which started in 1948 as an FM radio station, became a television station the following year. It was the second television station in North Carolina. Its original owner was the Greensboro News Company, which owned Greensboro's two daily newspapers. With facilities at 1615 Phillips Avenue, it has always been the Triad's CBS affiliate. The FM station was dropped in the early 1950s, and WQMG-FM eventually took its place on the dial. Gannett Company, a media conglomerate out of Tysons Corner, Virginia, purchased WFMY in 1988. Sandra Hughes, shown on the left at a blood drive, was one of many news personalities the station has had over the years. (Left, courtesy of WFMY-TV.)

The Battle of Guilford Courthouse was fought on March 15, 1781. It took until the 20th century, long after the county seat was moved to Greensboro, in the center of Guilford County, but interest in making a park out of the battleground site eventually came to fruition. The park was established in 1917. By then, monuments had already been set up and graves were moved to the park, including those of former North Carolina governor and US senator Jesse Franklin and former congressman and general Joseph Winston. But the best-known monument at the park is the statue of Gen. Nathanael Greene, a major general in the Continental army. Pres. Gerald Ford (right) spoke in front of the Greene Monument in 1976, as did George H.W. Bush the same year, when he was director of the Central Intelligence Agency. An education center is located on the site, and reenactments of the battle occur every year on its anniversary. (Right, courtesy of National Park Service.)

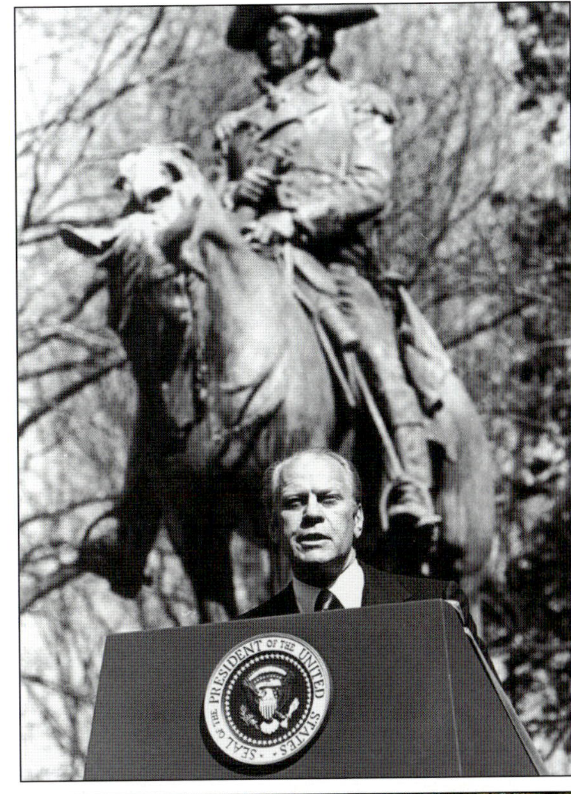

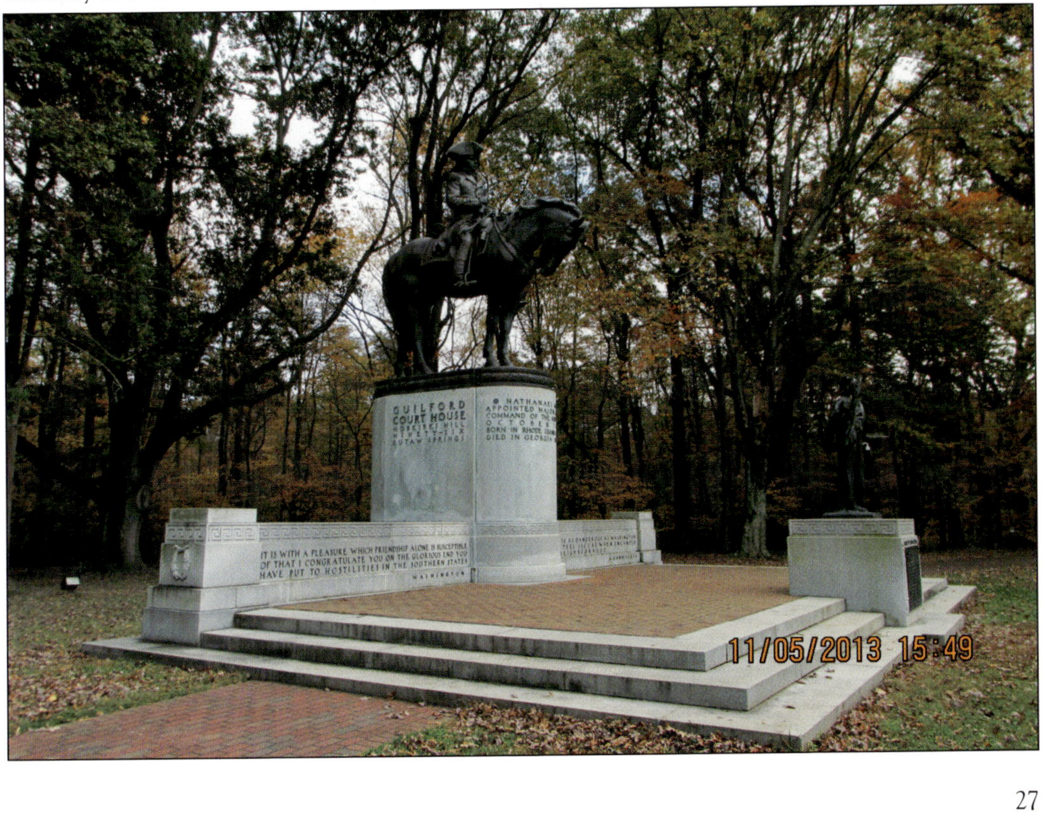

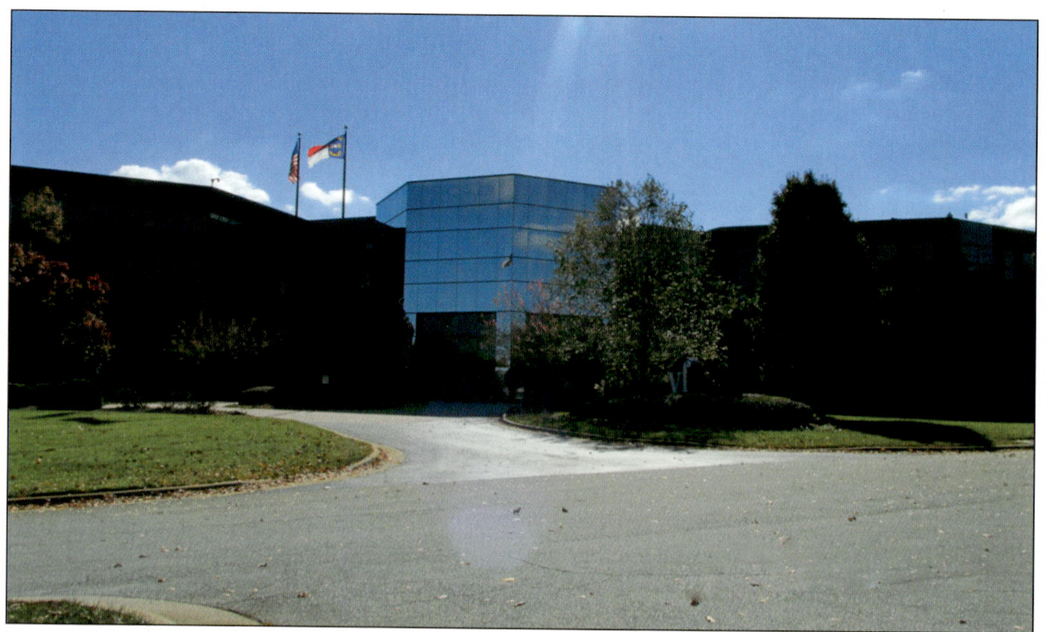

Founded by C.C. Hudson, Hudson Overall Company opened in 1904, changing its name to Blue Bell Corporation when it opened its own factory at South Elm and Lee Streets. After launching the Wrangler brand in 1943, it grew rapidly. In 1958, Blue Bell opened a $640,000, three-story office building at 335 Church Court. The company diversified, acquiring Jantzen and other brands. Blue Bell was acquired for $813 by VF Corporation in 1986, a move that laid off 300 employees in Greensboro. By 1996, one out of every five pairs of blue jeans sold was a pair of Wrangler jeans. In 1998, VF moved its headquarters from Wyomissing, Pennsylvania, to 105 Corporate Center Boulevard in Greensboro (above). It has also expanded the former Blue Bell headquarters, now listed at 400 North Elm Street (below). Other VF brands include Lee, Timberland, Nautica, and The North Face.

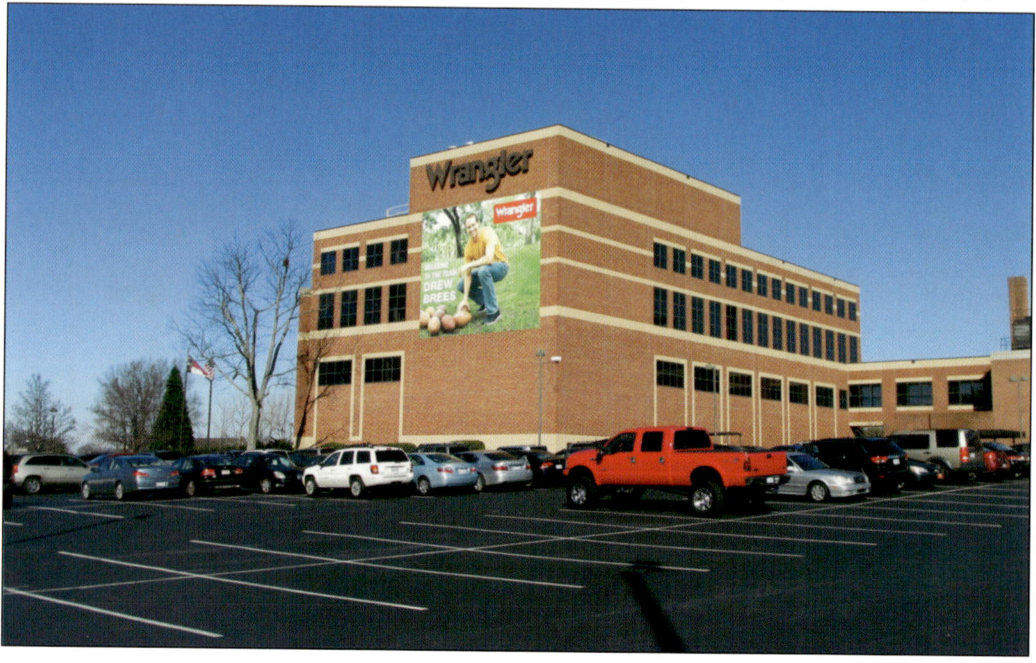

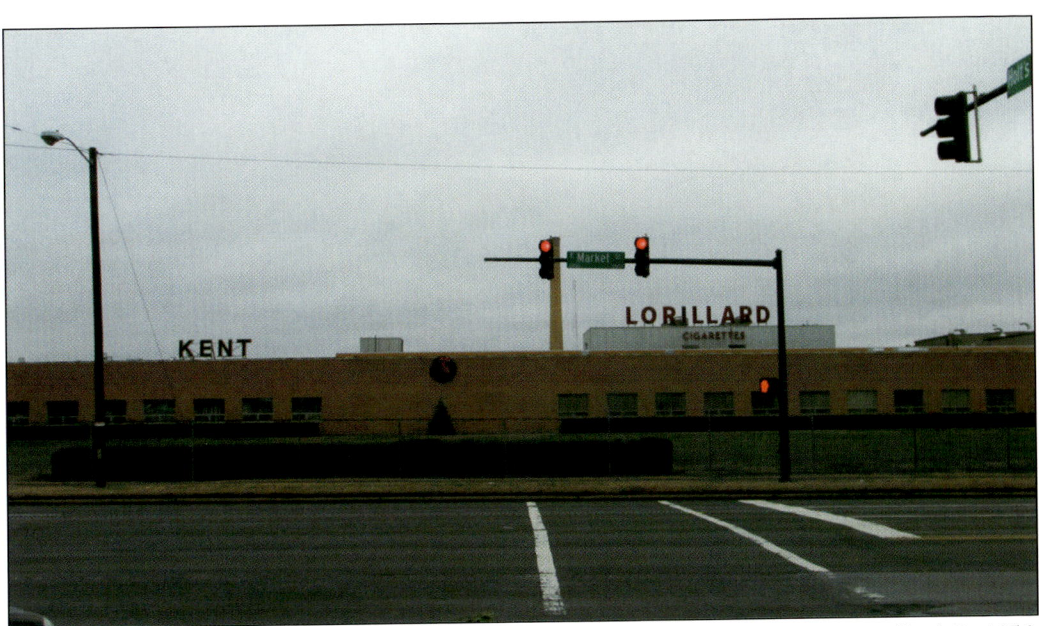

Lorillard Tobacco Company dates to 1760, when it was founded by Pierre Abraham Lorillard. By 1956, when it opened a manufacturing plant at 2525 East Market Street (above), it had its headquarters in New York. In 1967, the company was purchased by Loews Corporation, and 30 years later, it moved its headquarters to Greensboro, at 714 Green Valley Road (below). In 2008, Lorillard entered a separation agreement with Loews and became an independent, publically traded company. Its cigarette brands include Newport, Kent, and Old Gold. The company generated $6.46 billion in revenue in 2011. In 2014, word came out that R.J. Reynolds Tobacco Company was in merger talks with Lorillard.

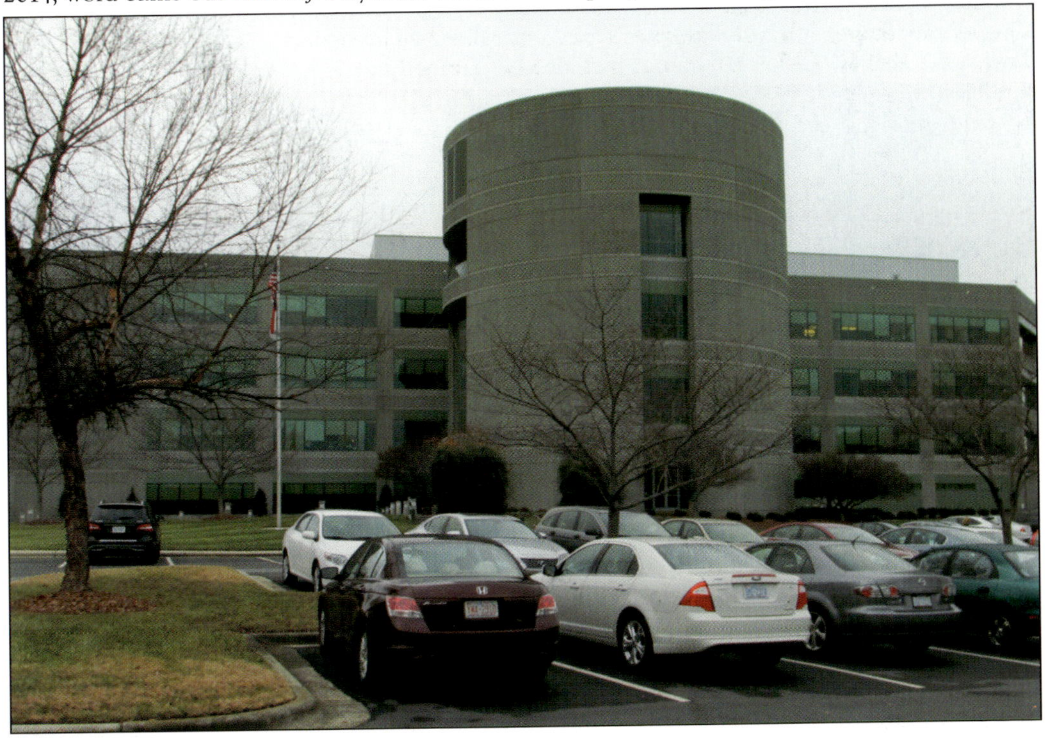

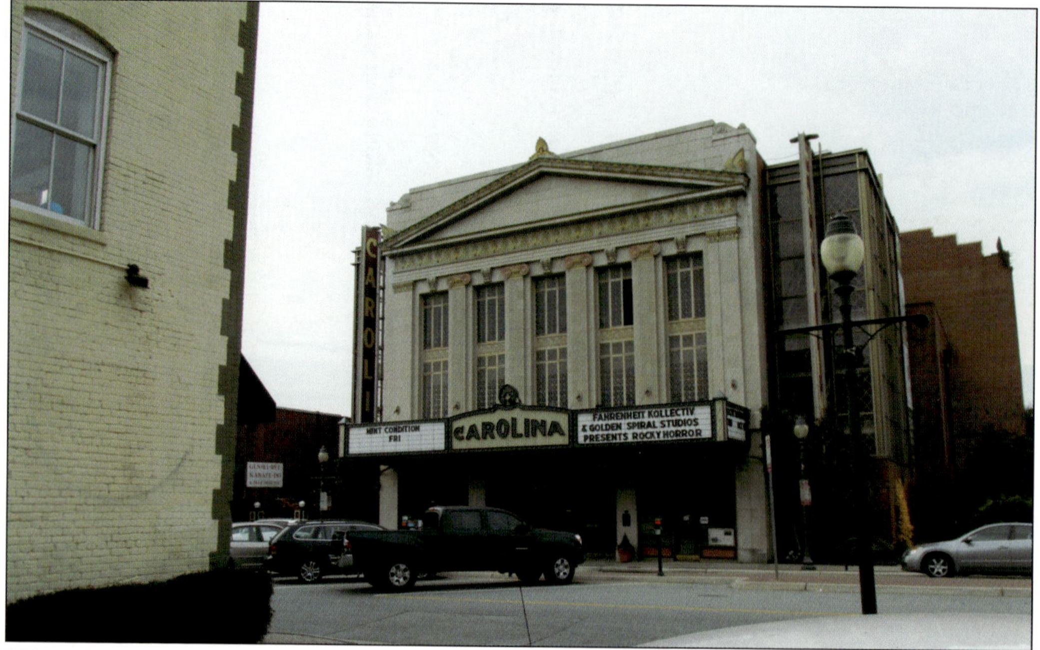

When the Carolina Theatre opened in 1927 at 310 South Greene Street, it was considered the finest theater between Washington, DC, and Atlanta. The structure was threatened by development in the 1970s. The United Arts Council raised over $550,000 for its restoration, bought the theater for $360,000, and opened it in February 1977 as a 1,200-seat performing arts center. In 2006, ownership passed to the Carolina Theatre of Greensboro, Inc.

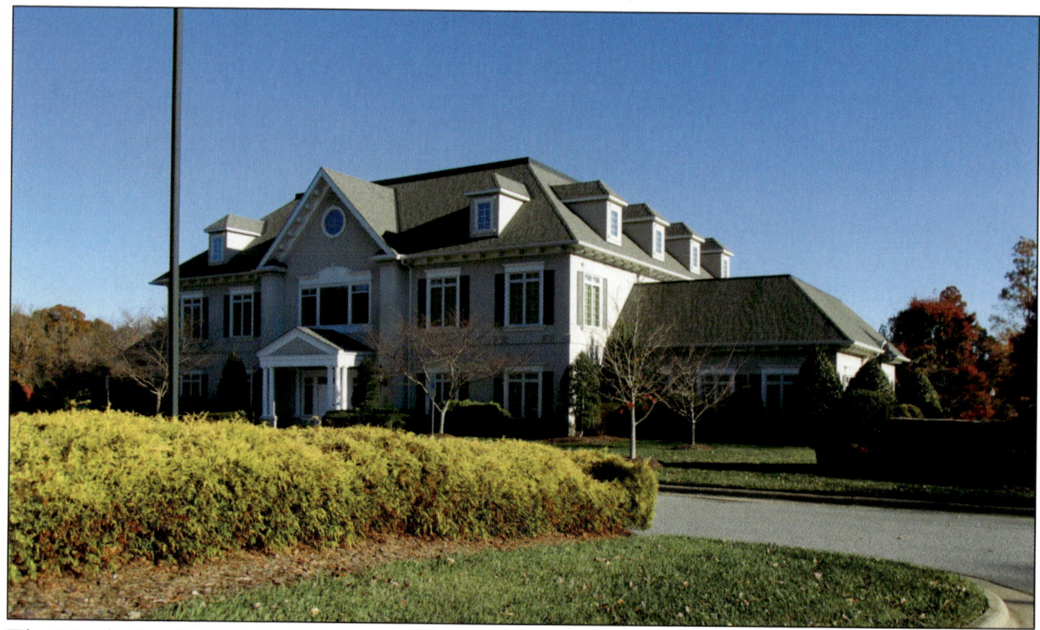

The North Carolina Association of Realtors was founded in 1921 in Greensboro. Its headquarters, at 1030 Homeland Avenue, opened in 1961. In the 1980s, the association moved to 2901 Seawell Road, and in 2002, it moved to its current location, 4511 Weybridge Lane (pictured). (Courtesy of North Carolina Association of Realtors.)

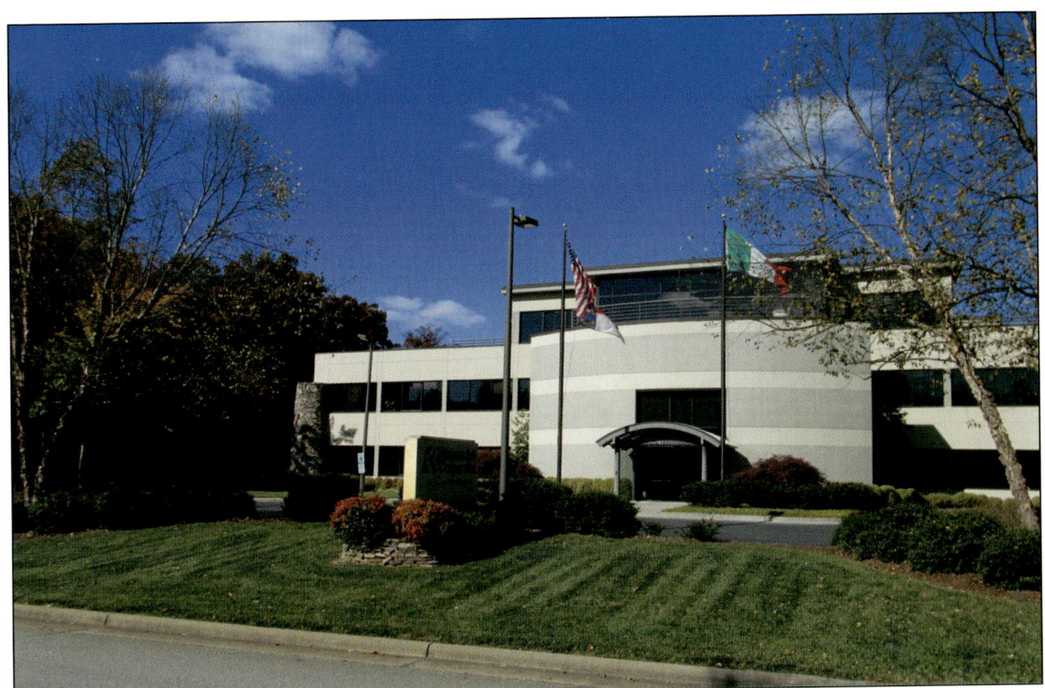

Kayser-Roth was formed in 1958 when Julius Kayser & Company, a half-century-old nylon-hose producer, purchased Chester H. Roth Company. With headquarters at 1004 Howard Street, it launched the No Nonsense hosiery brand in 1973. The company has had different owners, currently Golden Lady Company, Europe's largest hosiery company. The No Nonsense brand has been expanded to other products, and the corporate headquarters is now at 102 Corporate Center Boulevard (shown here).

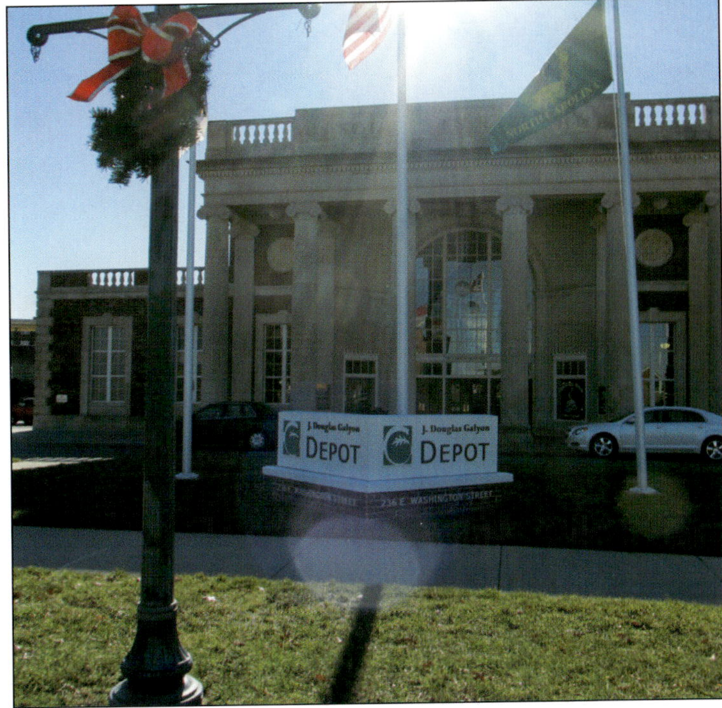

A facility for the Southern Railway was built in 1927 and closed in 1979. The building, then called The Depot, was transformed into a social center. Earlier this century, it was returned to its former use as a train station, as well as the city's bus station. In 2003, it was named J. Douglas Galyon Depot, after a former Greensboro city councilman and chairman of the North Carolina Board of Transportation.

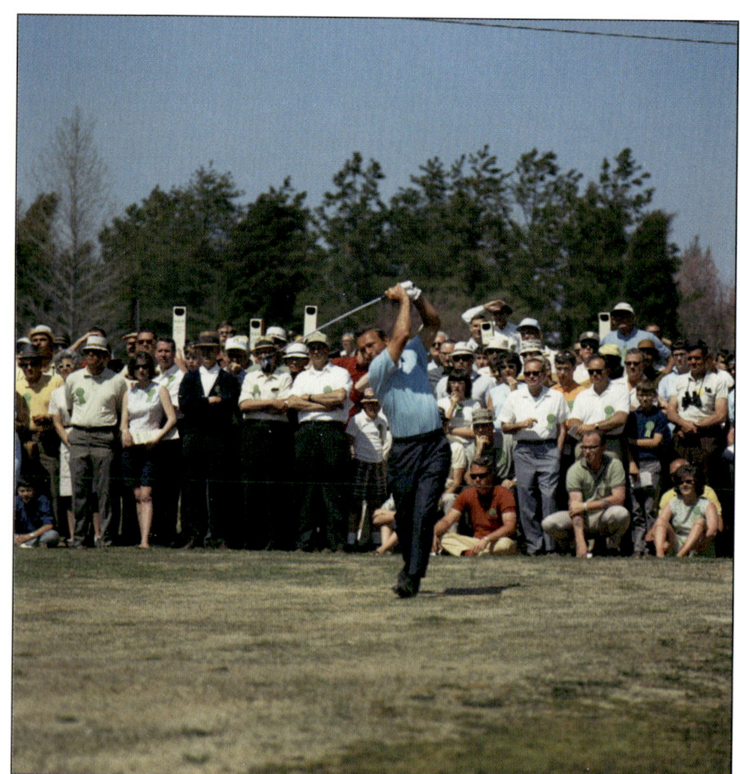

The Greater Greensboro Open (GGO) golf tournament debuted in 1938. Its name was later changed to Gate City Chrysler Classic. Traditionally played in April, the tournament switched to August in 2007. Its name changed again, to the Wyndham Championship. Besides Sam Snead, Arnold Palmer, pictured at the GGO in 1967, was probably the most popular golfer with the local fans. (Courtesy of Carol Martin/Greensboro Historical Museum Collection.)

Kress Department Store was one of several such retailers in downtown Greensboro for most of the 20th century. Kress closed around 1970. Shortly after the beginning of the 21st century, developer John Lomax bought the Kress building. He created a penthouse apartment in it for himself; constructed Kress Terrace on the roof, which is rented out for parties; and established office space in the building.

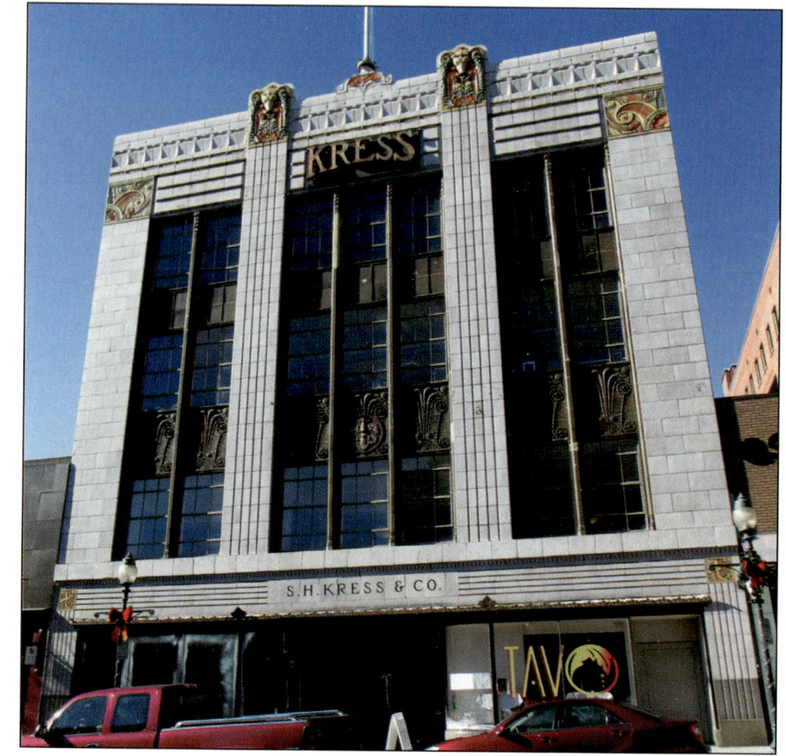

Schiffman's was founded in 1893 by Simon Schiffman at 326 South Elm Street. By 1936, the jeweler was at its third location, 225 South Elm Street, where it still operates today. Arnold Schiffman Jr., grandson of the founder, runs the company along with his sons. In 1971, Schiffman's opened a location at the Friendly Shopping Center. It also operates a Schiffman's in Winston-Salem and five jewelers under different names.

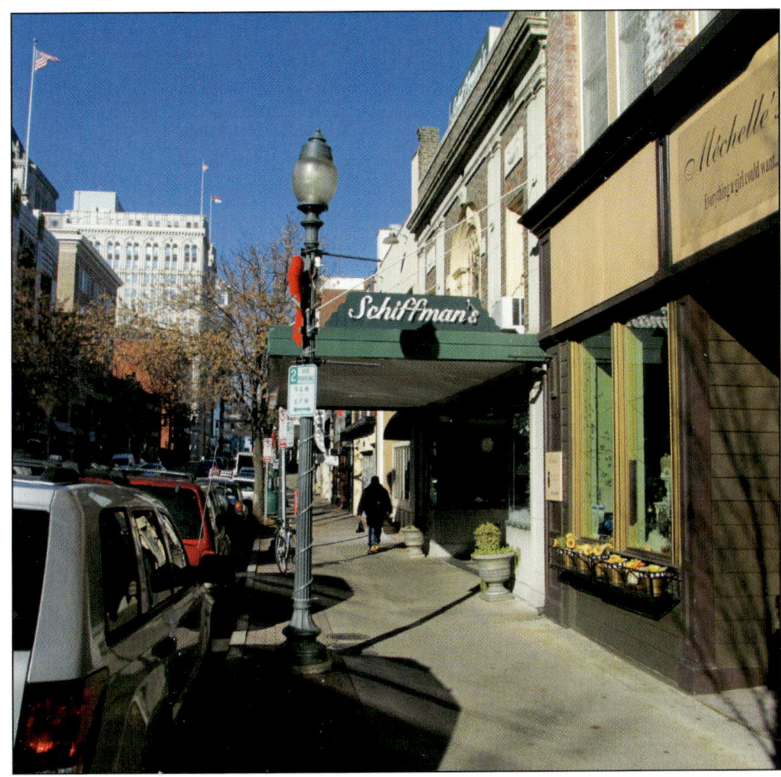

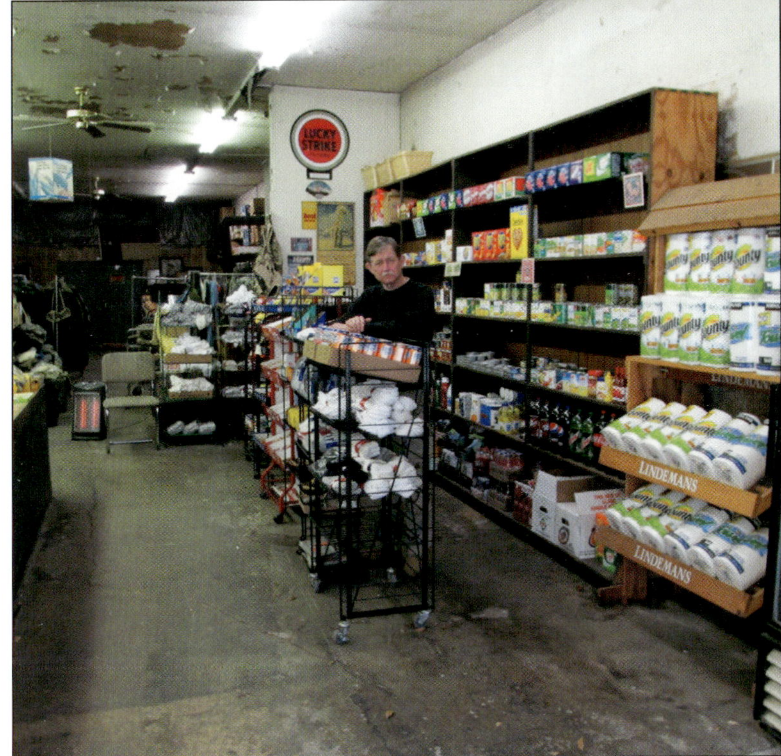

Coe Grocery was started by three brothers in that family in 1902. The company changed location during the early years, but it was always downtown on South Elm Street. By the 1950s, it was at 527 South Elm Street, and it was still there when Charles Coe Jr. sold the store in 1979 to Carlton Fields. In 1998, Fields sold Coe Grocery & Seed to Bill Brooks (shown here), who still owns the store.

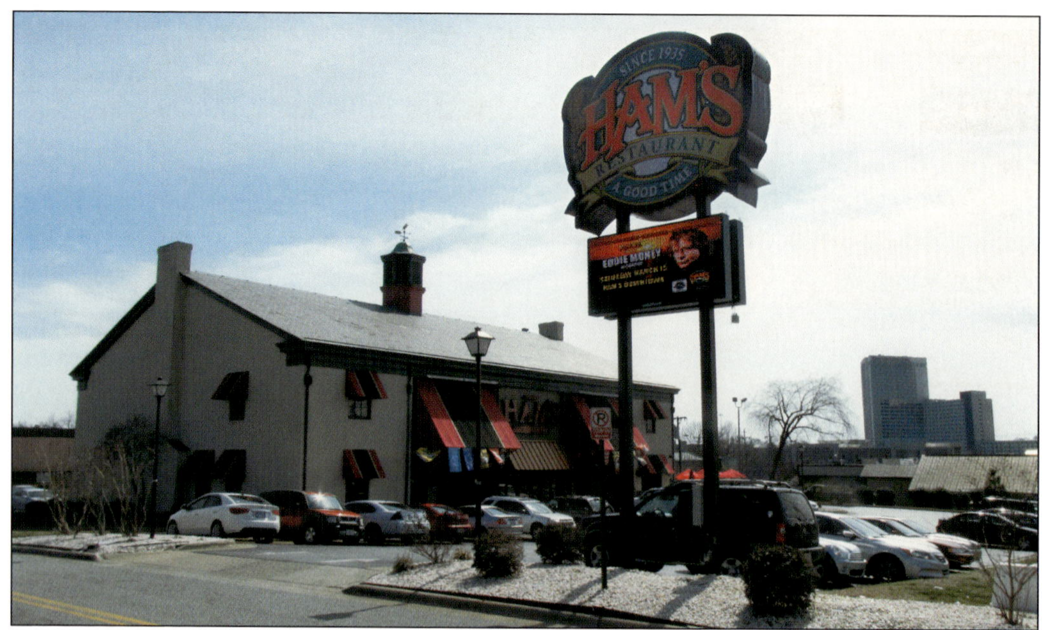

Founded as Ham Drug Company in 1935 by Frank Ham at 201 North Aycock Street, the establishment became Ham's Sundries Store a few years later, when it was sold to Alfred Frieberg and Carl Herbst. A succession of owners followed, and Ham's became a chain. Currently owned by Rocco Scarfone, there are seven Ham's Restaurants, including the one pictured here at 3017 High Point Road. The original is now the Mad Hatter Bar and Grill, specializing in craft beers.

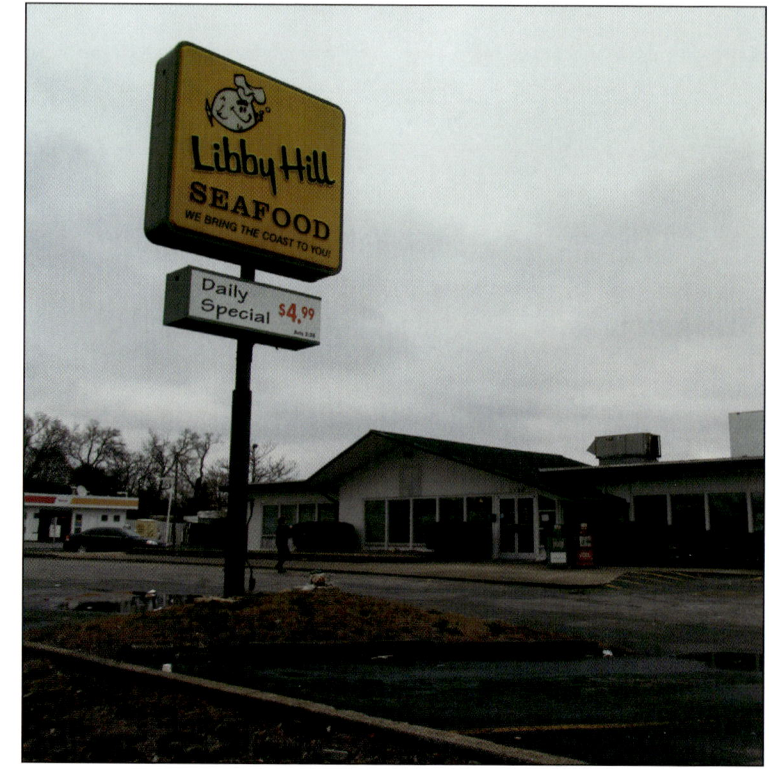

In 1953, Luke Conrad opened the first Libby Hill Seafood Restaurant in an old roadhouse on the corner of US 220 and New Garden Road. Now in the third generation of managemet, with Justin Conrad as president, there are nine Libby Hills, including the one shown here at 1100 Summit Avenue. The original Libby Hills was replaced by one at 3920 Cotswald Avenue. Justin's father, Marshall "Ken" Conrad, is the chairman of the company and president of the National Restaurant Association.

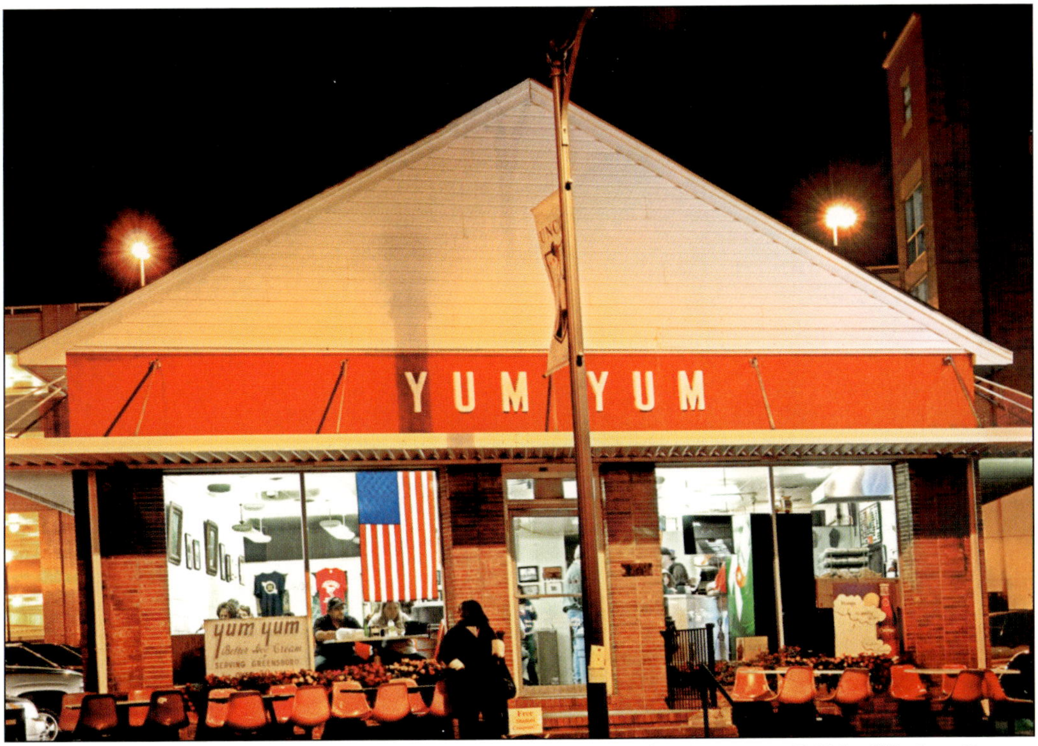

Yum Yum Better Ice Cream was founded at 1200 Spring Garden Street in 1921 by Wisdom Brown Aydelette. In 1972, an expanding University of North Carolina at Greensboro forced Yum Yum to move nearby to 1219 Spring Garden Street, where it continues to prosper, selling its ice cream and hot dogs. It is now operated by Clint Aydelette, the family's third generation in the business. (Courtesy of Greensboro Historical Museum.)

Stamey's Old Fashioned Barbecue was founded in Lexington in 1930. In 1953, founder C. Warner Stamey opened a location at 2216 High Point Road (pictured). There have been Stamey's in other cities, but the only other current location is at 2812 Battleground Avenue. The barbecue is cooked over hardwood hickory coals in a facility behind the High Point Road restaurant. Chip Stamey, grandson of the founder, is now in charge.

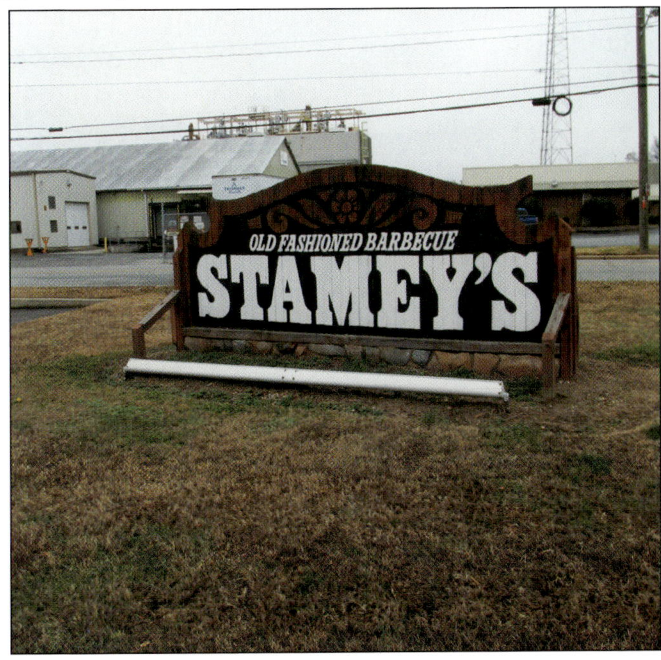

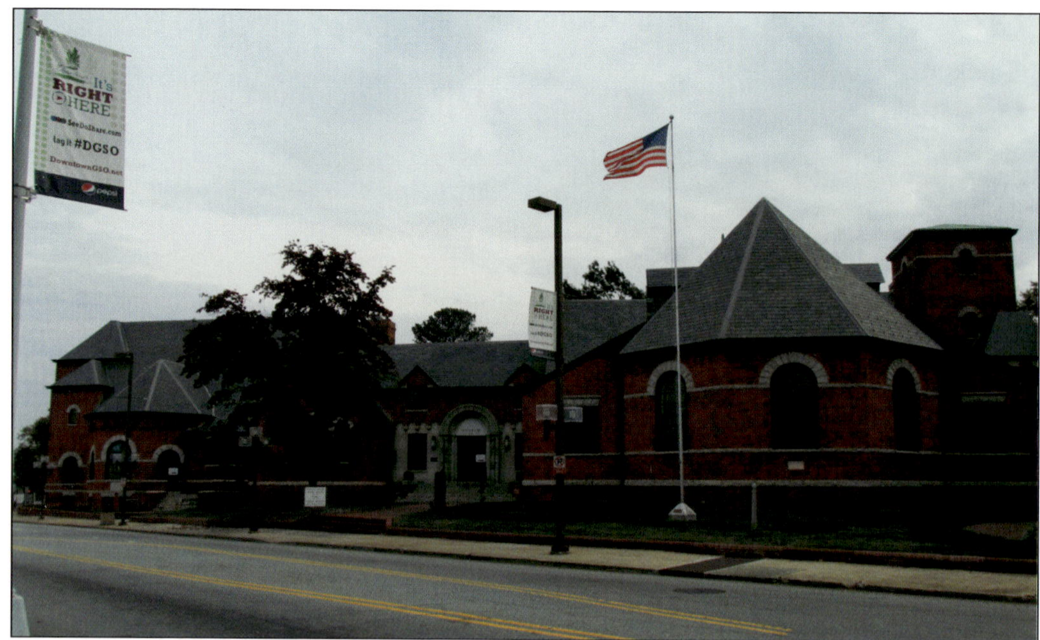

The Greensboro Historical Museum occupies the building at 130 Summit Avenue (above), constructed originally for the First Presbyterian Church. Used as a hospital for the wounded at the Battle of Bentonville during the Civil War, it was abandoned by the church when it built at nearby Fisher Park. The widow of Lunsford Richardson and her three daughters purchased the building in 1939, changed its name to the Richardson Center, and set up the Greensboro Historical Museum, Greensboro Public Library, and other organizations there. Eventually, it was exclusively used for the museum. In addition to displays on Greensboro's history, the museum offers various activities and has hundreds of thousands of photographs and other items in its archives. In 2010, the museum opened the David and Rachel Caldwell Historical Center (below) at 3211 West Cornwallis Drive.

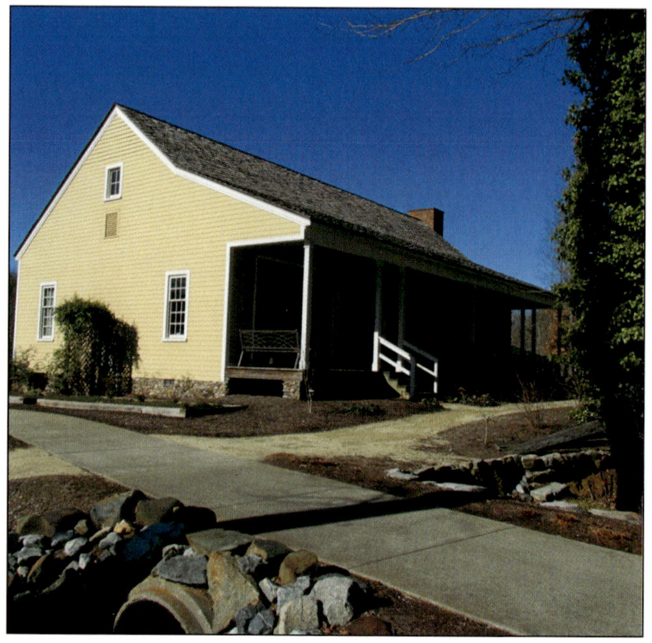

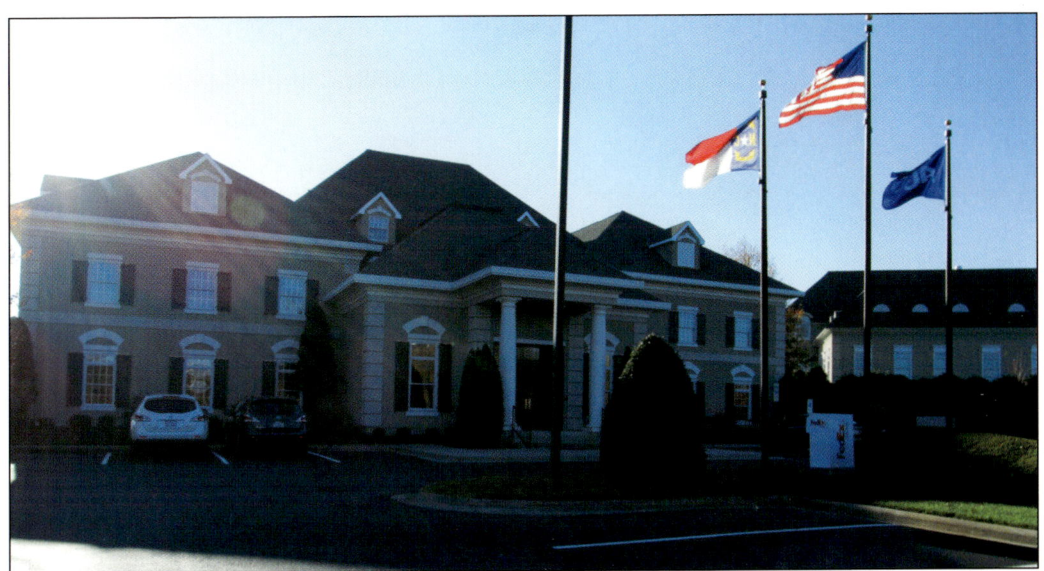

The Atlantic Coast Conference (ACC), founded in 1953 at the Sedgefield Inn, was originally composed of seven schools. As members of the Southern Conference, these institutions felt that the conference was too big, and they disagreed with its ban on postseason play. The ACC's offices were in the King Cotton Hotel (101 South Davie Street) and later the old Wesley Long Hospital. The conference was also located at Cornwallis Square and 6011 Landmark Court Boulevard before moving to its current home at 4512 Weybridge Lane (pictured).

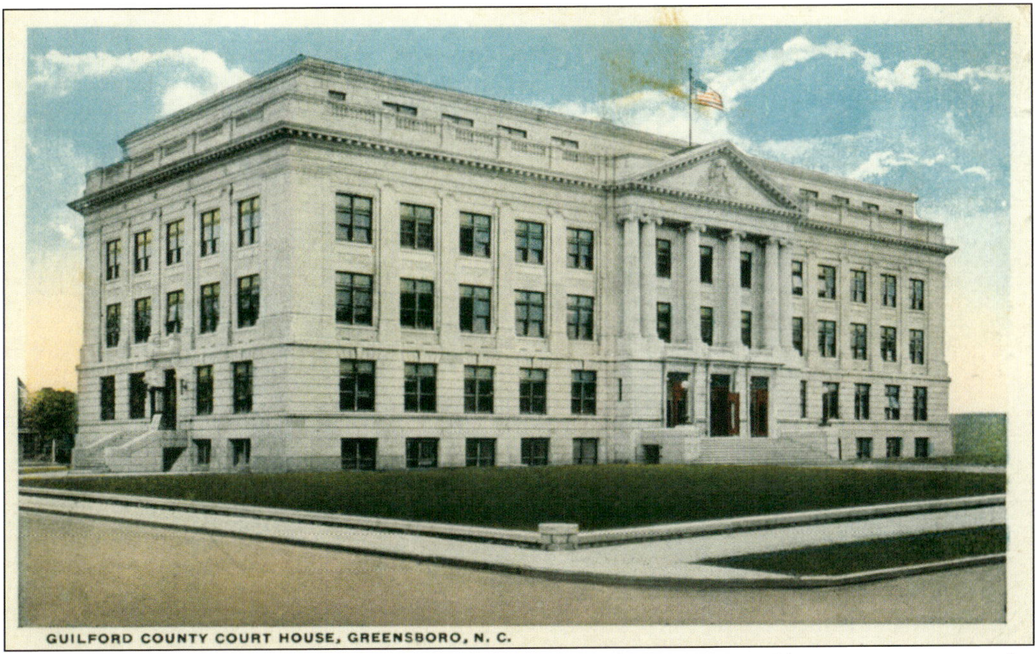

The old Guilford County Court House was at 221 West Market Street. In addition to courtrooms, the building housed the sheriff, the Guilford County Commissioners, the jail, and the engineer. While this courthouse no longer stands (a BB&T Bank building stands there now), a Guilford County Courthouse was the reason Greensboro was created in 1808—and it still has one. The current courthouse is in the governmental complex on Greene Street. (Courtesy of Bill Burris.)

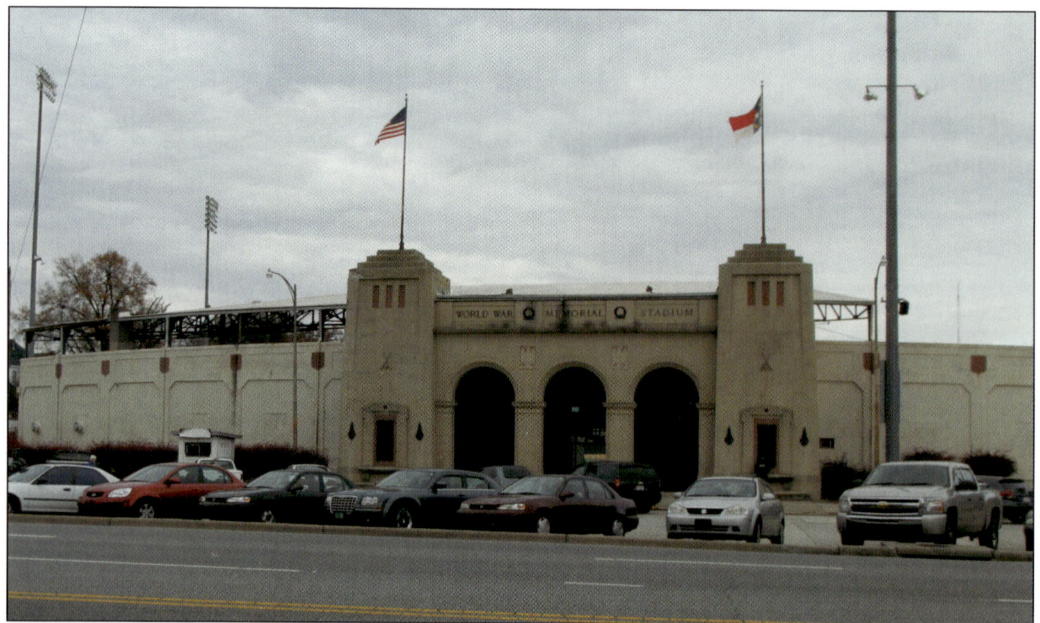

World War Memorial Stadium opened in 1927 with funds raised by the American Legion. Minor-league baseball started there in 1932. An original member of the Carolina League, Greensboro professional baseball left after the 1968 season. In 1979, professional baseball returned with the Greensboro Hornets of the Western Carolina League, which changed its name to the South Atlantic League a year later. Today, the stadium is home to A&T and Greensboro College baseball.

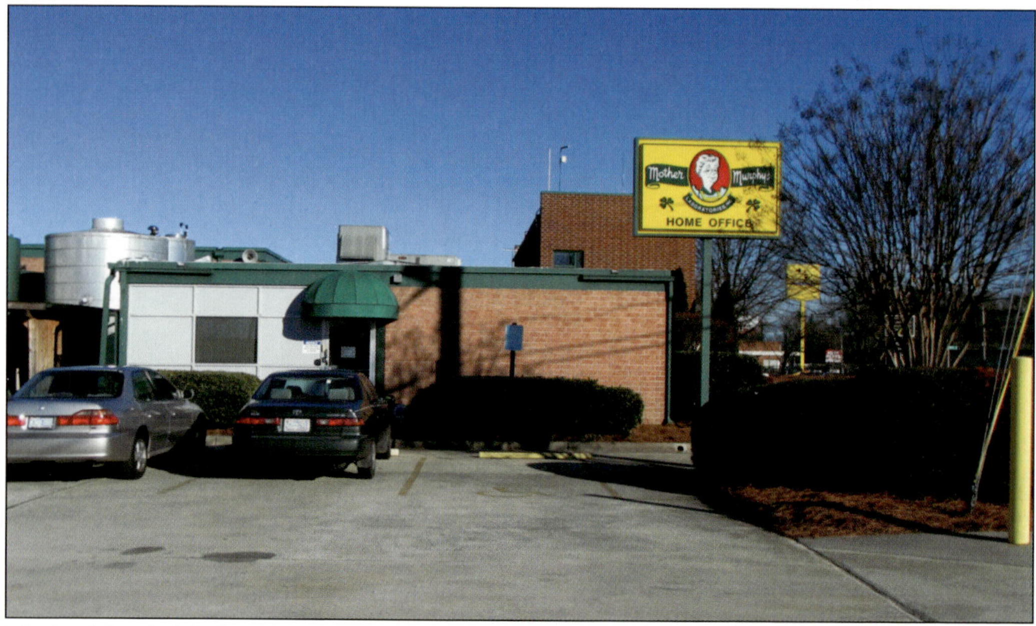

Mother Murphy's Laboratories, cofounded by insurance salesman Kermit Murphy in 1946, moved to its current location, 2826 South Elm-Eugene Street, in 1965. A major producer of vanilla flavorings, it is now operated by the second generation of the Murphy family. It has entered the markets of sweet flavorings and flavorings for dairies, specific drinks, ice cream, tobacco products, and pharmaceutical products.

The Southeastern Building was erected at 102 North Elm Street in 1919 as home to American Exchange National Bank. It has since then housed many businesses and is now owned by developers Barry Siegel and Willard Tucker, who plan to turn the nine-story, 100,000-square-foot building into a combination of offices, apartments, restaurants, and retail establishments. Renovation began in the spring of 2013.

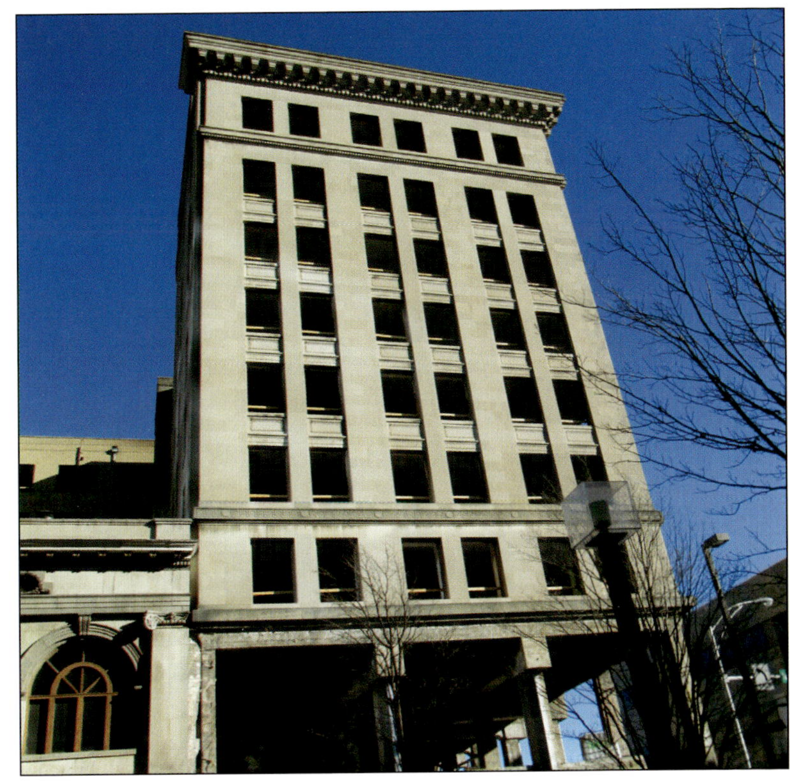

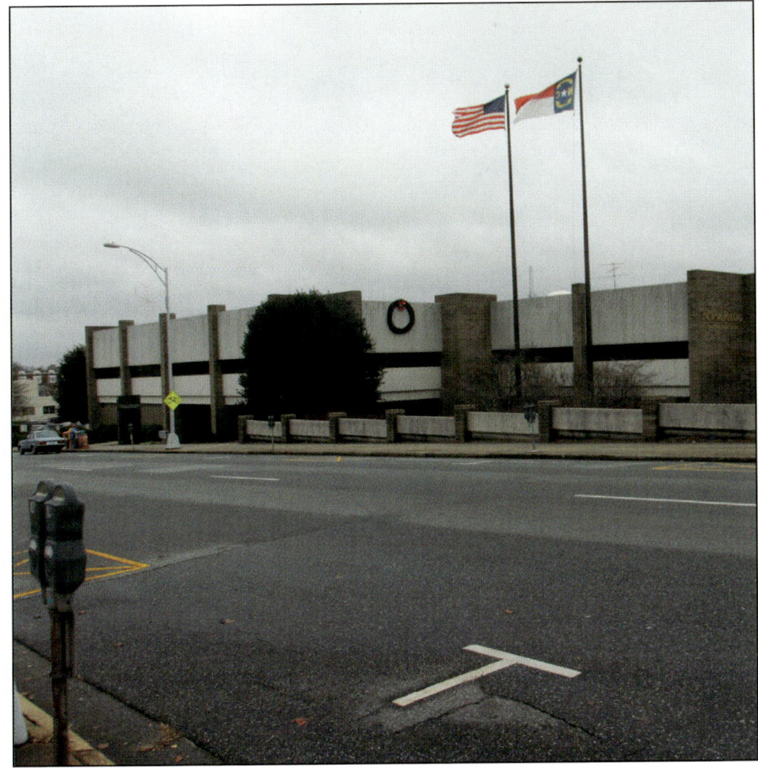

The *Greensboro Daily News*, a morning newspaper, and the *Greensboro Record*, which put out papers six afternoons per week, were sold in 1965 to a Norfolk, Virginia, company, which became Landmark Communications in 1967. During the 1970s, it moved to a building at 200 East Market Street (shown here). In 1984, Landmark consolidated the two newspapers into the *News & Record* and ceased afternoon publication. In 2013, the newspaper was sold to BH Media Group, a Berkshire Hathaway Company.

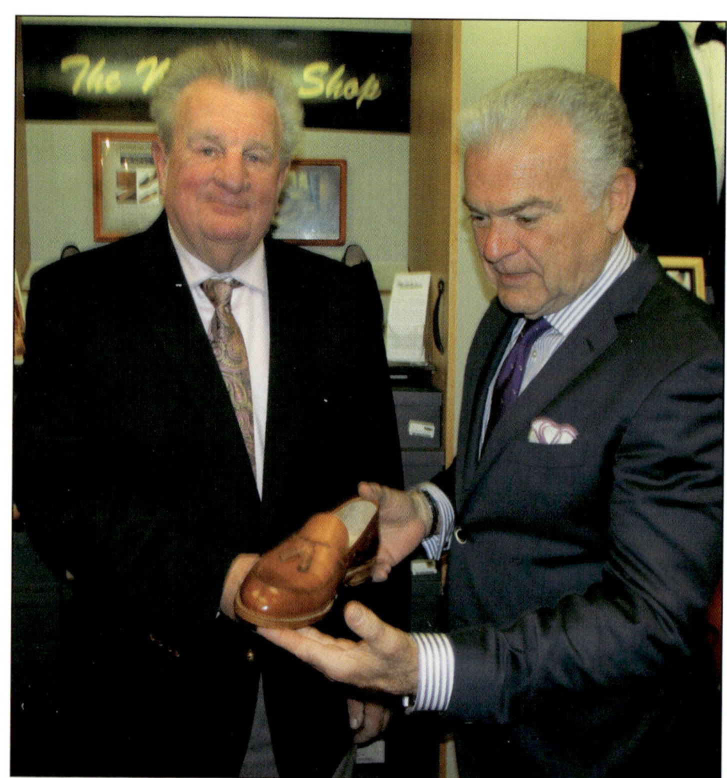

Gordon Turner (left), owner of Gordon's Menswear (3712 Lawndale Drive), and Ed Tognoni, president of the Nettleton Group, examine a Nettleton shoe. Thousands of pairs of this style of Nettleton shoe were sold in the 1960s and 1970s. The shoe was originally known as the Nassau, then employees at the Nettleton factory in Syracuse, New York, started calling it the Greensboro, as over 95 percent of its sales came from there. The Nettleton brand was dormant for a number of years, but Tognoni revived it. Turner then encouraged Tognoni to reintroduce the Greensboro model.

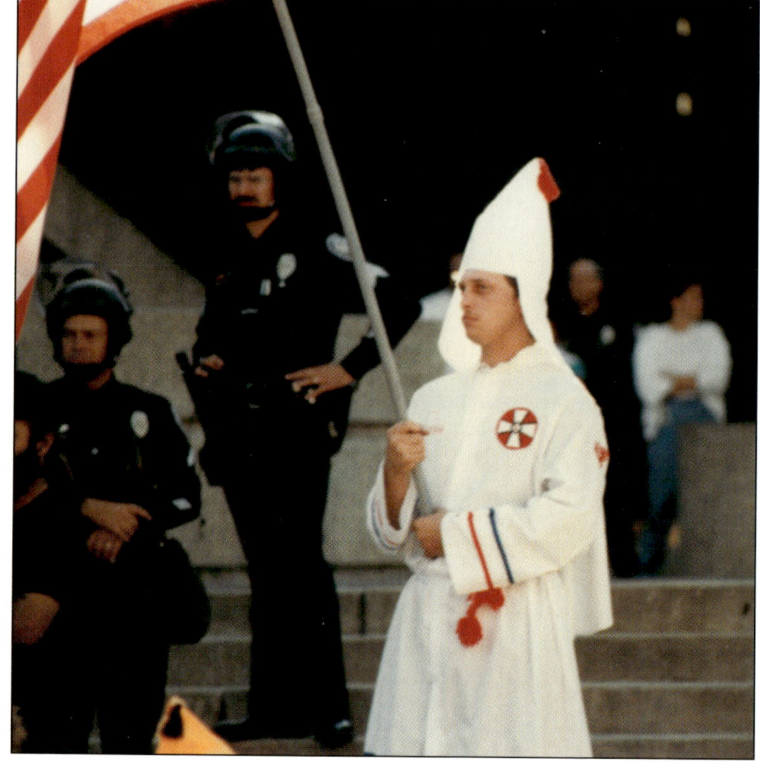

The Ku Klux Klan began in the late 1860s and continues today. In 1979, the Communist Workers Party (CWP) sponsored a "Death to the Klan" rally at Morningside Homes in Greensboro. This led some Klan and Nazi groups from out of town to show up and engage with the workers party. The ensuing encounter left five CWP members dead, four of them white and one of them African American. The mid-1990s demonstration shown here has not been repeated as of this writing. (Courtesy of Gregory Haas.)

Three

ARRIVING

While Greensboro has lost key industry, there have been enough additions to completely change the city's chemistry.

As cell phones became part of everyday life, not only in the United States but worldwide, entrepreneurs found a way to manufacture parts for most of these devices. Also, a forward-looking man in the food-retail business chose Greensboro as the place to try out his idea of the type of supermarket he thought America was ready for. Another local entrepreneur started a chain of factory outlets, the beginning of a major industry in this country. Yet another startup has gone on to become one of the world's leading providers of mortgage insurance.

While Greensboro was not awarded the headquarters for the future Bank of America, it has several branches of that bank here. It is also home to a bank created by the merger of two established banks that had headquarters nearby. A nationally known financier has rescued two well-known companies that had led Greensboro through the 20th century before falling on hard times. Greensboro has also been fortunate enough to gain headquarters of some major truck manufacturers, as well as the leading producer of gasoline pumps.

Perhaps the most significant breakthrough of new companies has occurred near the airport. Among the firms is TIMCO, a world-renowned center for airline maintenance and repair. It also attracted the headquarters of a major new airplane producer. And FedEx set up its mid-Atlantic hub here, something that could snowball as far as Greensboro's future goes.

Retail, residential, and commercial development has changed the looks of the city and the use of its land. Like most cities of Greensboro's size, it has gained a hospice and has developed cultural additions, including a science center and a children's museum. Always a leader among cities its size in park space, Greensboro has added many parks over the years, including Tanger Family Bicentennial Garden, Barber Park, and Price Park. But the key addition on the part of the government has to be the Greensboro Coliseum.

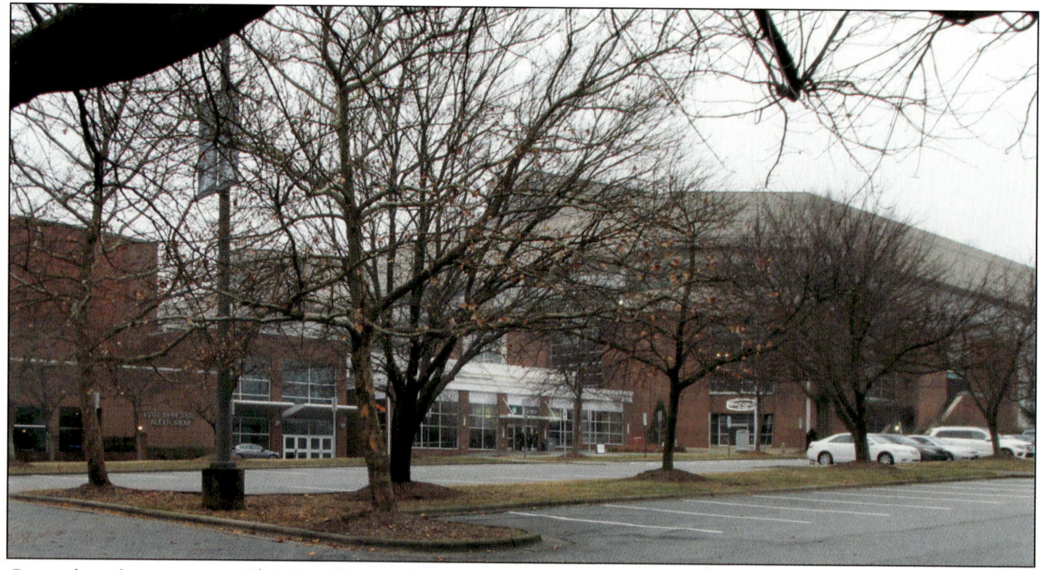

Completed at a cost of $4.5 million, the Greensboro Coliseum opened October 29, 1959, with a seating capacity of 7,100. It now seats more than 23,000. In addition to the aforementioned Cougars and Hurricanes, the coliseum has been home to the minor-league hockey teams Greensboro Generals and Greensboro Monarchs. It has also been host to National Basketball Association exhibition games, as well as college basketball, including ACC tournaments. Currently, the coliseum serves as the home court for UNCG men's basketball. It regularly hosts conventions and concerts. The 1921 West Lee Street site includes several other buildings.

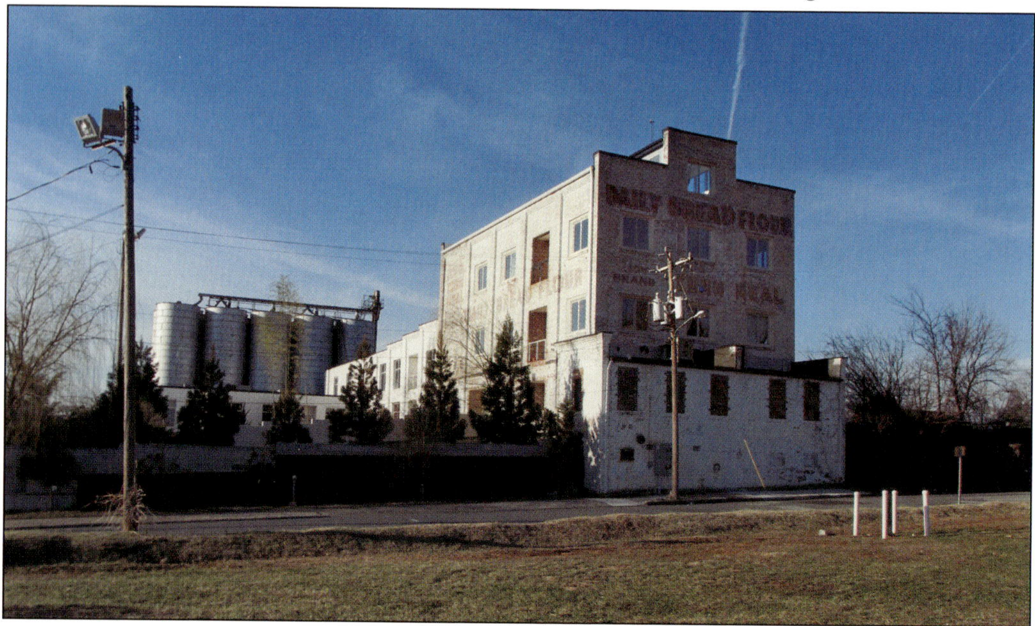

Prospect Brands, which had been in Stoneville, is already listing the pictured address, at 816 South Elm Street, as its headquarters. The former site of a flour manufacturer is being converted to offices as well as retail space to sell the brands. Prospect acquired Duck Head Apparel, a company that has been in business since 1865, in November 2013. Its other brand is Gerbing, a line of heated clothing for outdoor enthusiasts. Manufacturing will continue in Stoneville.

Greensboro Cultural Center is at 200 North Davie Street, in the building that housed the daily newspapers for many years. It was opened in 1988 after a $2 million renaissance campaign to give art organizations in the city a downtown home. Operated by the Greensboro Parks & Recreation Department, it provides studio, gallery, classroom, administrative, and meeting space for 15 local arts organizations.

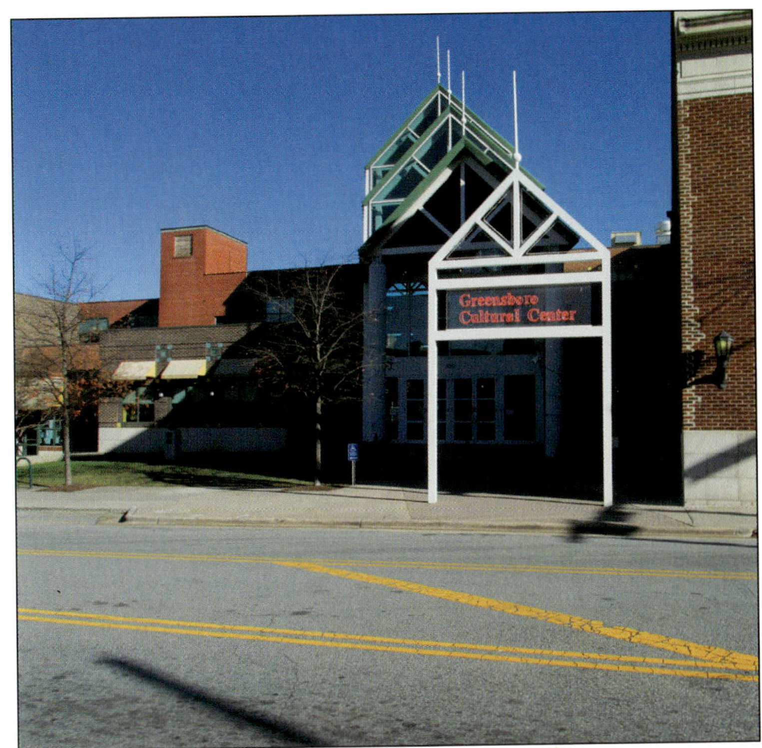

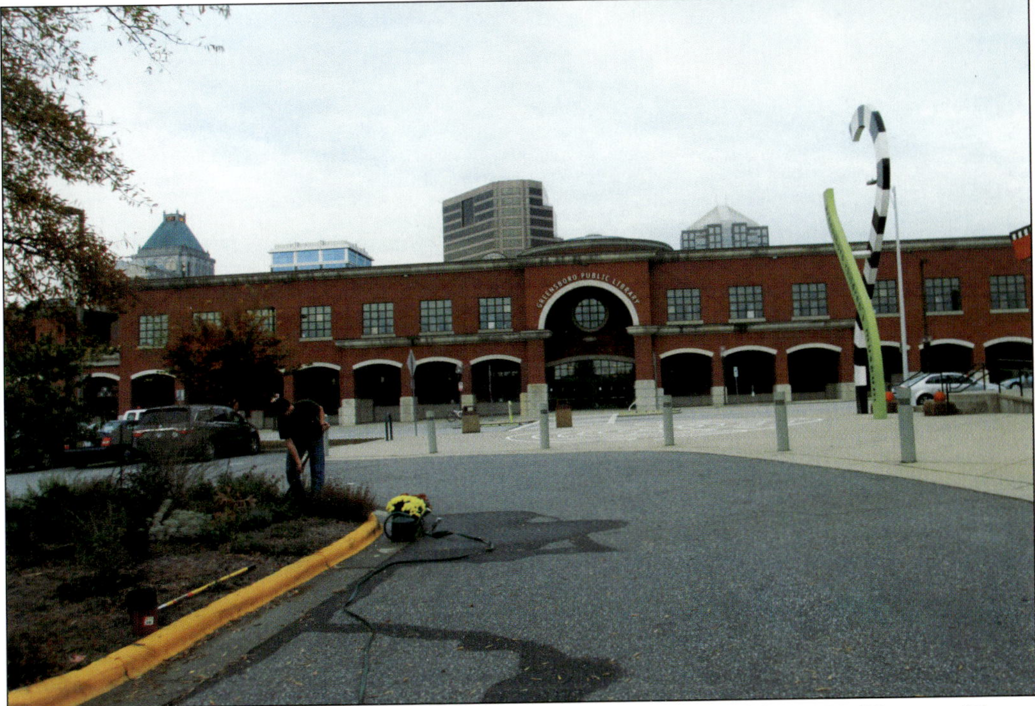

Greensboro Central Library's Greene Street location was outdated by 1974. The new library opened in 1998 at 219 North Church Street. Public space went from 21,800 to 62,000 square feet. The extra space allowed for more public-access computers and other amenities.

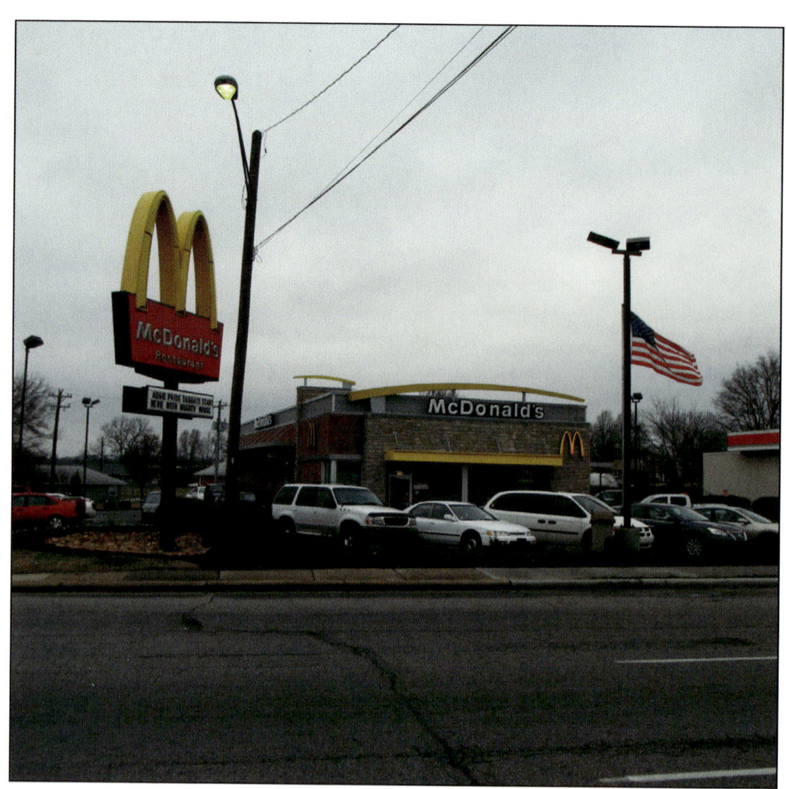

This McDonald's has been remodeled several times, but when it opened at 1101 Summit Avenue in 1959, it was the first McDonald's in North Carolina. On the day it opened, Wilbur Hardee brought an engineer to Greensboro. After studying the new McDonald's, they stayed at the nearby Oaks Motel and designed a similar building. This led to the opening of the first Hardee's restaurant in Greenville, North Carolina, in 1960.

Biff (Best In Fast Food) Burger had three locations in Greensboro by 1962. Biff Burger once had 3,400 restaurants, but the company developed financial difficulties. That did not stop Ralph Havis from continuing his restaurant at 1040 West Lee Street. When his franchise fee was returned in 1972, Havis changed the name of his operation to Beef Burger, and he has been operating as an independent restaurateur ever since.

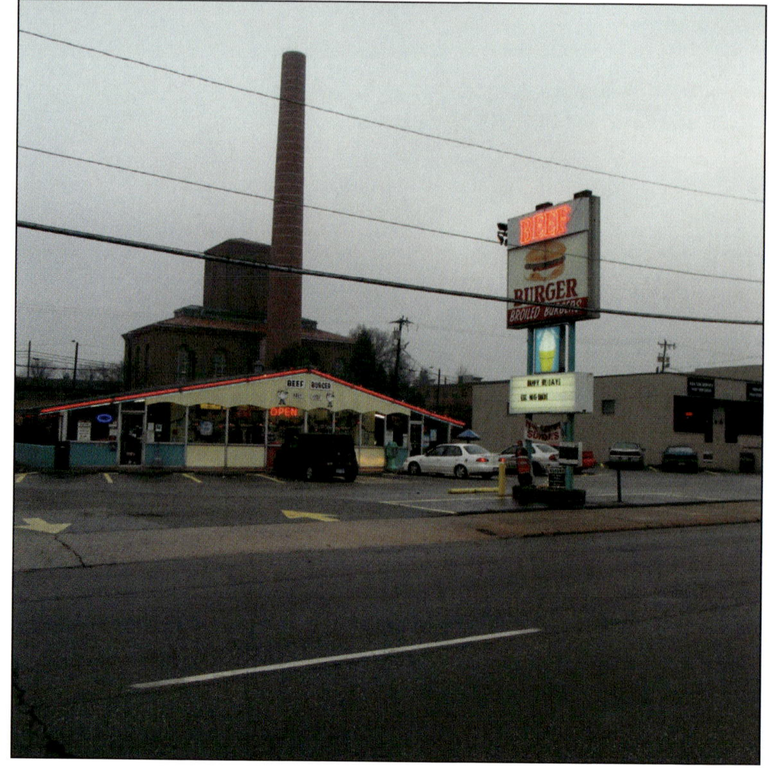

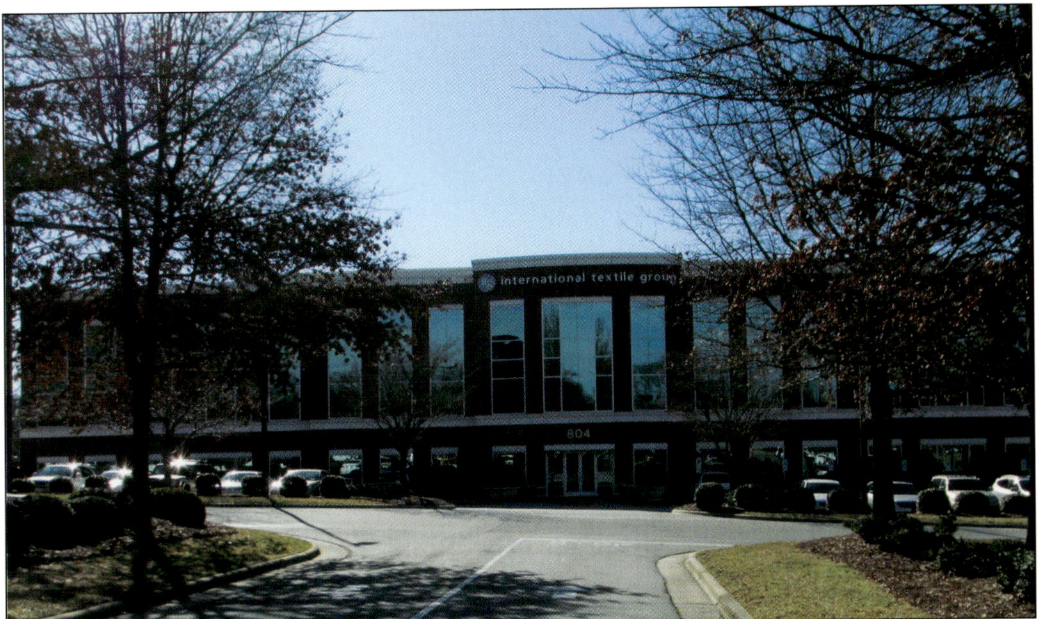

Financier Wilbur Ross purchased the assets of Burlington Industries in 2003 and Cone Mills in 2004, combining them to form International Textile Group, located at 804 Green Valley Road. The White Oak plant still produces denim for Cone Mills. The Burlington division has nearby plants producing denim, specialty nylon products used in automotive airbag systems, and specialty military products. (Courtesy of ITG Corporation.)

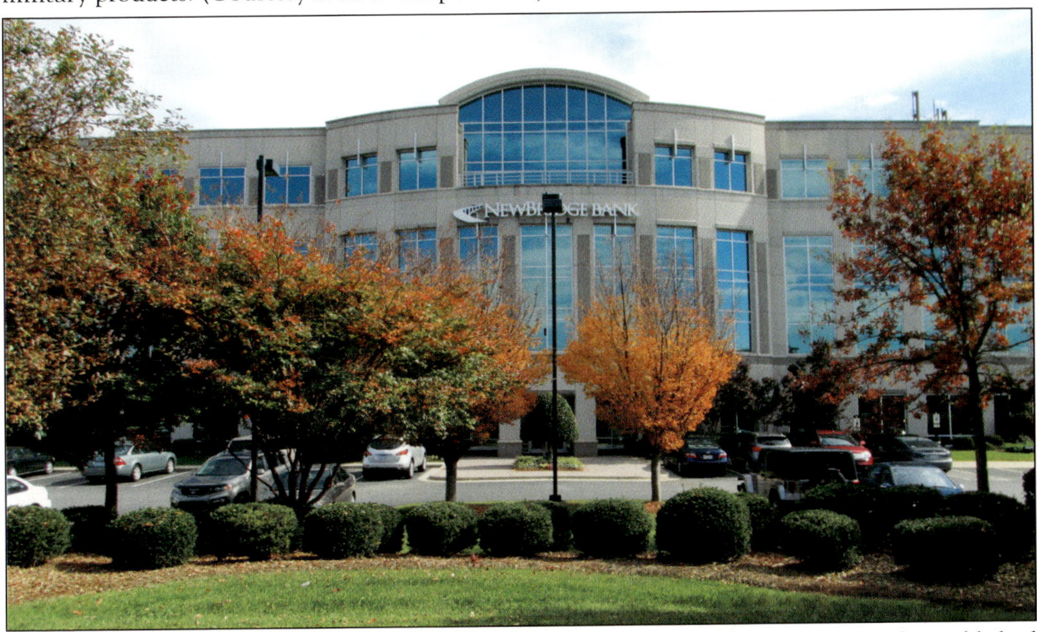

NewBridge Bank was formed in November 2007 by the merger of Lexington State Bank, established in Lexington in 1949, and FNB, founded in Reidsville in 1910. The headquarters was set up at 1501 Highwoods Boulevard (shown here). The new company became the largest bank with a Greensboro headquarters and one of the largest community banks in North Carolina. It has assets of about $2.4 billion and about 40 locations throughout the state.

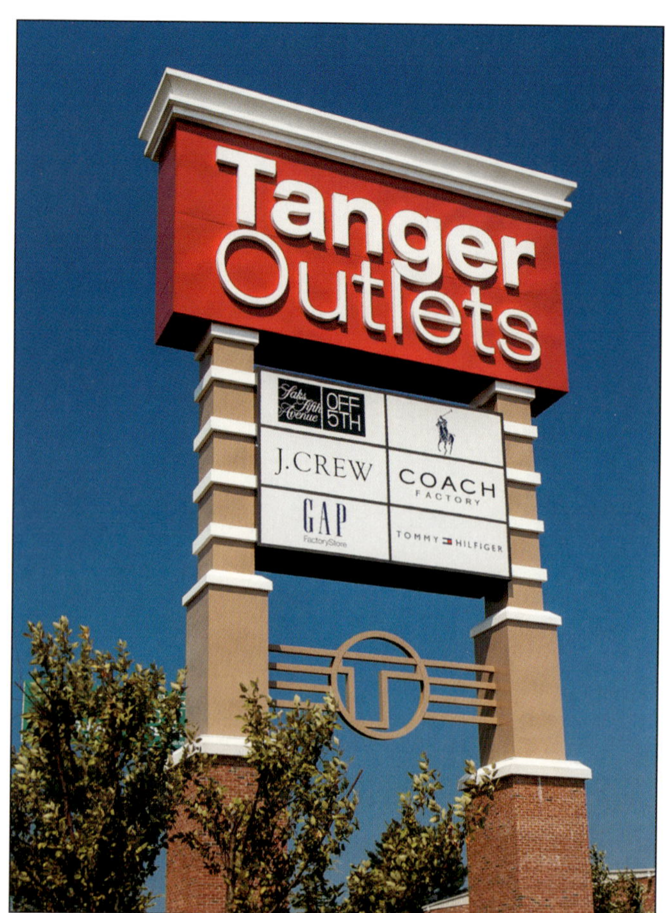

Tanger Factory Outlet Centers has its headquarters at 3200 Northline Avenue. Stanley Tanger operated Creighton Shirt Manufacturers out of Reidsville. Creighton had an outlet store at the plant and, at the opening of Cotton Mill Square, opened an outlet in Greensboro. In 1981, Tanger, leaving manufacturing for the outlet business, started the first authentic outlet center in the United States, Burlington Manufacturers Outlet Center. In 1993, Tanger was the first outlet center real estate investment trust (REIT) to be listed on the New York Stock Exchange. Stanley's son Steven Tanger replaced his father as CEO in 2009. He is seen below at the stock exchange, holding the gavel. As of this writing, the company operates 43 outlets throughout the United States, the closest one to Greensboro being in Mebane. (Both, courtesy of Tanger Factory Outlet Centers, Inc.)

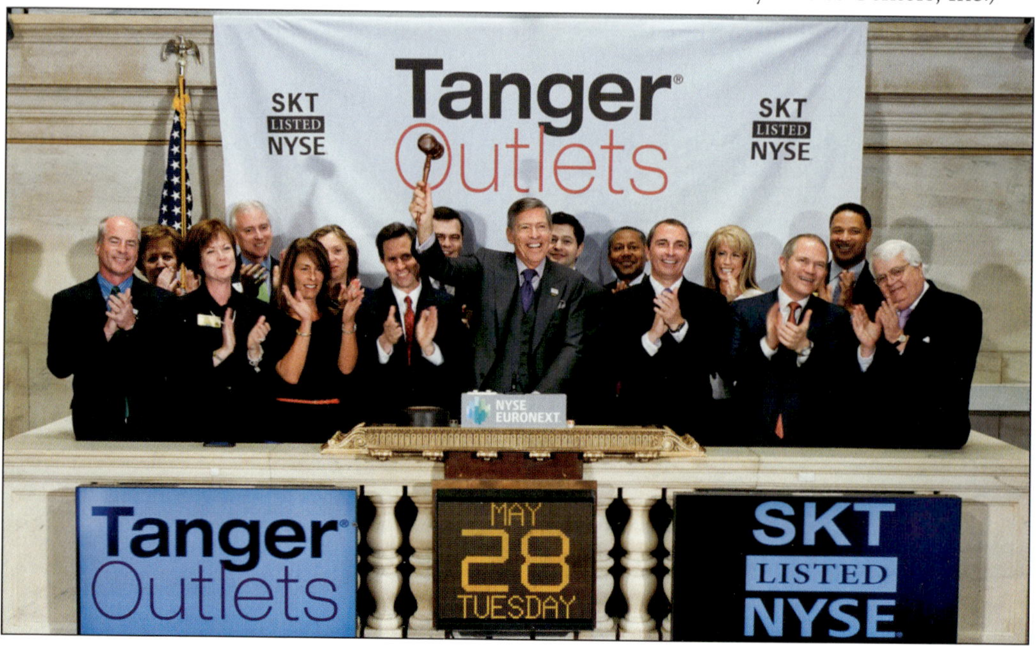

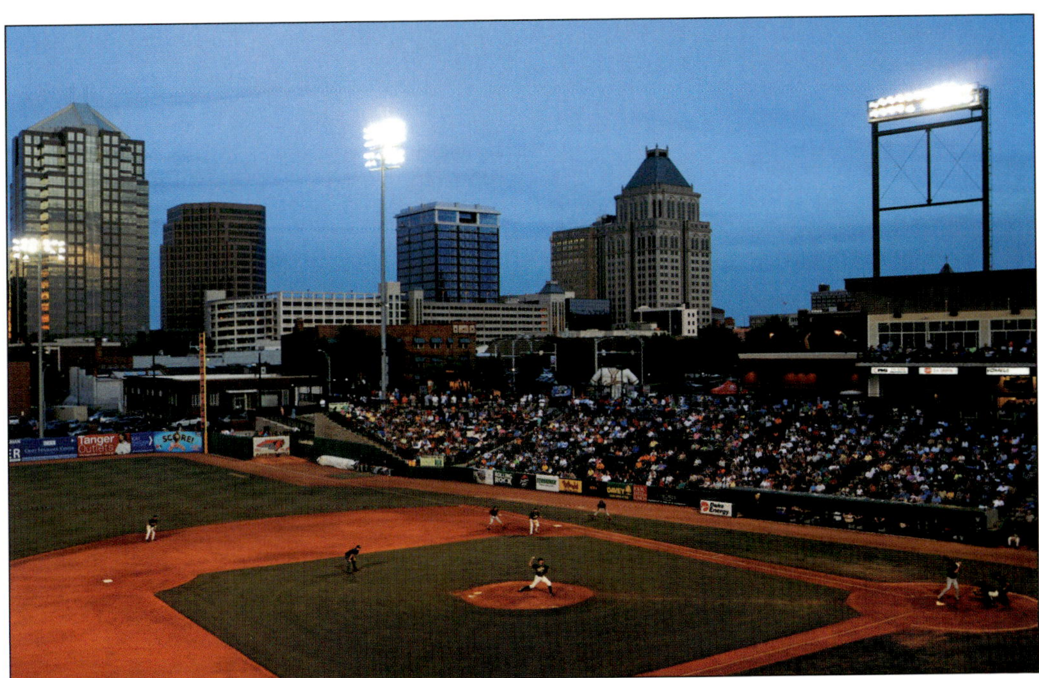

Greensboro minor-league baseball owners had expressed their desire for a new stadium since the 1980s. Initially, there was interest in building a stadium in the airport area, but that would have been blocked by the Winston-Salem baseball franchise because of its territorial rights. Then came the effort to lure a Major League Baseball team, which failed in 1998. Finally, E.S. "Jim" Melvin, who headed the Joseph M. Bryan Foundation, assembled a group of 200 people to buy the Greensboro Bats. He also worked in acquiring the land and arranging the construction for a ballpark. There was an effort to change the zoning to keep the proposed stadium out of the downtown district, but that referendum failed. The Bryan Foundation built the new stadium, at 408 Bellemeade Street, in time for the 2005 South Atlantic League season. Today, it is known as NewBridge Bank Park. The team changed its name to Greensboro Grasshoppers when it moved into the new stadium (Above, courtesy of Lynn Donovan.)

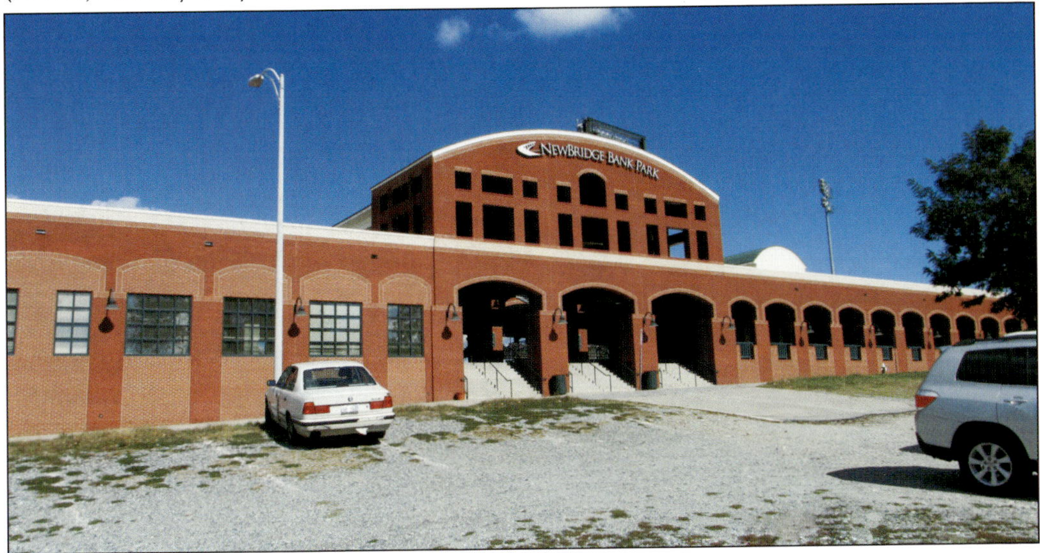

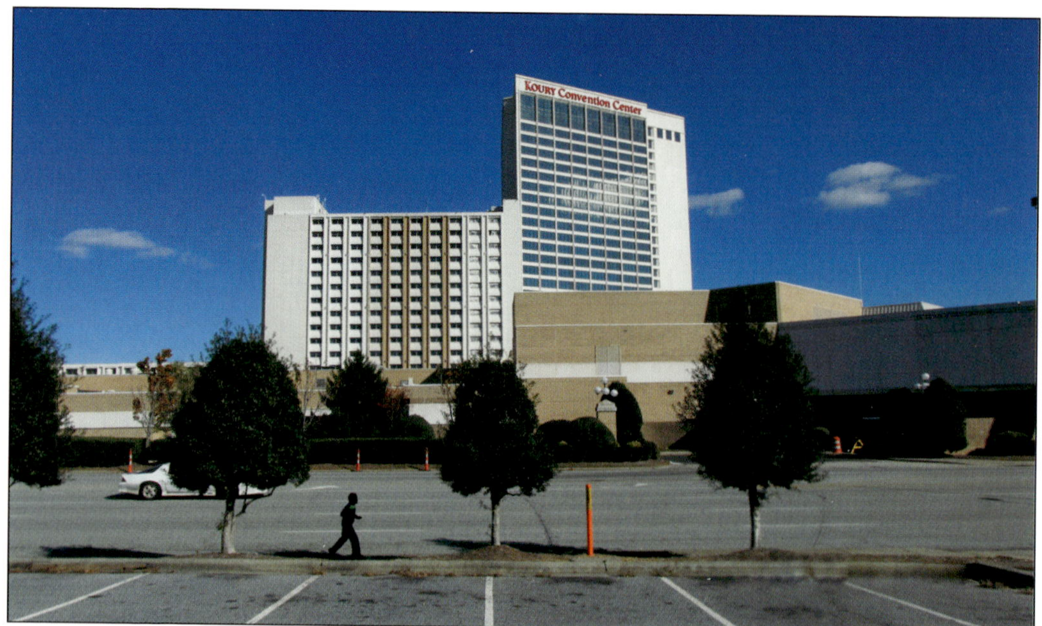

Joseph Koury was the most prolific developer in the history of Greensboro. He is credited with building more than 8,000 homes, 14 residential neighborhoods, 7 shopping centers, and 9 major office buildings. Starting in 1952, Kirkman & Koury began building the homes and neighborhoods. Koury opened the Holiday Inn Four Seasons at the corner of High Point and Pinecroft Roads. By 1974, he had established the Four Seasons Mall (below), now known as Four Seasons Town Centre. In the 1980s, he built the Joseph S. Koury Convention Center (above), the largest such facility between Atlanta and Washington. The Holiday Inn eventually became a Sheraton. (Below, courtesy of Carol Martin/Greensboro Historical Museum Collection.)

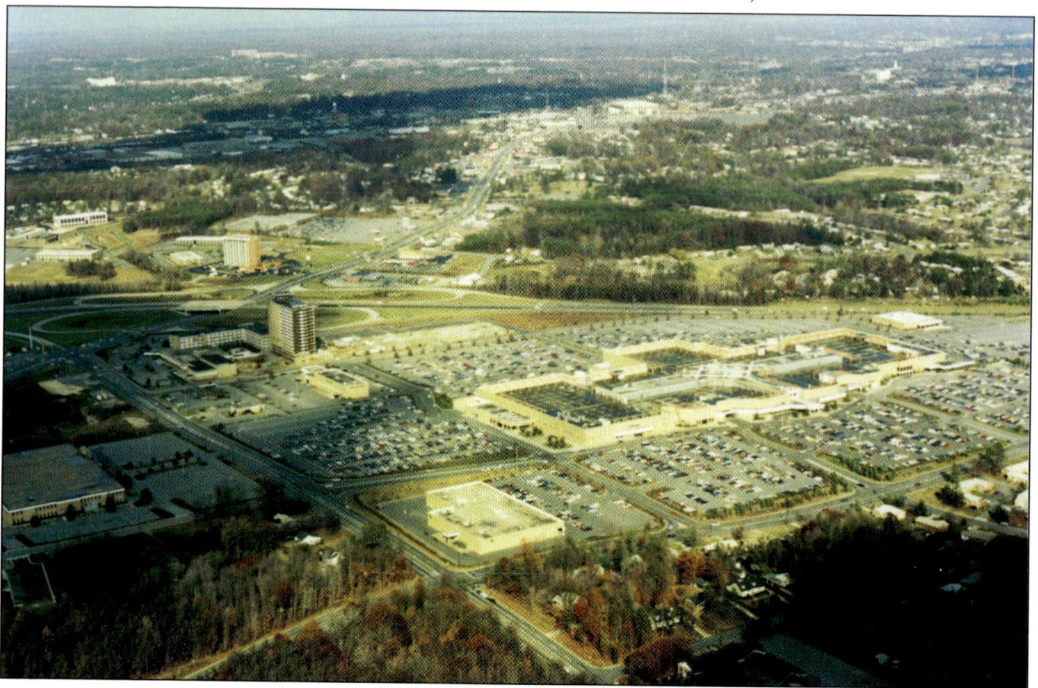

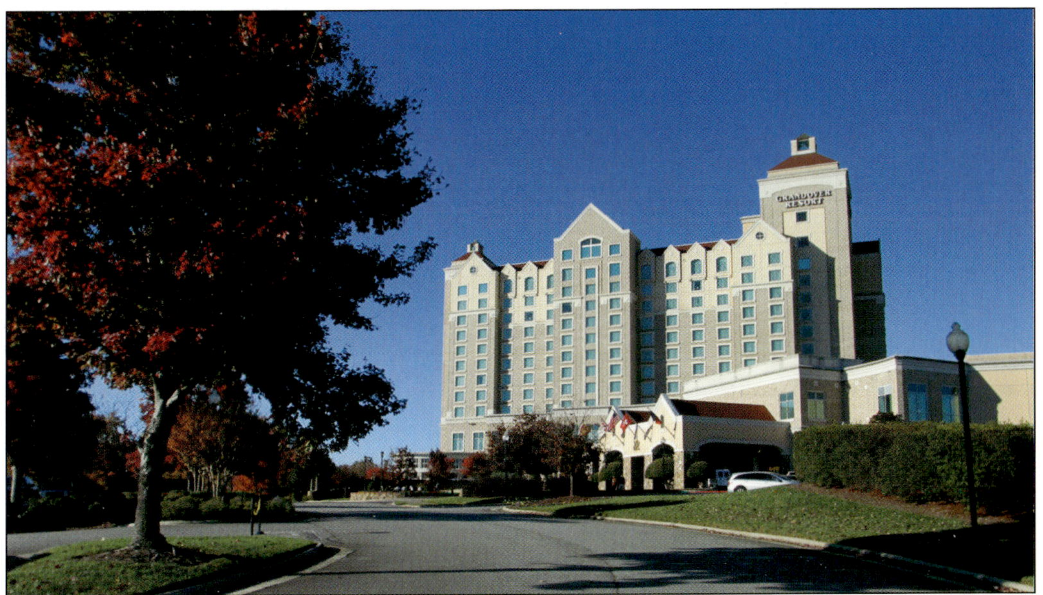

Koury's last major project was Grandover Resort. In the late 1960s, a major tract of land was being put together in hopes of landing an Anheuser-Busch plant in Greensboro. When that did not pan out, Koury worked to acquire the land, eventually the site of Grandover Resort, built around a top-flight golf course and a luxury hotel.

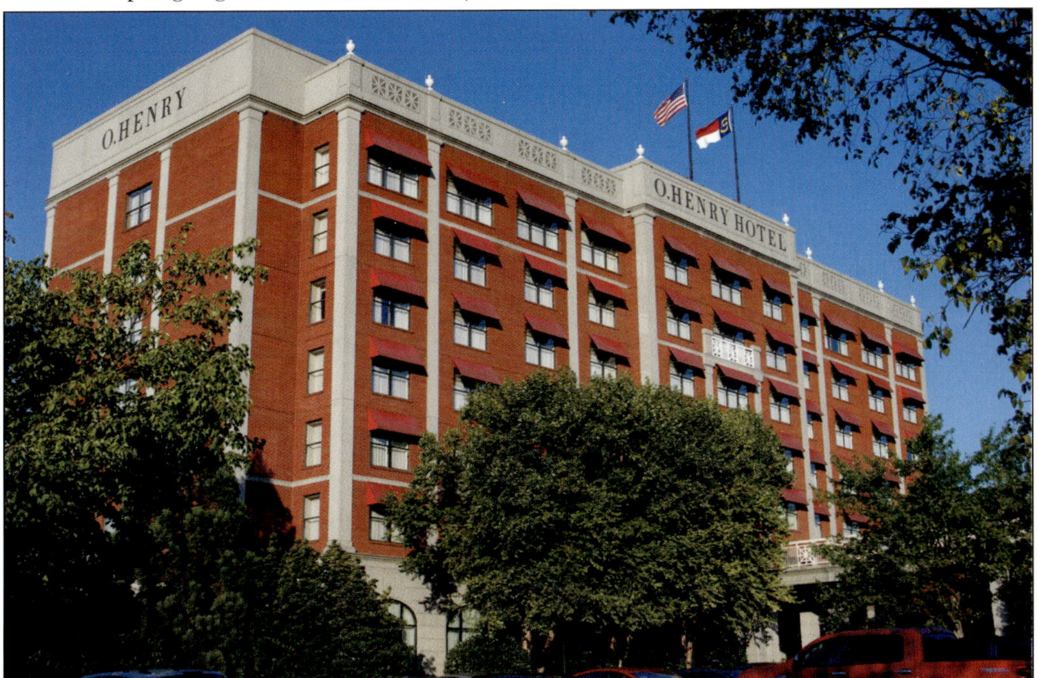

Another builder and operator of fine hotels in Greensboro is Dennis Quaintance, who, along with Mike Weaver, operates a newer version of the O. Henry Hotel, which opened in 1998 at 624 Green Valley Road; the Proximity Hotel opened in 2007 at 724 Green Valley Road. Quaintance and Weaver also operate the Green Valley Grille at the O. Henry, the Printworks Bistro by the Proximity, and other upscale restaurants. (Courtesy of O. Henry Hotel.)

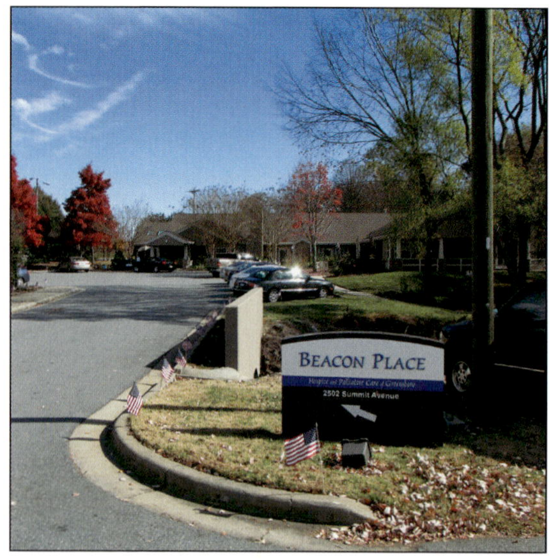

Hospice and Palliative Care of Greensboro opened in 1984 at Moses Cone Hospital. After using a facility at 706 North Greene Street, it opened Beacon Place (left) at 2500 Summit Avenue in 1996. Beacon Place serves patients at the end of their lives. In addition, the hospice offers care in the patient's home as well as other facilities in and around Greensboro. In 2001, alongside Beacon Place, Kids Path (below) opened for the care of terminally ill children and children losing someone. Recently, the hospice staff announced plans to build a 15,000-square-foot education and administration building on 6.75 acres of land it has acquired across the street.

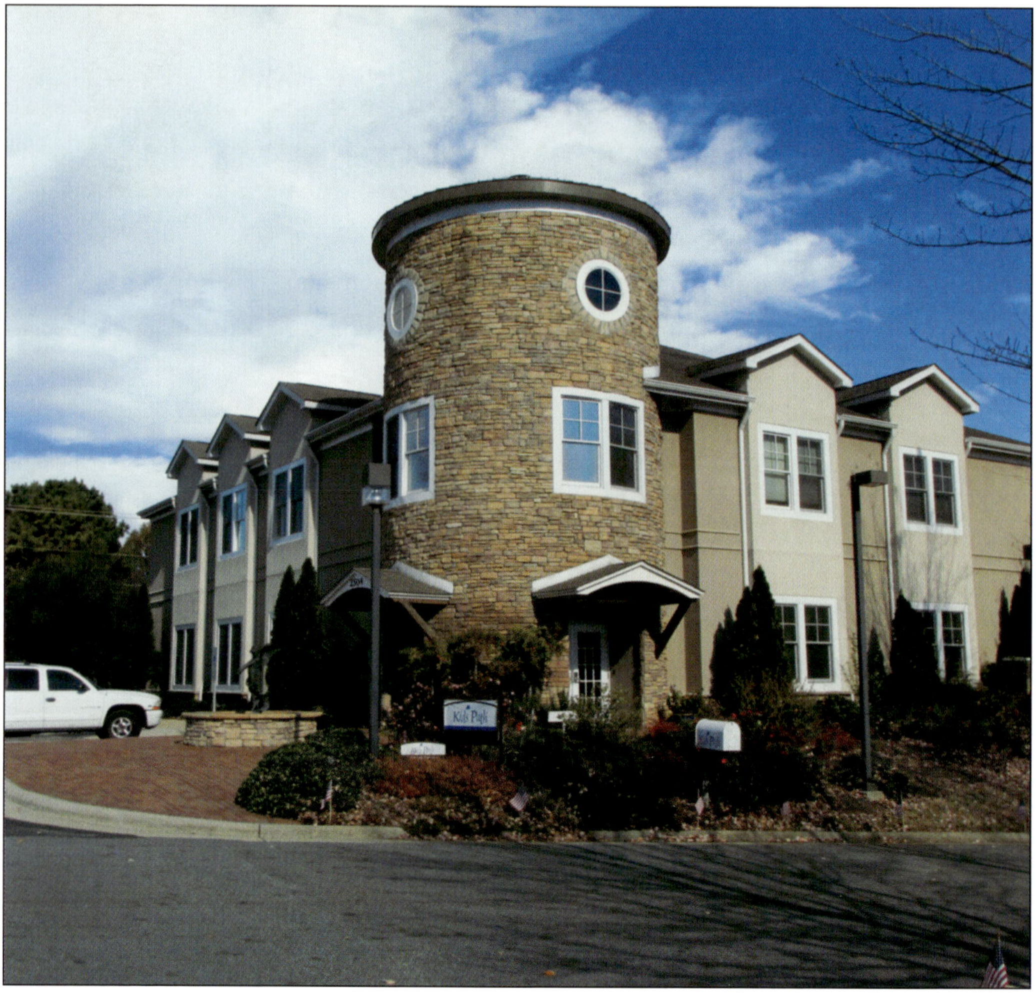

In 2006, Honda
Aircraft began
taking orders for
the new HondaJet.
It set up world
headquarters at 6430
Ballinger Road,
near Piedmont
Triad International
Airport, and
production is
just now getting
underway. As of
this writing, the
company expects
its first plane to
be delivered in
early 2015.

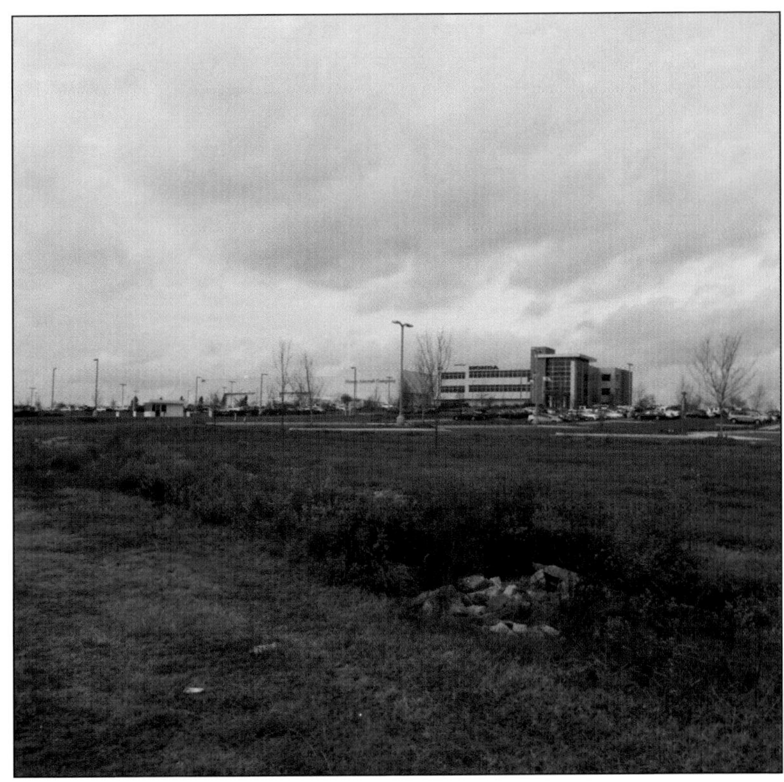

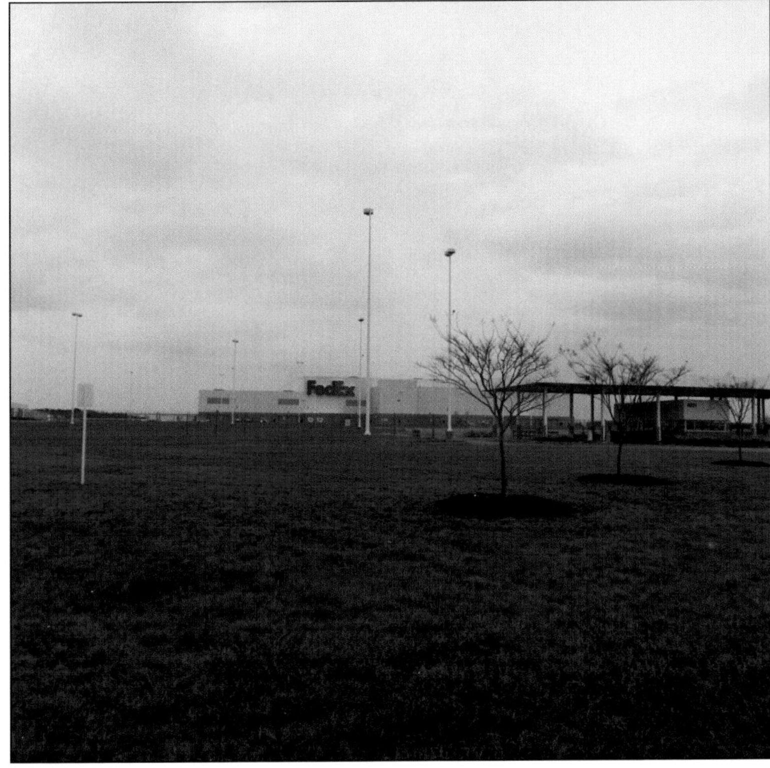

In 1998, Federal
Express chose
Piedmont Triad
International Airport
(PTIA) as the site
of its new Mid-
Atlantic Regional
Hub. A third runway
was built at PTIA
to accommodate
the new activity.
It opened in 2009,
at 6035 Old Oak
Ridge Road. It has
yet to reach hub
capacity, but this
facility is considered
a major reason
why Greensboro
may develop into
an aerotropolis.

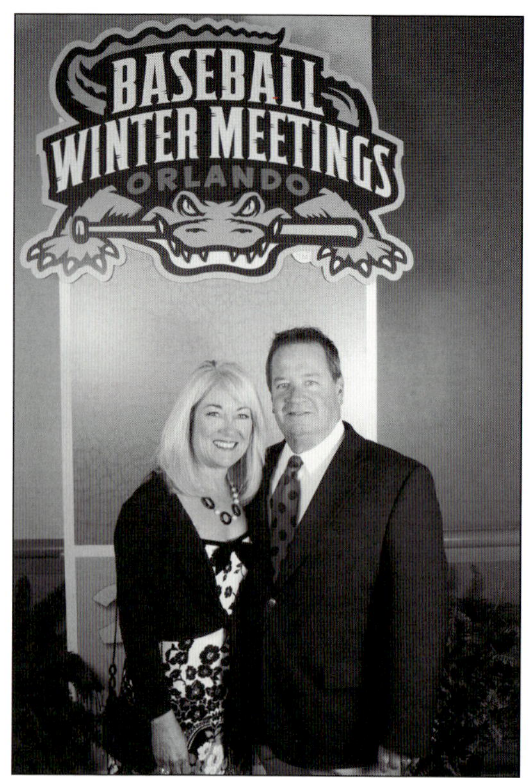

The Carolina League, formed in 1945, is classified as a High-A baseball league. Greensboro was a charter member of the league, staying through 1968. Greensboro resident John Hopkins, who had been general manager of the Greensboro Hornets, became the Carolina League's president in 1984 and set up his office at 1806 Pembroke Road. Seen here are Hopkins and his wife, Dru, at the Baseball 2010 Winter Meetings in Orlando, Florida. (Courtesy of Minor League Baseball.)

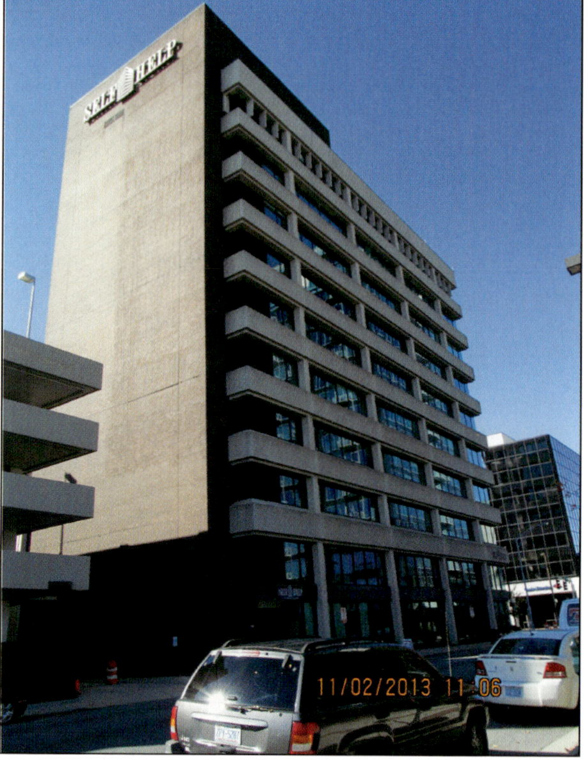

Self Help, at 100 South Elm Street, is a full-service, 10-story office building that rents exclusively to nonprofits. It is the old First Union Building, originally constructed in 1970. Self Help took over the building in 1996. The organization, based in Durham, rents to nonprofits and counsels them. Amenities for tenants include free conference rooms, access to copiers and postal equipment, and counseling. (Courtesy of Self Help.)

The Millennium Gate at Phill G. McDonald Plaza illustrates a variety of events that happened, mostly in this area, during Greensboro's history. The government complex, which includes the Melvin Municipal Building as well as courthouses and state and county government agencies, was named in 1988 after the first person from Greensboro to be killed in the Vietnam War. (Courtesy of Lynn Donovan.)

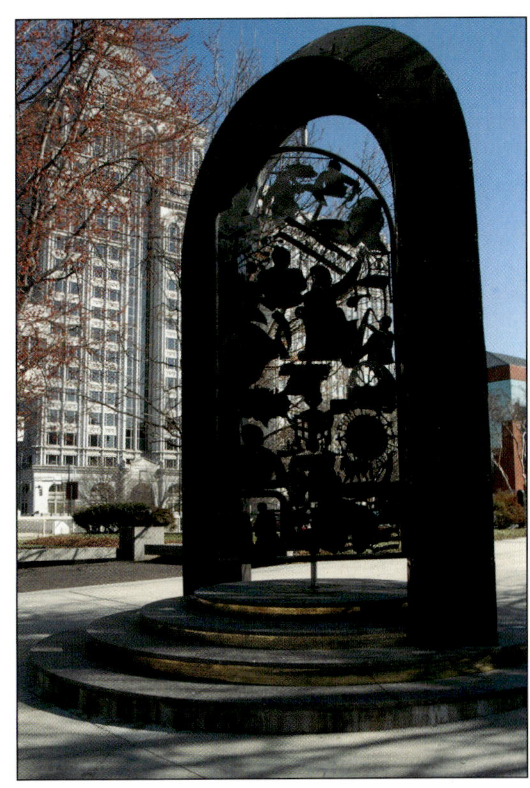

War Memorial Auditorium opened in 1959, along with other original segments of the Greensboro Coliseum Complex. A smaller venue than the coliseum itself, the auditorium was used for concerts. On March 26, 2008, presidential candidate Barack Obama held a town meeting there. It is now said to be in need of repair and outdated, and it is slated to be replaced by the Steven Tanger Performing Arts Center in downtown Greensboro.

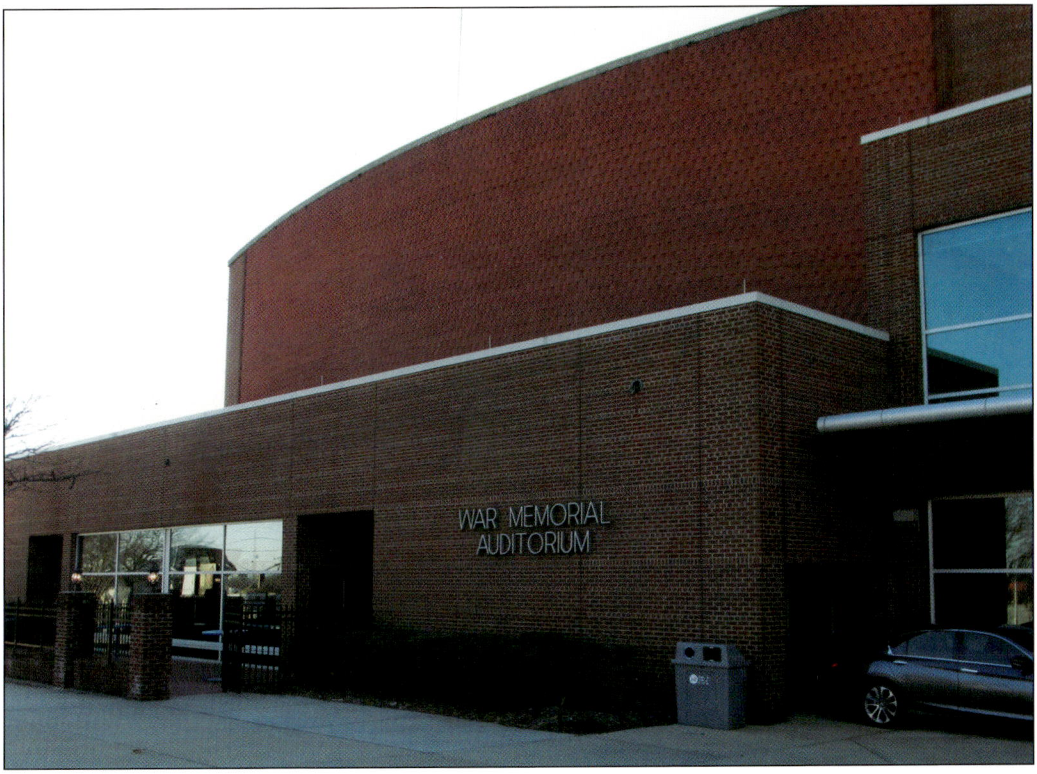

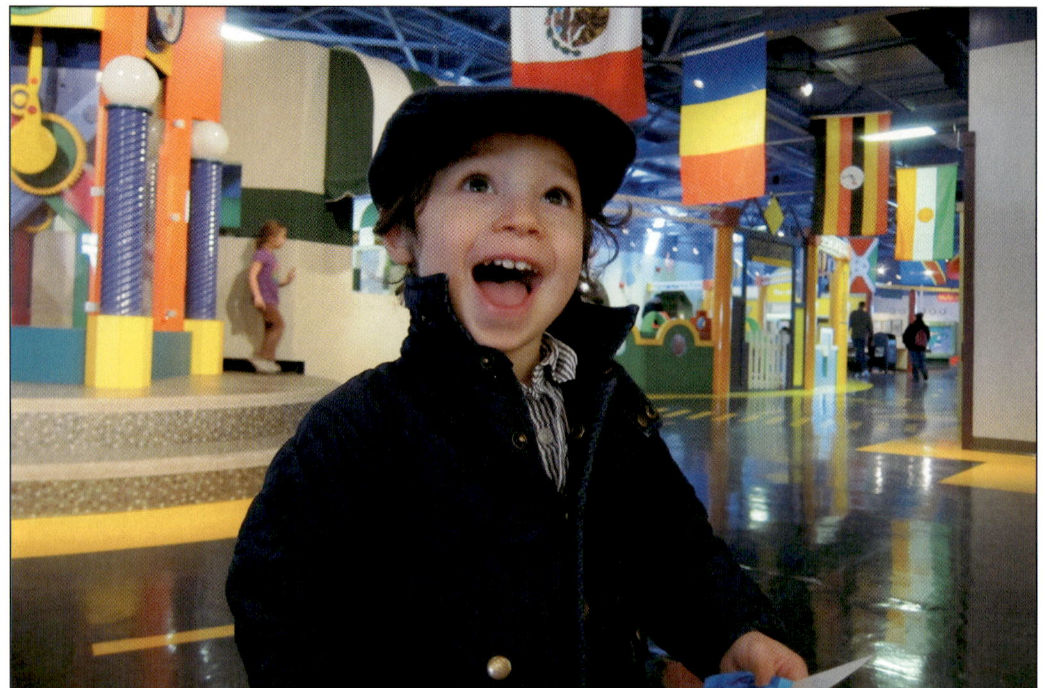

The Greensboro Children's Museum is a hands-on, interactive museum for children and their parents, guardians, and teachers. Greensboro resident Jerry Hyman began traveling around the country, looking at children's museums in other cities. After he shared his findings with leaders in the community, alumni from Leadership Greensboro launched a capital campaign, which resulted in the 1999 opening of the Greensboro Children's Museum in the converted Gate City auto dealership at 220 North Church Street. In addition to 37,000 square feet of floor space for indoor activities, it boasts an Edible Schoolyard outside as well as other amenities. (Above, courtesy of Greensboro Children's Museum.)

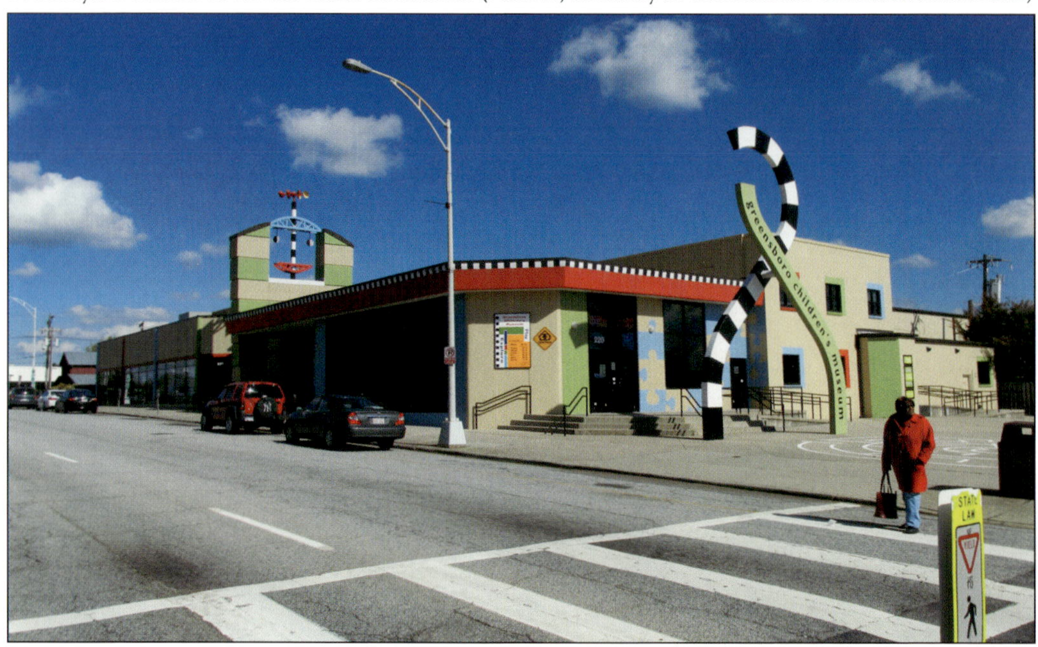

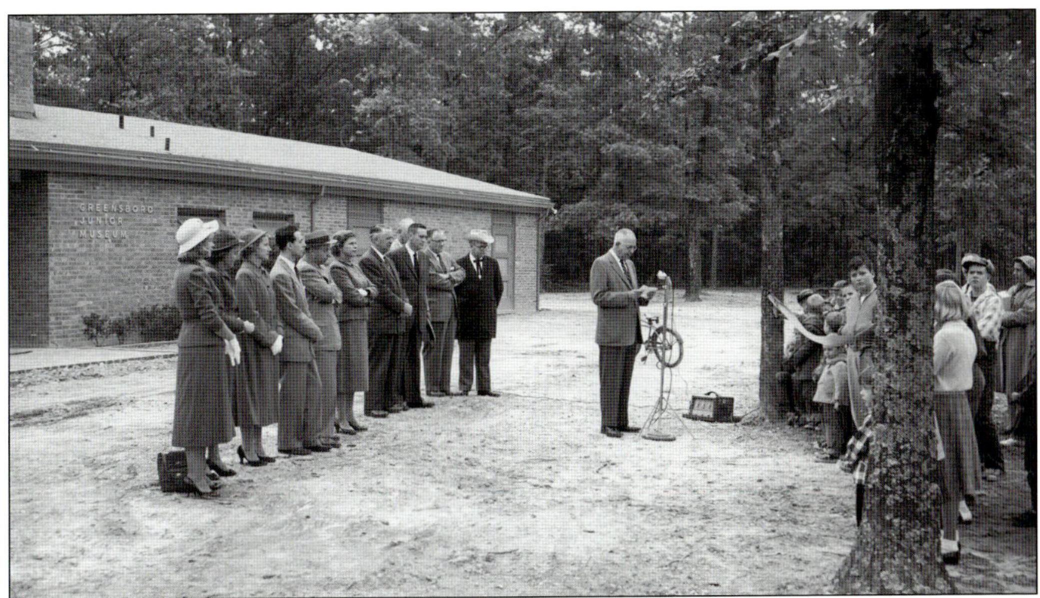

The Greensboro Science Center opened on October 5, 1957, as the Greensboro Junior Museum (above). Located at 4301 Lawndale Avenue, it housed reptiles and a few other animals. In 1989, the Natural Science Center became a public-private partnership between the City of Greensboro and the Greensboro Science Review Board. It added features, such as a petting zoo, an aquatics lab, and classrooms. Following a $20 million bond approval in 2009, the Greensboro Science Center is in the midst of a three-phase, seven-year plan. When completed in 2020, the center will be a state-of–the-art, accredited science museum with a high-tech OmniSphere Theater, an accredited zoological park, and an improved aquarium. (Above, courtesy of Greensboro Historical Museum; below, courtesy of Lynn Donovan.)

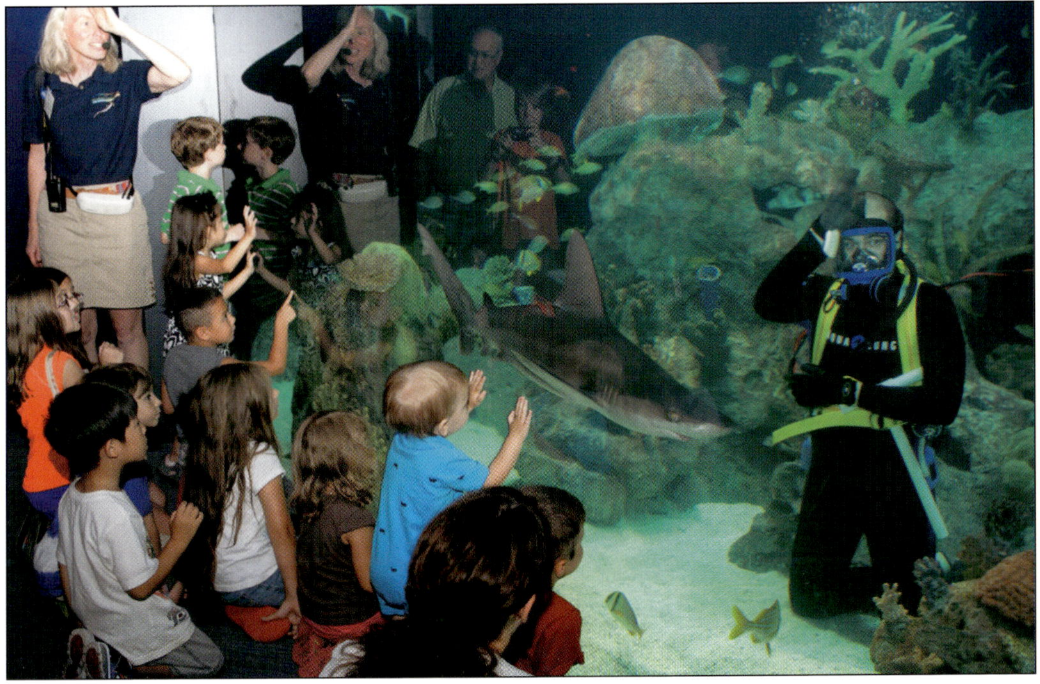

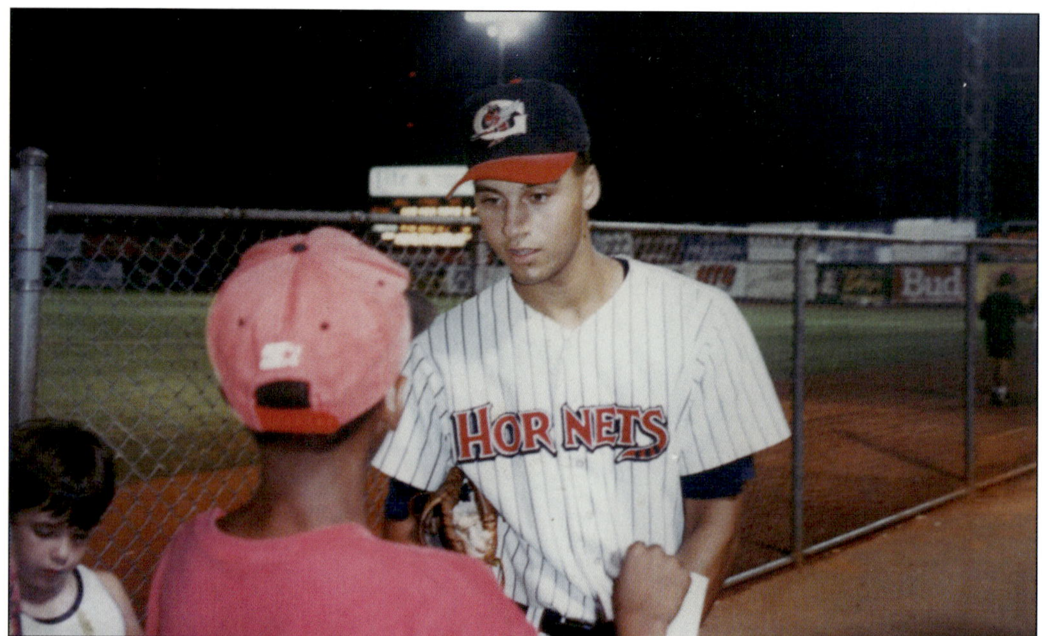

After the city had 10 seasons without professional baseball, the Greensboro Hornets came to War Memorial Stadium in 1979. Shortstop Derek Jeter (above), who played for the Hornets in 1993, has had a hall-of-fame career with the New York Yankees. So did Mariano Rivera, the Yankees star closer who pitched for the Hornets in 1991. The South Atlantic League team changed its name to the Bats in 1994, and, upon moving to the new ballpark in 2005, began calling itself the Grasshoppers. José Fernandez (below), who pitched for the Grasshoppers in 2012, was the 2013 National League Rookie of the Year, pitching for the Miami Marlins, now the parent club of the Hoppers. (Above, courtesy of Ann Cook; below, photograph by Amanda Williams, courtesy of the Greensboro Grasshoppers.)

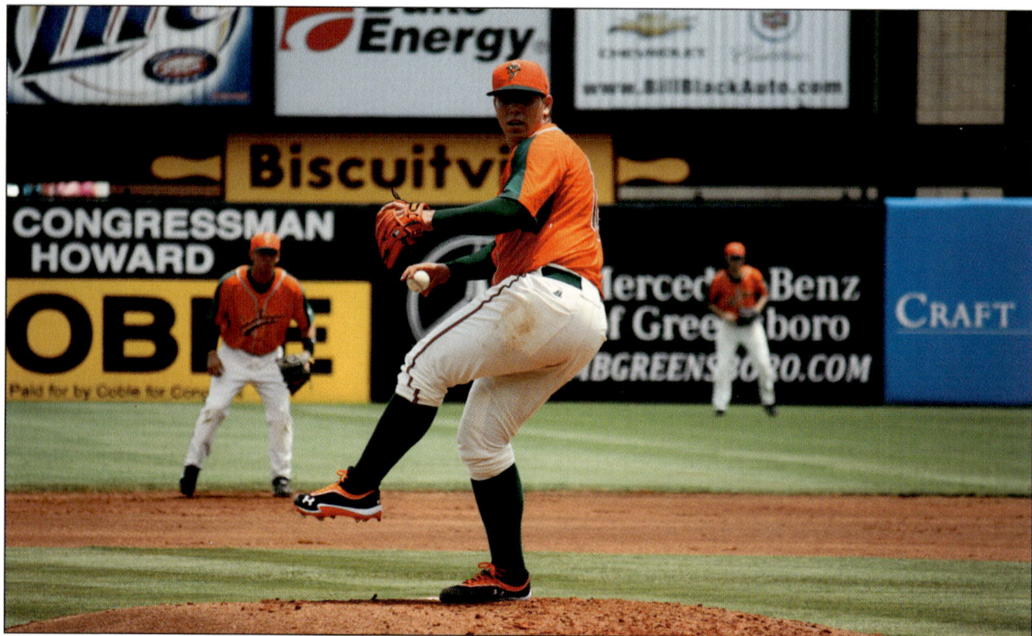

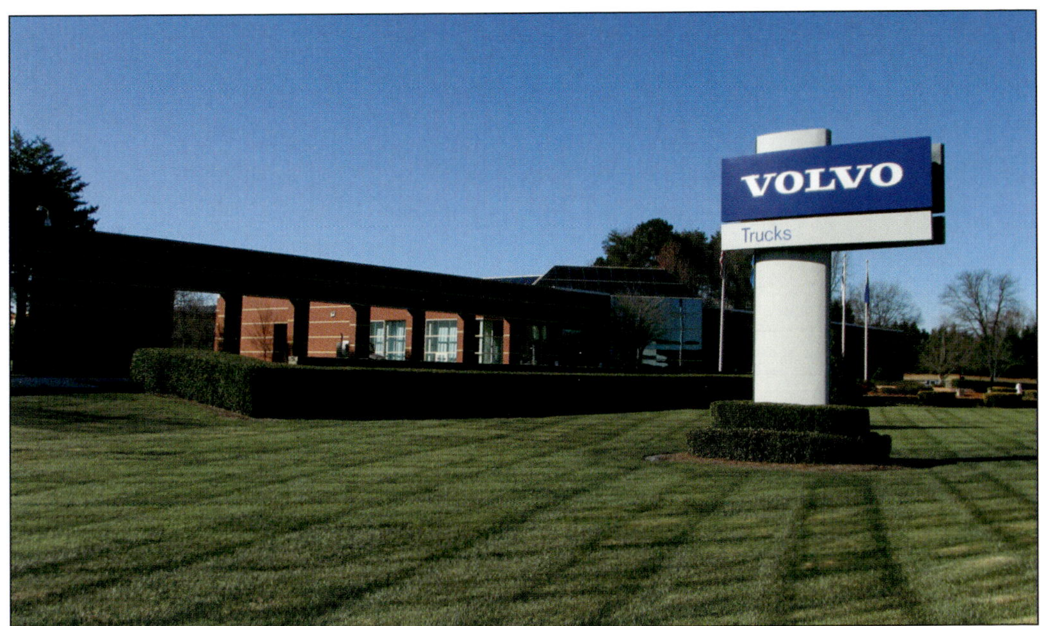

In 1980, AB Volvo, the Swedish automobile company, purchased the assets of White Motor Company for $70 million. The company announced it would set up North American headquarters in Greensboro and that it would manufacture White, Western, Autocar, and small-to-medium-sized Volvo trucks. In July 1982, it purchased 35 acres near I-40 West and NC 68 and built a facility at 7900 National Service Road. It now operates as Volvo Trucks North America.

Mack Trucks, Inc., which had its headquarters in Allentown, Pennsylvania, since 1905, moved to Greensboro in 2009, where it operates as a subsidiary of AB Volvo, which purchased Mack and Renault Trucks in 2000. Mack keeps a sample truck parked at its headquarters, where it can be viewed along Interstate 40. Mack products are still produced in Macungie, Pennsylvania, with other assembly plants in Pennsylvania, Maryland, Australia, and Venezuela.

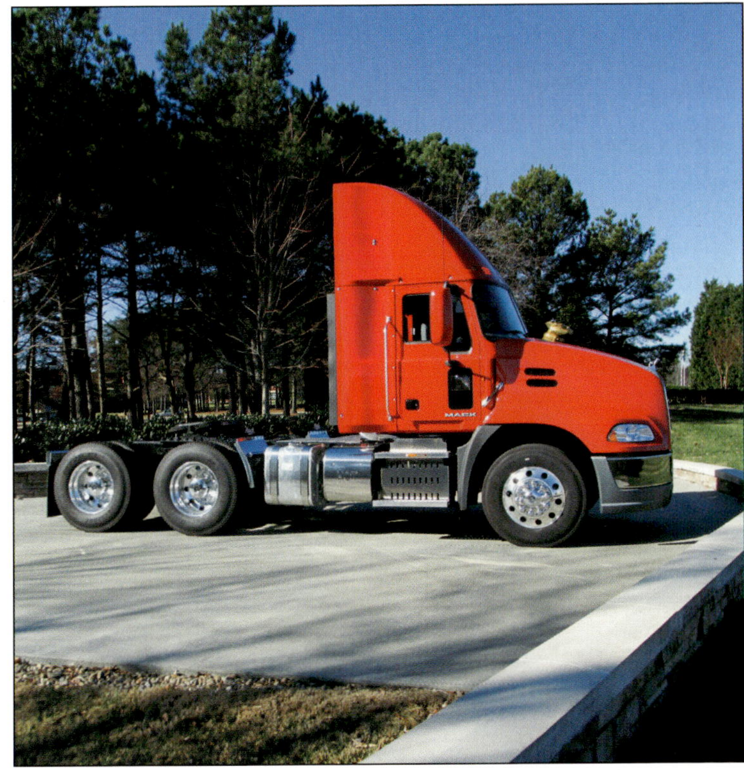

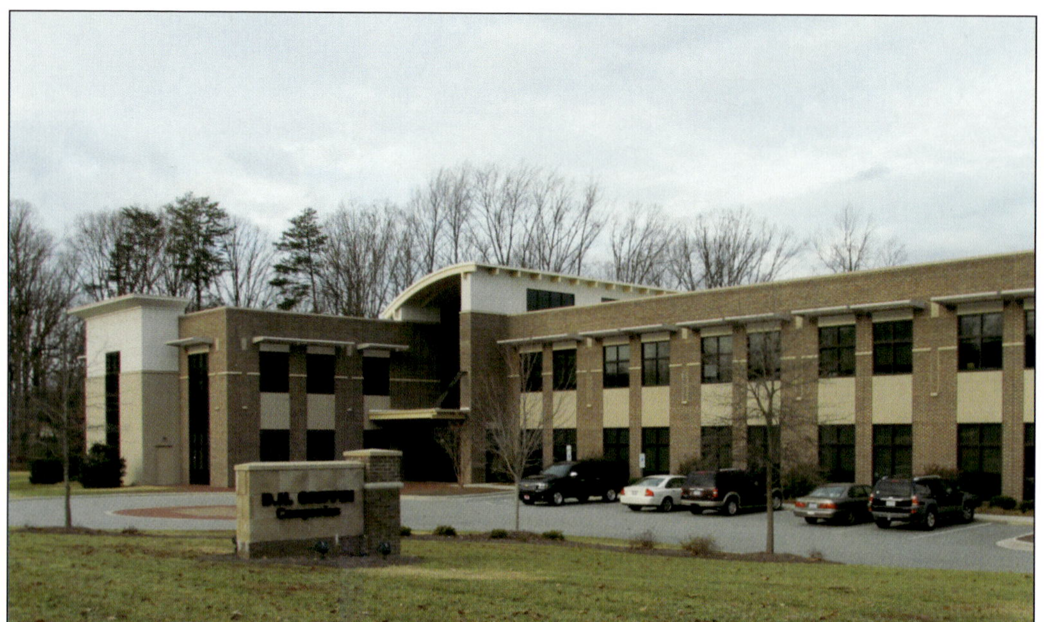

D.H. Griffin Companies, at 4916 Hilltop Road, started in 1959, when David H. Griffin Sr. coordinated the demolition of an old church building. That has led to a group of six independently owned, but integrated, companies that formed around its demolition projects. Among D.H. Griffin's projects was cleaning up at the World Trade Center following the September 11, 2001, attacks. The firm was the largest contractor on that project.

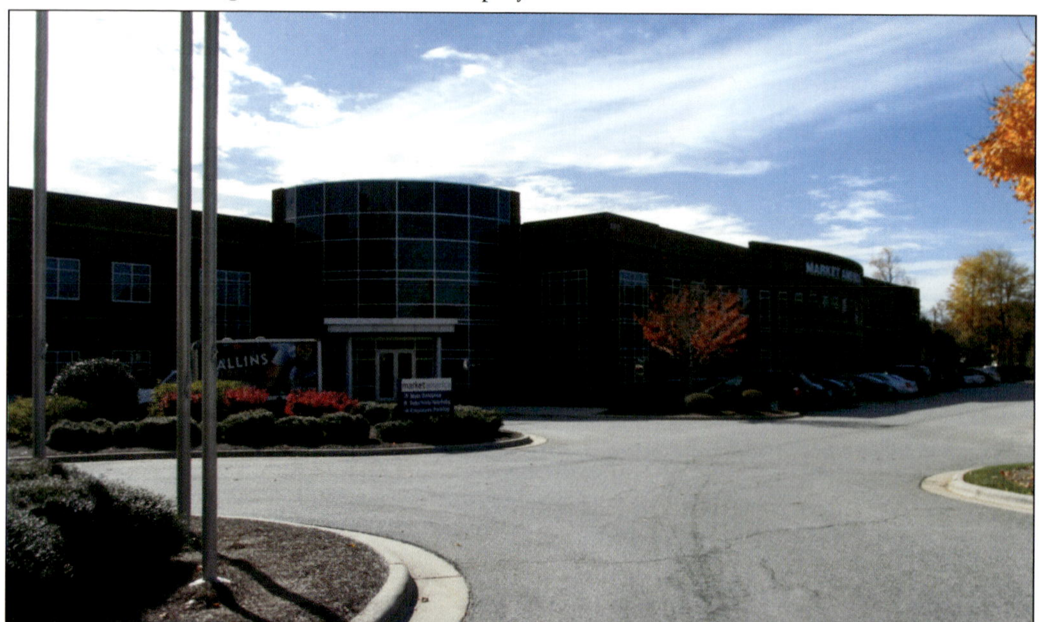

Market America is one of the world's largest online retailers and one of the most prosperous private companies in North Carolina. Founded in 1992 by former Amway distributor J.R. Ridenger, along with his wife and her brother, it generated $1 million in sales the next year and moved into an 8,400-square-foot building. Sales increased to $250 million in 2006, and the company increased the size of its headquarters, at 1302 Pleasant Ridge Road, by 30,000 square feet.

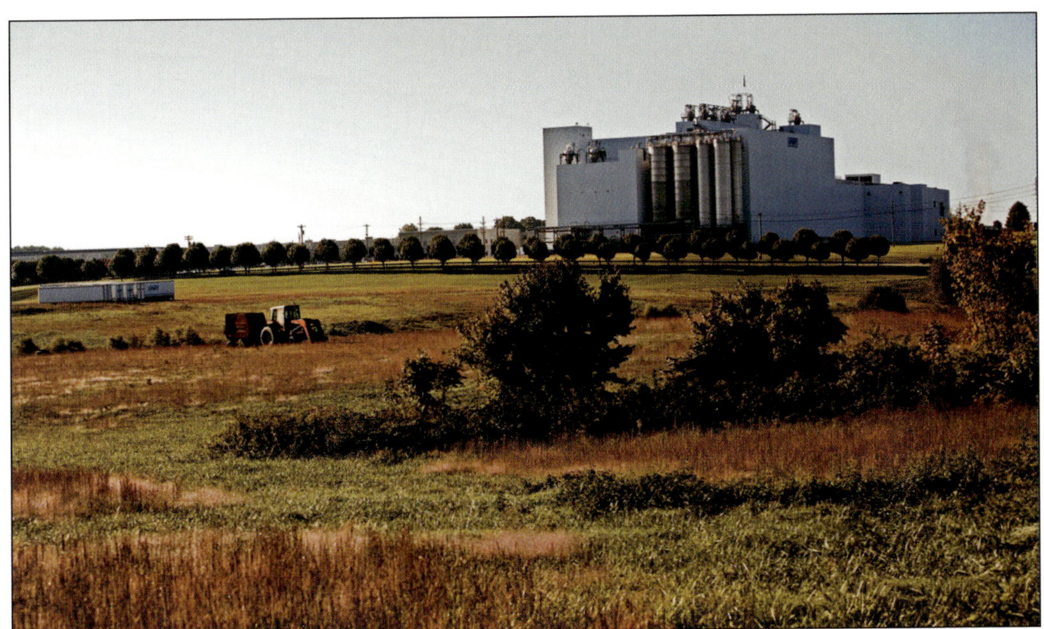

Unifi, Inc., is a leading producer and processor of multifilament polyester and nylon-textured yarns. Founded in 1971, at 7201 West Friendly Avenue, it diversified into nylon, became a niche producer of hosiery, and, by 1991, was one of the world's largest polyester and nylon manufacturers. Unifi yarns can also be found in automotive textiles, industrial applications, and home and contract furnishings. (Courtesy of the Quixote Group.)

United Guaranty was founded in 1963 as First Mortgage Insurance Company, with three employees working in the Piedmont Building, at 114 North Elm Street. The company provides insurance against defaults on mortgages. It moved to a three-story office building on Beamon Street in 1973 and changed its name. Now located at 230 North Elm Street, in Renaissance Plaza, it is one of the world's largest mortgage-insurance companies. A division of AIG, it has more than 1,200 employees.

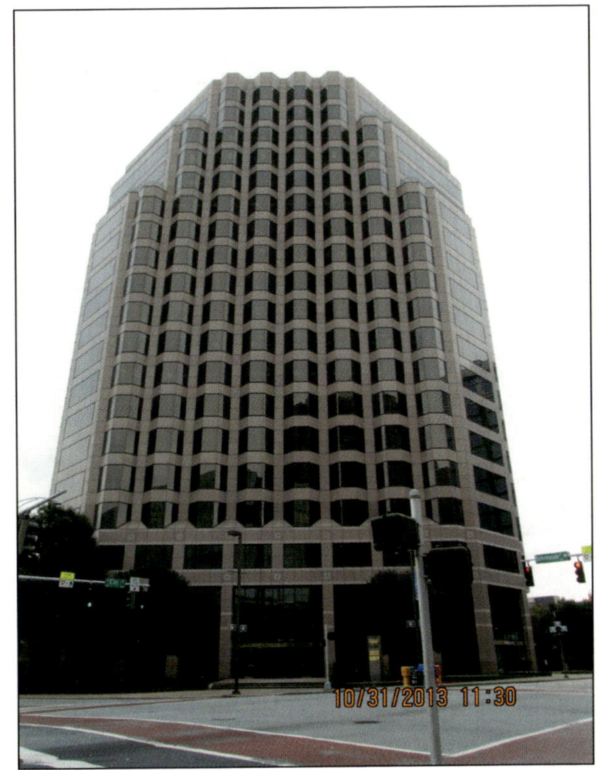

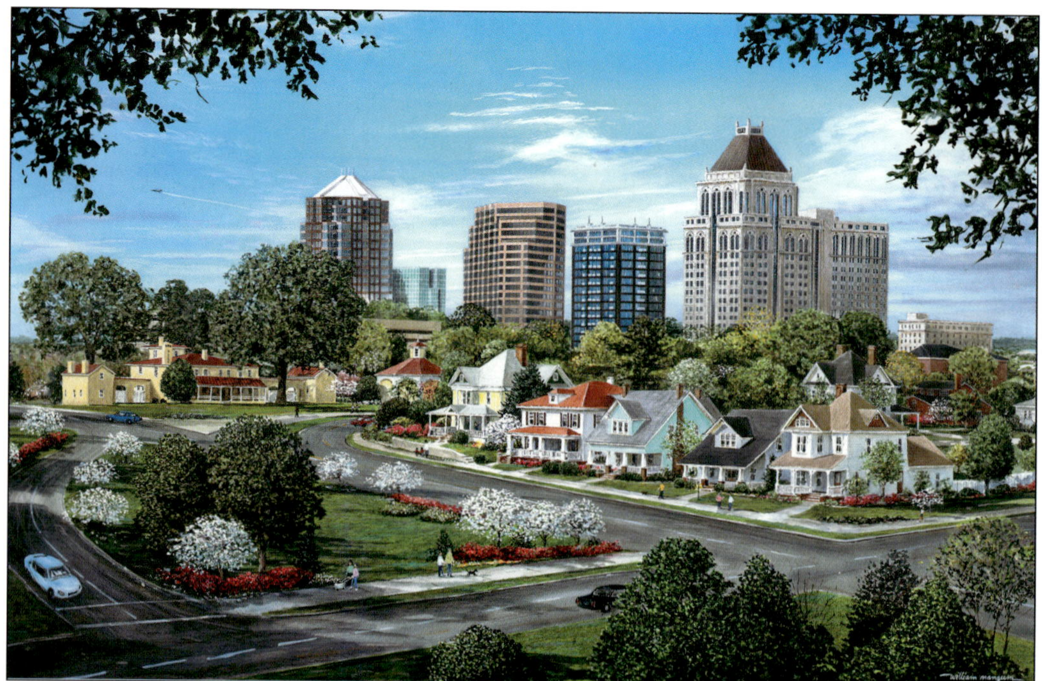

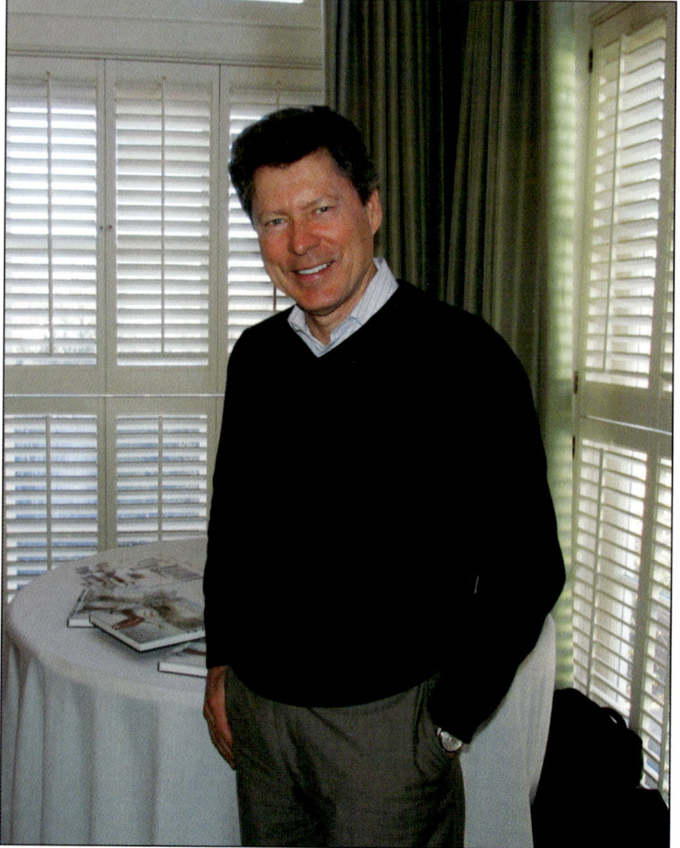

While working on a master of fine arts degree at UNC-Greensboro, William "Bill" Mangum held an exhibition, which sold out. Settling in Greensboro, in 1982, he opened Carey-Mangum Gallery, at 2166 Lawndale Drive, where it still operates with William Mangum Fine Art. He has become one of the most popular and respected watercolor artists in this area. His painting *Gate City* is used at the front of his book *Greensboro: Roots & Renaissance*, published in 2008 by the Joseph M. Bryan Foundation as part of Greensboro's bicentennial. Since 1988, Mangum has offered his service with his Honor Cards, holiday cards that raise money for Greensboro's homeless. (Above, courtesy of William Mangum Fine Art.)

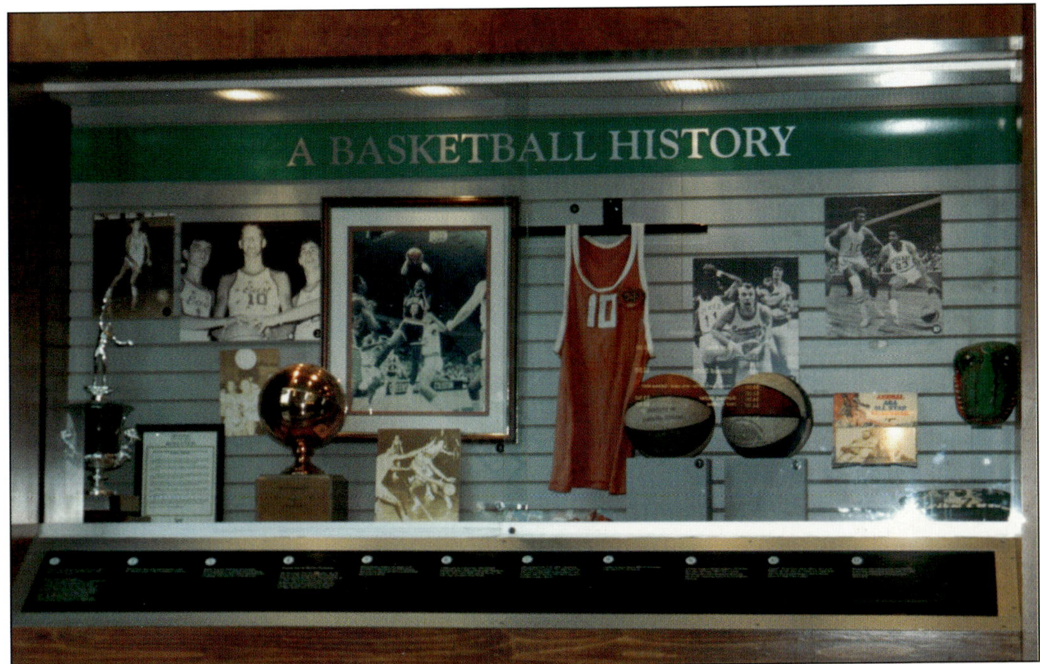

The ACC Hall of Champions opened in March 2011, as the Greensboro Coliseum continued its expansion. Through interactive displays and multipurpose programming, it showcases the Atlantic Coast Conference's history. Still in its first phase, with 8,100 feet of exhibition space, it also features member-school memorabilia, a historical time line, and high-tech exhibits that promote the ACC. (Courtesy of Lynn Donovan.)

The Greensboro Aquatic Center, just beyond the ACC Hall of Champions, is also part of the expanding Greensboro Coliseum Complex. Also opening in 2011, the 78,323-foot indoor facility incorporates leading concepts of aquatic design. Open to the public, the center meets or exceeds the highest standards in competitive swimming-related sports. Recently, it was named to host the 2014 USA Swimming AT&T Winter National Championships.

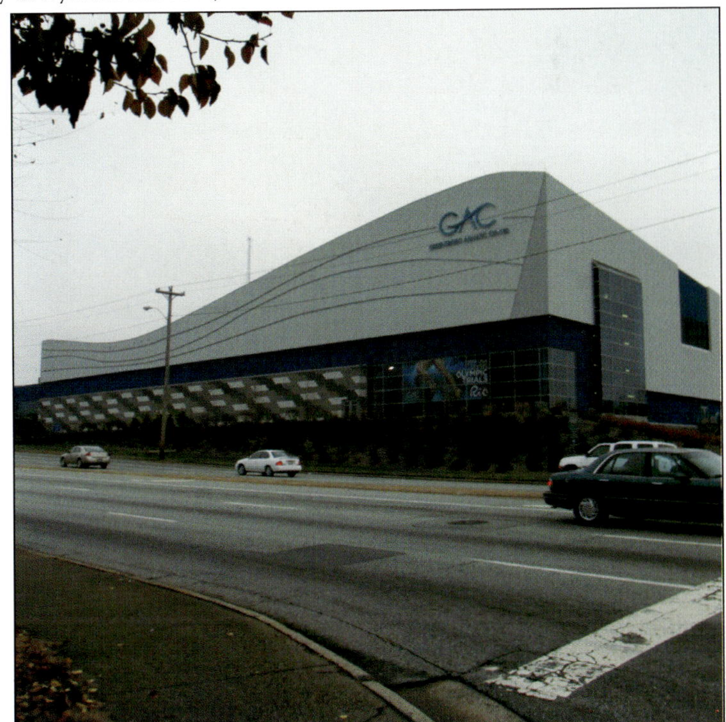

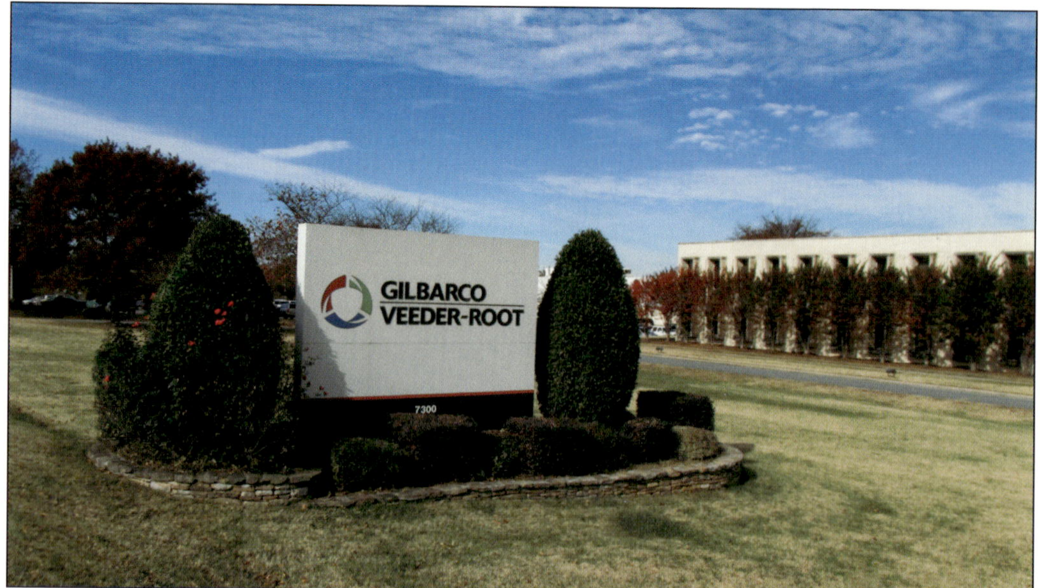

Gilbarco, originally Gilbert & Barker Company, was founded in 1865 by Charles Gilbert and John Barker in Springfield, Massachusetts, as a gas-lighting company. The leading producer of gasoline pumps, it was acquired by Standard Oil, changed its name, and, in 1965, moved its headquarters and US manufacturing to 7300 West Friendly Avenue. In 2002, it was acquired by Danaher Corporation, which merged Gilbarco with its own brand, Veeder-Root.

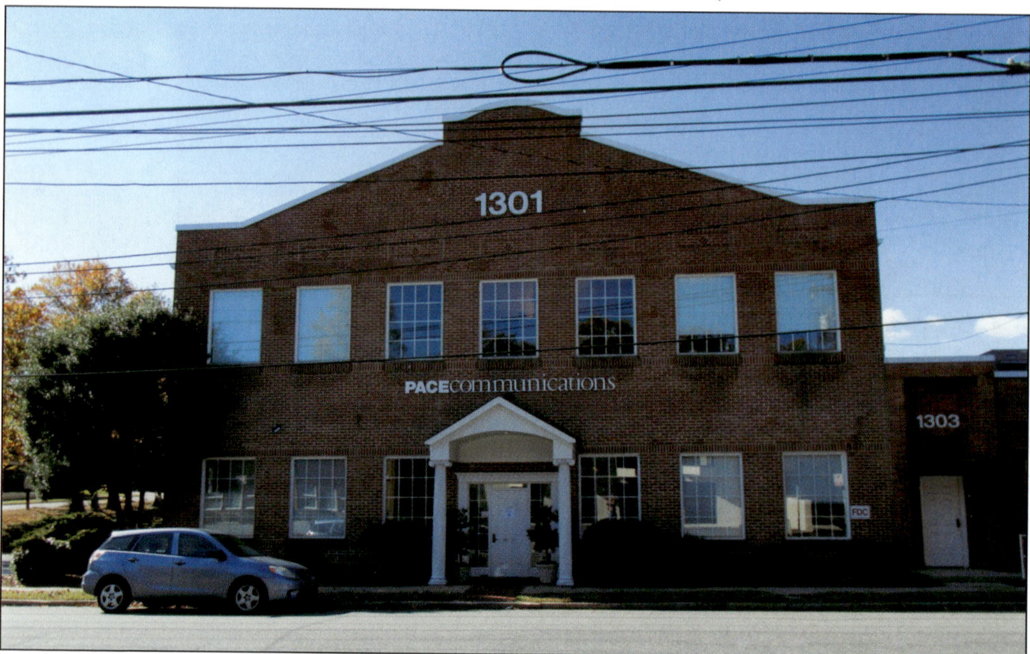

Pace Communications, at 1301 Carolina Street, was founded by Bonnie McElveen-Hunter. As Bonnie McElveen, she moved to Greensboro to publish a new magazine for Fisher-Harrison Printing Company, *PACE*, the in-flight magazine for Piedmont Airlines. Other titles followed, and in 1983, Fisher-Harrison Publications spun off from the printing company, leaving McElveen-Hunter as president. The company's first newsstand magazine, *Southern Bride*, debuted in 1988. It became *Elegant Bride* in 1990.

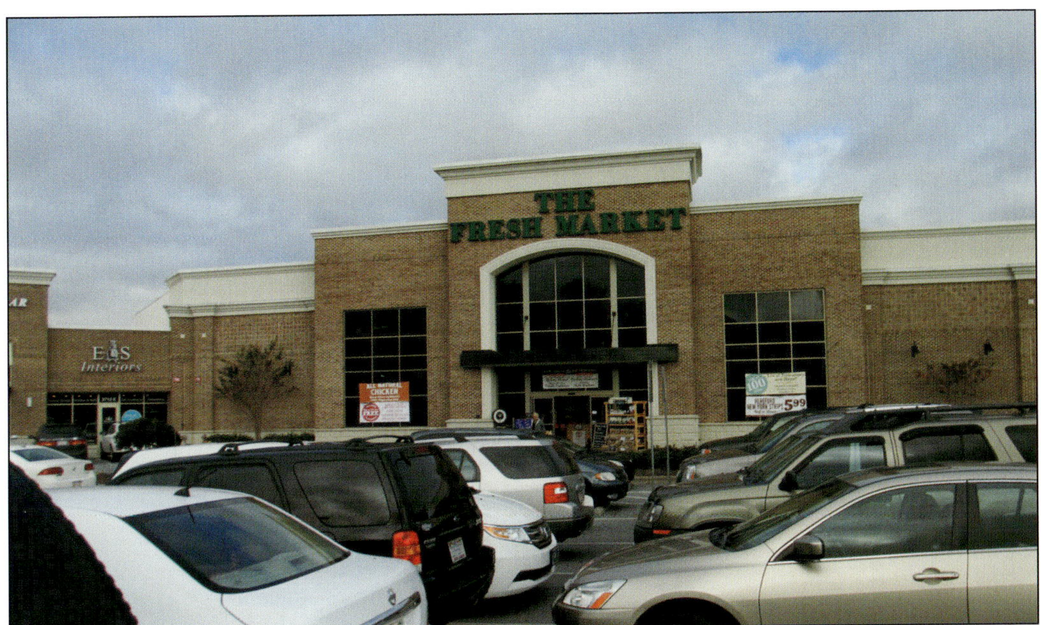

As an executive with 7-Eleven Corp., Ray Berry conceived the idea of a grocery store with the feeling of an open, European-style market. He moved to Greensboro, purchased a supermarket building on Lawndale Drive, and started the Fresh Market in 1982. The store was replaced with one built in the immediate vicinity in 2010 (pictured). The company is now a national chain with more than 130 stores and continued plans for expansion.

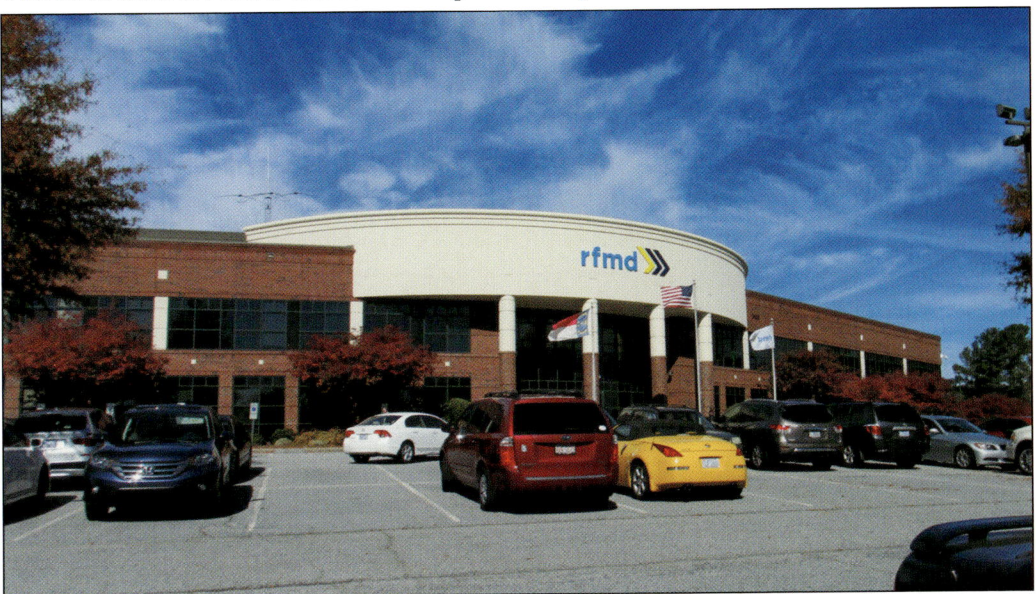

RF Micro Devices, founded in 1991, designs and manufactures solutions for applications that drive wireless and broadband communications. Most cell-phone owners have a product by this company within their devices. Located near the airport, at 7628 Thorndike Road, the company announced it had joined TriQuint Semiconductor, Inc., of Hillsboro, Oregon, in a "merger of equals" on February 24, 2014. A new company name will be announced at a later date. The location of the headquarters (Greensboro or Oregon) has yet to be revealed.

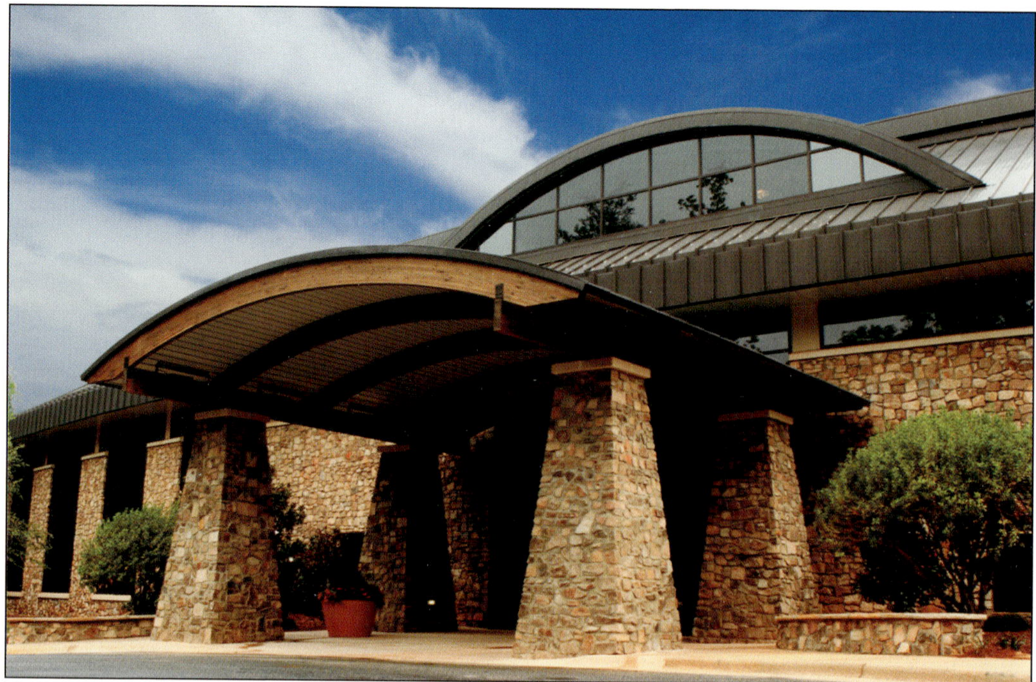

Smith Richardson, longtime CEO of Vicks, was concerned about how businesses could remain successful over time during changes in management and fluctuations in the market. This inspired him to start the Smith Richardson Foundation, which led to the creation of the Center for Creative Leadership, at 1 Leadership Place, just off Battleground Avenue in northwest Greensboro, in 1970, two years before his death. Today, the center operates at the 19-acre campus, as well as at nine other locations around the world. Leadership development, whether for individuals, groups, or entire organizations, is the prime focus of its activity. (Both, courtesy of Center for Creative Leadership.)

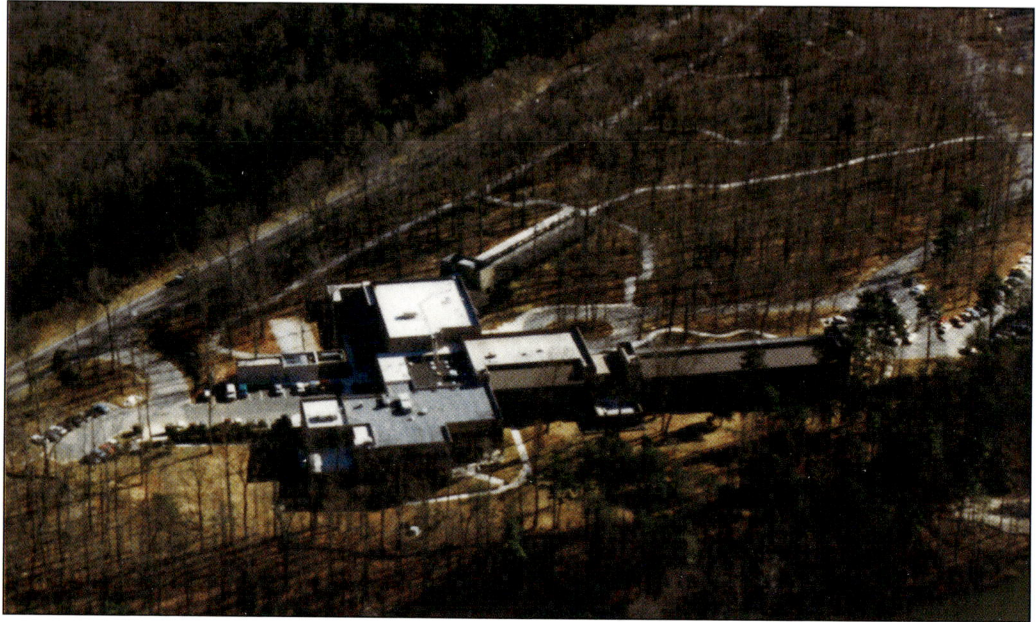

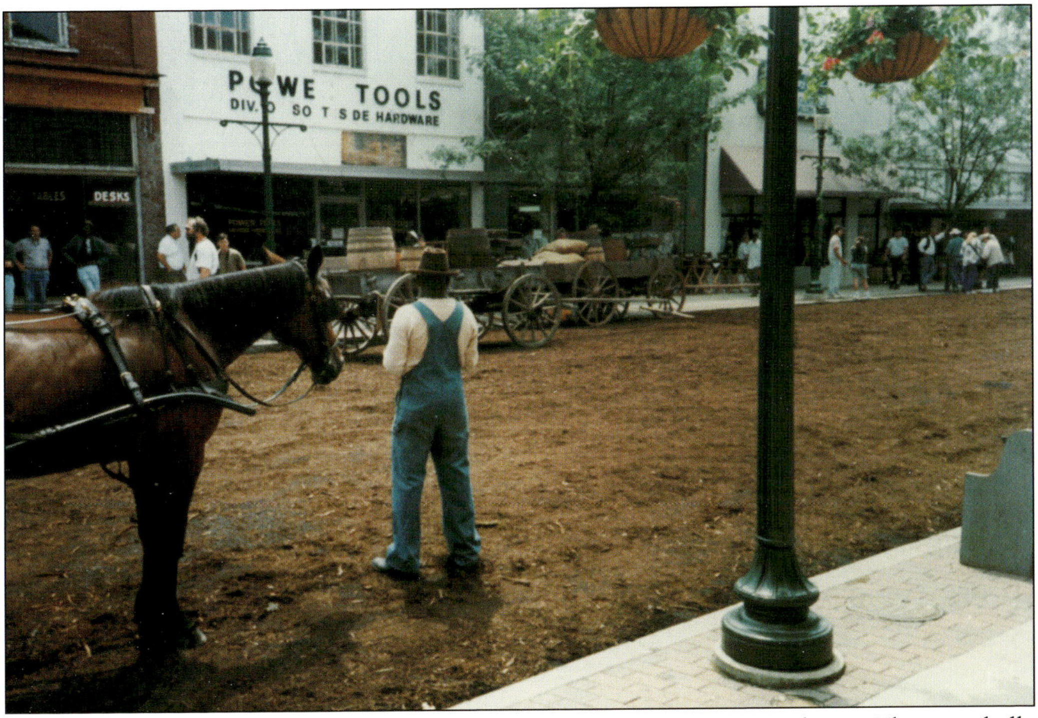

Like the rest of North Carolina, Greensboro has embraced the movie industry. The city gladly makes adjustments and accommodations to film producers. This photograph is a perfect example of that. During filming of *The Other Anna*, a made-for-television movie, dirt was placed on the 500 and 600 blocks of South Elm Street, lending the street the appearance of a scene from the 1800s. (Courtesy of Gregory Haas.)

The Greensboro city logo was designed by Harry Blair and adopted in the late 1980s. The city flag, designed by Chuck Hodgin, shows the Nathanael Greene monument inside an oak wreath. It was adopted in 1965. That same year, the Greensboro red Camellia japonica was named the city flower. (Courtesy of City of Greensboro.)

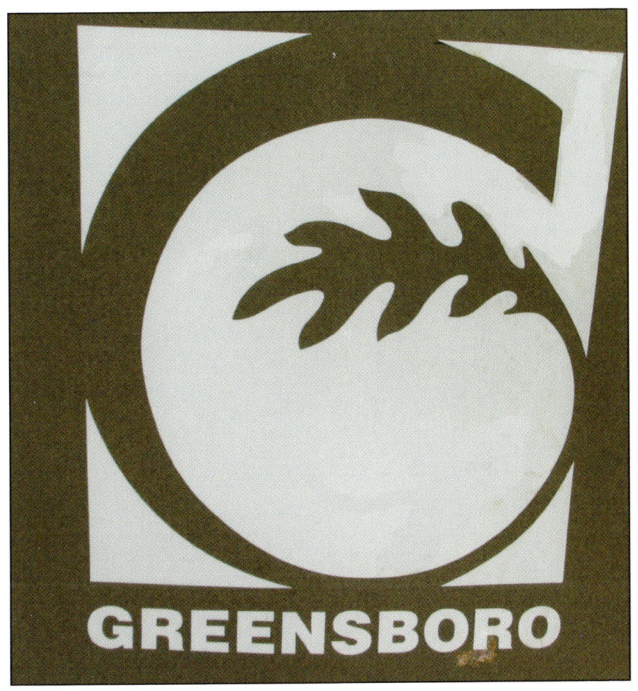

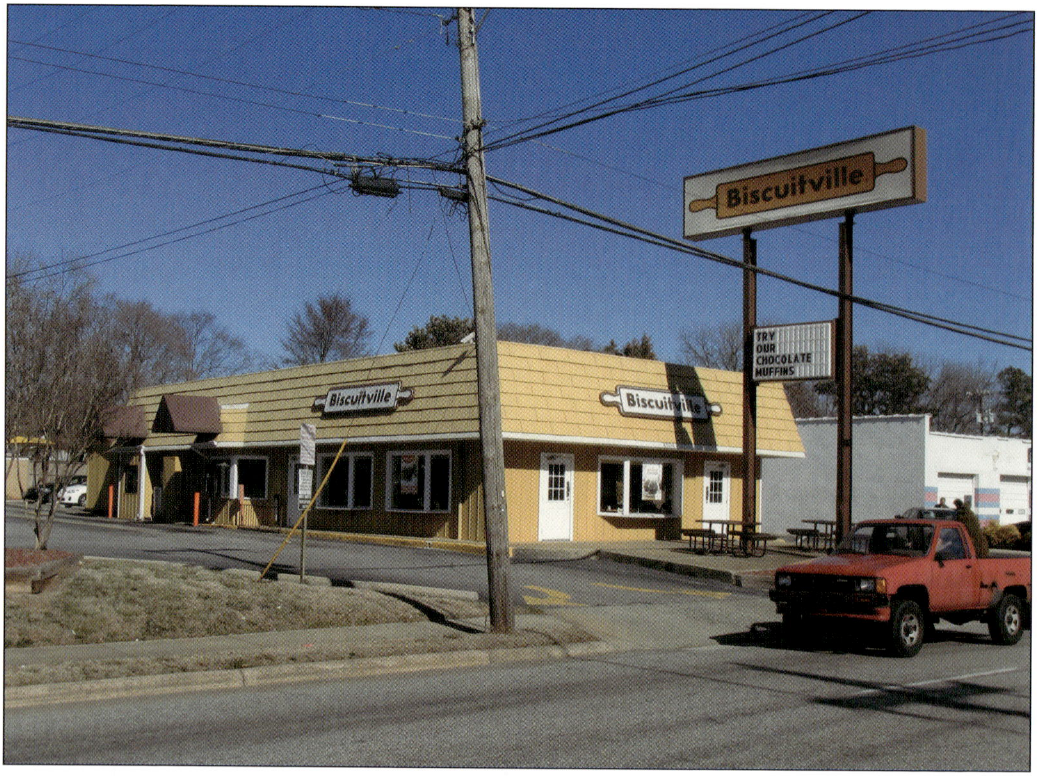

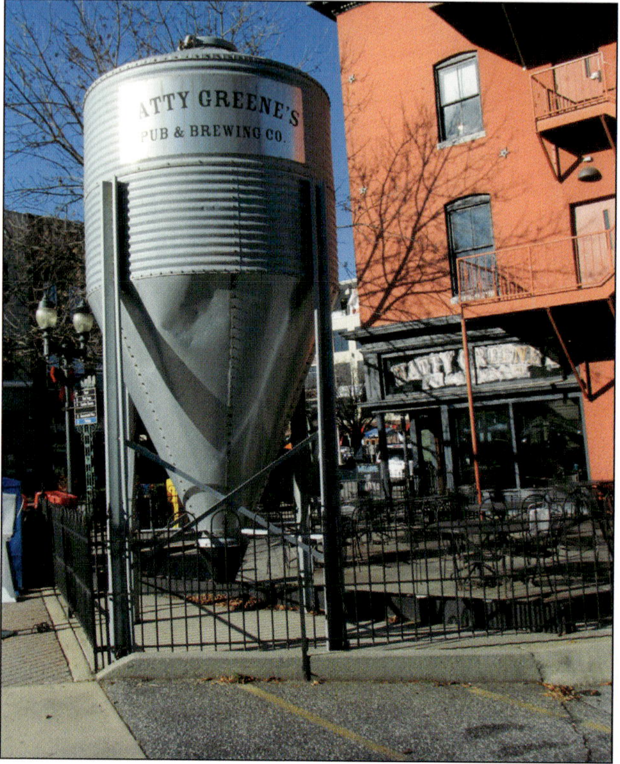

The first Biscuitville opened in 1975, when the headquarters for the company was in Burlington. In May 2007, the company moved its headquarters to 1414 Yanceyville Street at Maple Corporate Park. It operates 54 breakfast-oriented restaurants in North Carolina and Virginia, including the one pictured at 4504 West Market Street. The family-owned company has just introduced a lunch menu and is updating its logo.

Perhaps the biggest reminder these days of the Revolutionary War general is a restaurant and nightspot called Natty Greene's, at 345 South Elm Street. The establishment has another location in Cary. In addition, Natty Greene's Brewing Company brews a line of ales and beers at the Greensboro restaurant and at a separate brewery at 3121 High Point Road.

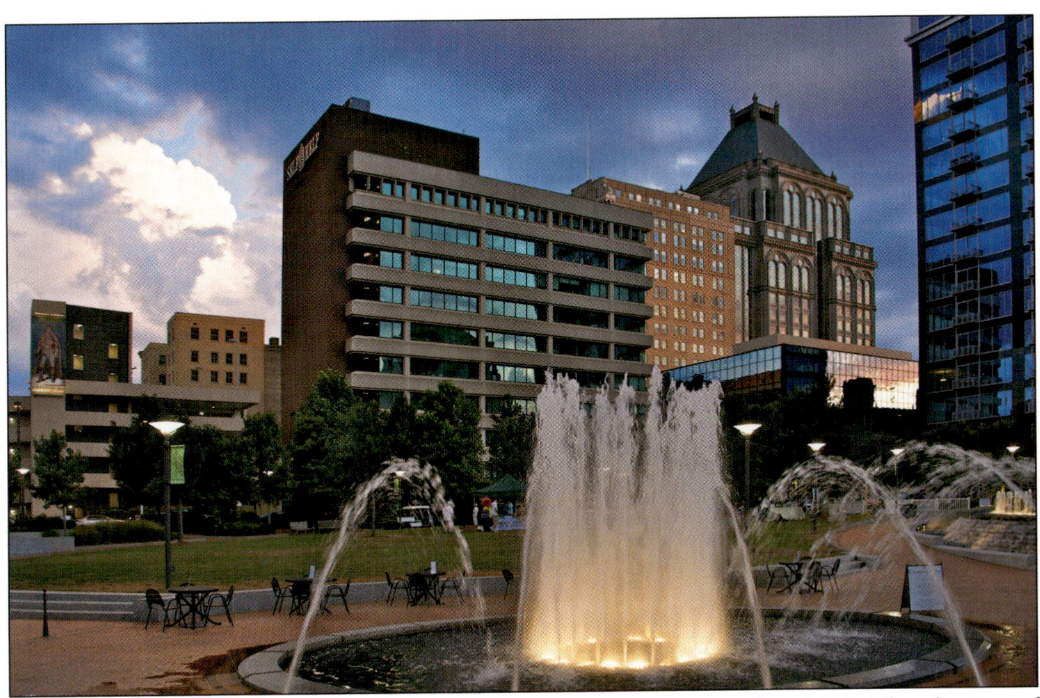

The idea for Center City Park, at 200 North Elm Street, got started in 2002. The clearing of land began the next year, when an interim park was set up. While not quite at the exact center of Guilford County, the park is closer to the area that was chosen to start the city than the downtown center is. Competed in 2007, the park, with its magnificent fountains, is often the site of festivities. (Courtesy of Lynn Donovan.)

Center Pointe was built at 201 North Elm Street as the Wachovia Building in the late 1960s. At the time, it was the only building that came close to the Jefferson Standard Building in height. After Wachovia moved out of the building, it stood vacant for several years before developer Roy Carroll bought it. He transformed it into condominiums, all of which have balconies. The balconies on the east side overlook Center City Park.

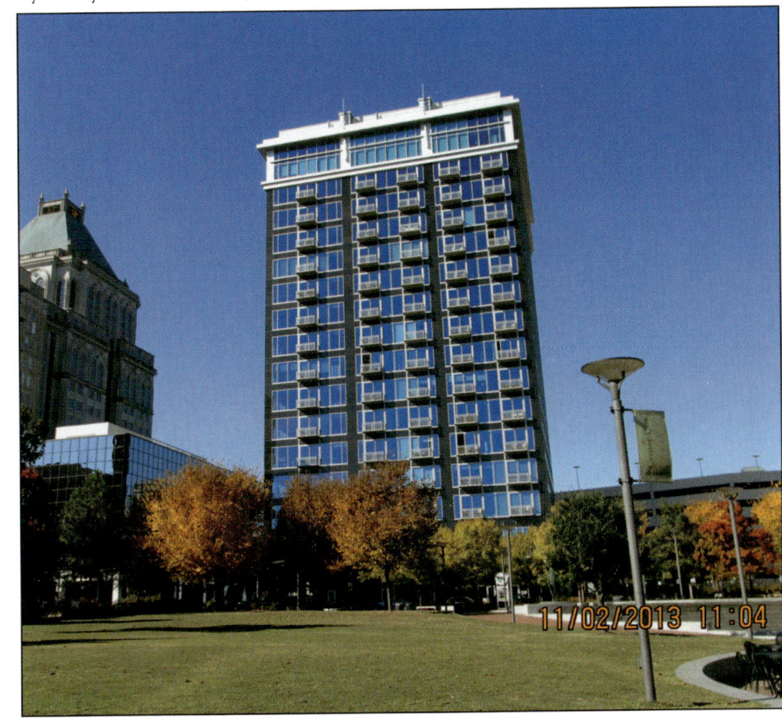

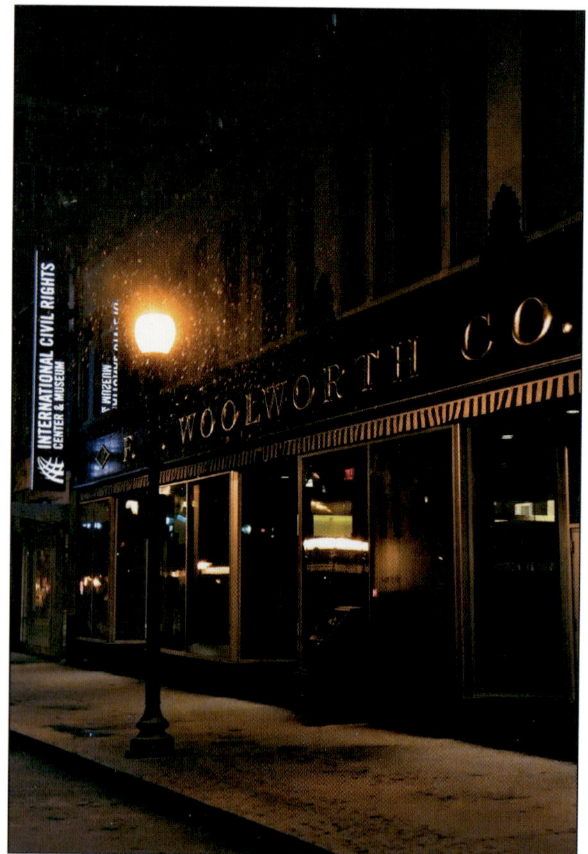

When Woolworth closed its store at 134 South Elm Street in 1993, it announced plans to tear down the building. Because of the structure's role in civil rights history, members of the African American community, including Guilford County commissioner Melvin "Skip" Alston and Greensboro city councilman Earl Jones, worked to save the building for the purpose of establishing a civil rights museum. The International Civil Rights Center & Museum opened on February 1, 2010, the 50th anniversary of the sit-ins. The display includes stools at the lunch counter used 50 years previously, on the day of the first sit-ins. The three surviving original participants attended the grand opening. (Both, courtesy of Lynn Donovan.)

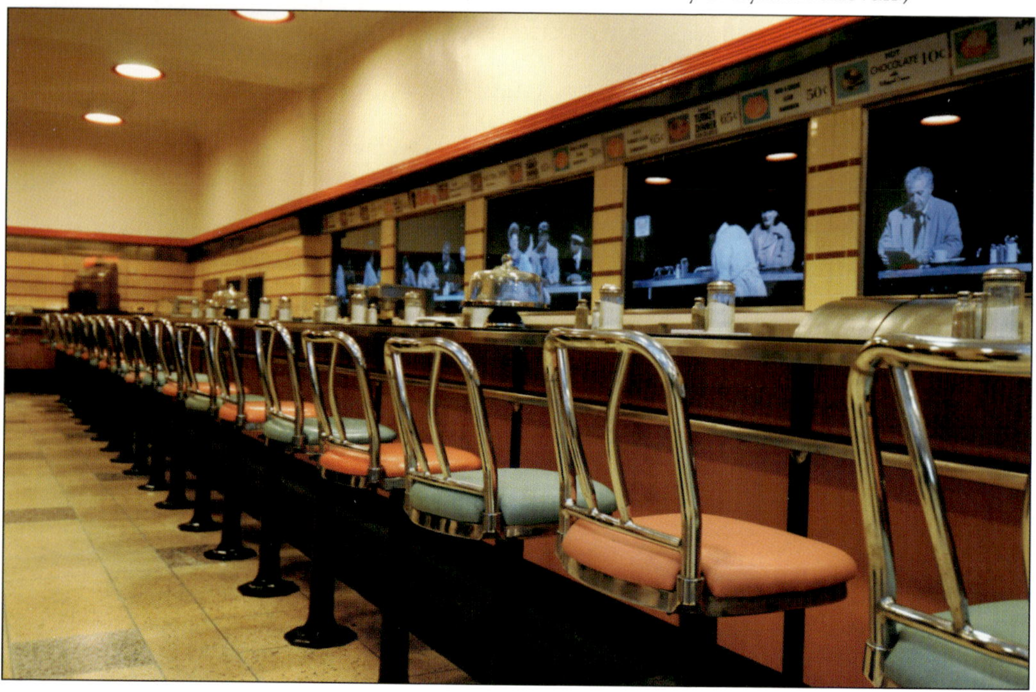

Four

CHANGING

Greensboro has not only changed itself during the last half century, but activities here have led to social change, particularly integration, in the South. On a fateful day in 1960, four freshmen at A&T—Franklin McCain, Joseph McNeil, Ezell Blair, and David Richmond—who had already purchased items at the downtown Woolworth store, made it plain that the custom of not serving people at lunch counters because of the color or their skin was no longer acceptable. A&T student body president Jesse Jackson continued with similar causes and went on to be a national figure, making race relations his life's work. Other breakthroughs in racial advancement are highlighted in the following pages, as are those who worked to change Greensboro for the better.

The philanthropists on these pages were able to make a difference because of their generous gifts to causes. Some, such as the Joseph M. Bryan Foundation, enable operators of the foundation to distribute money to projects exclusively in Greensboro. Among other foundations in Greensboro is the Weaver Foundation, which also targets Greensboro causes.

Action Greensboro, a relatively new organization, strives to come up with ways to help the Gate City become a better place. Greensboro's cooperation with Winston-Salem and High Point, as well as other nearby cities, particularly through the Piedmont Triad Partnership, should lead to more opportunity for people in this area.

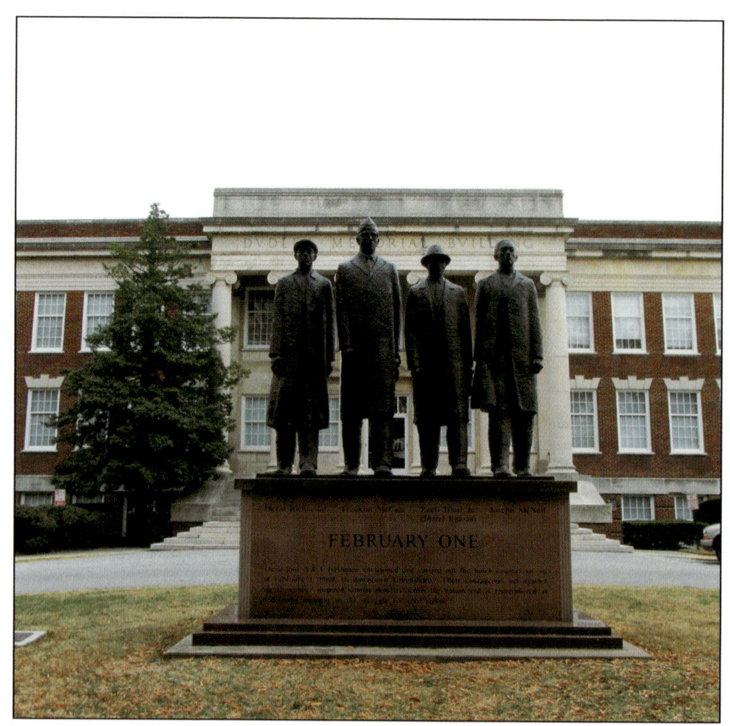

On February 1, 1960, four African American freshmen from North Carolina A&T College, now a university, sat at the counter in the downtown Woolworth, asking for coffee. They were denied service, but two of them returned the next day, and 18 others joined them. The movement continued to evolve and, by July, Woolworth opened its lunch counter to all races. The statue of the four pioneers is on the A&T campus.

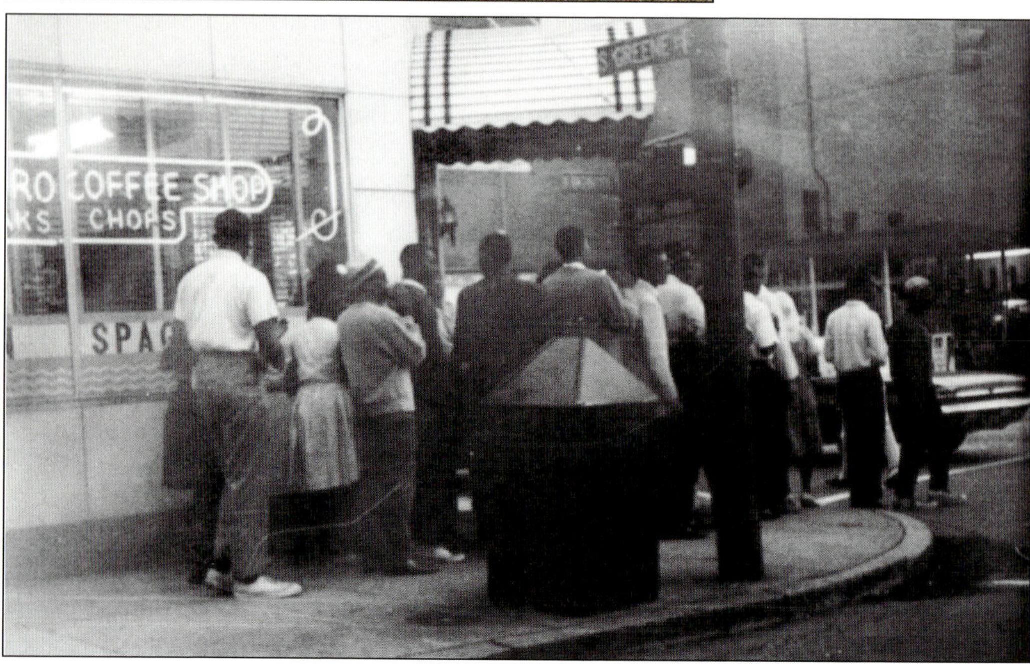

In 1963, Jesse Jackson, then president of the North Carolina A&T College student body, led a demonstration in downtown Greensboro. This photograph shows members of the group heading to the Carolina Theater, which had segregated seating at the time. This and further demonstrations led Greensboro mayor David Schenk, the Greensboro Chamber of Commerce, and the Greensboro Merchants Association to ask all public places to integrate. By this time, most businesses complied. (Courtesy of Bill Brooks.)

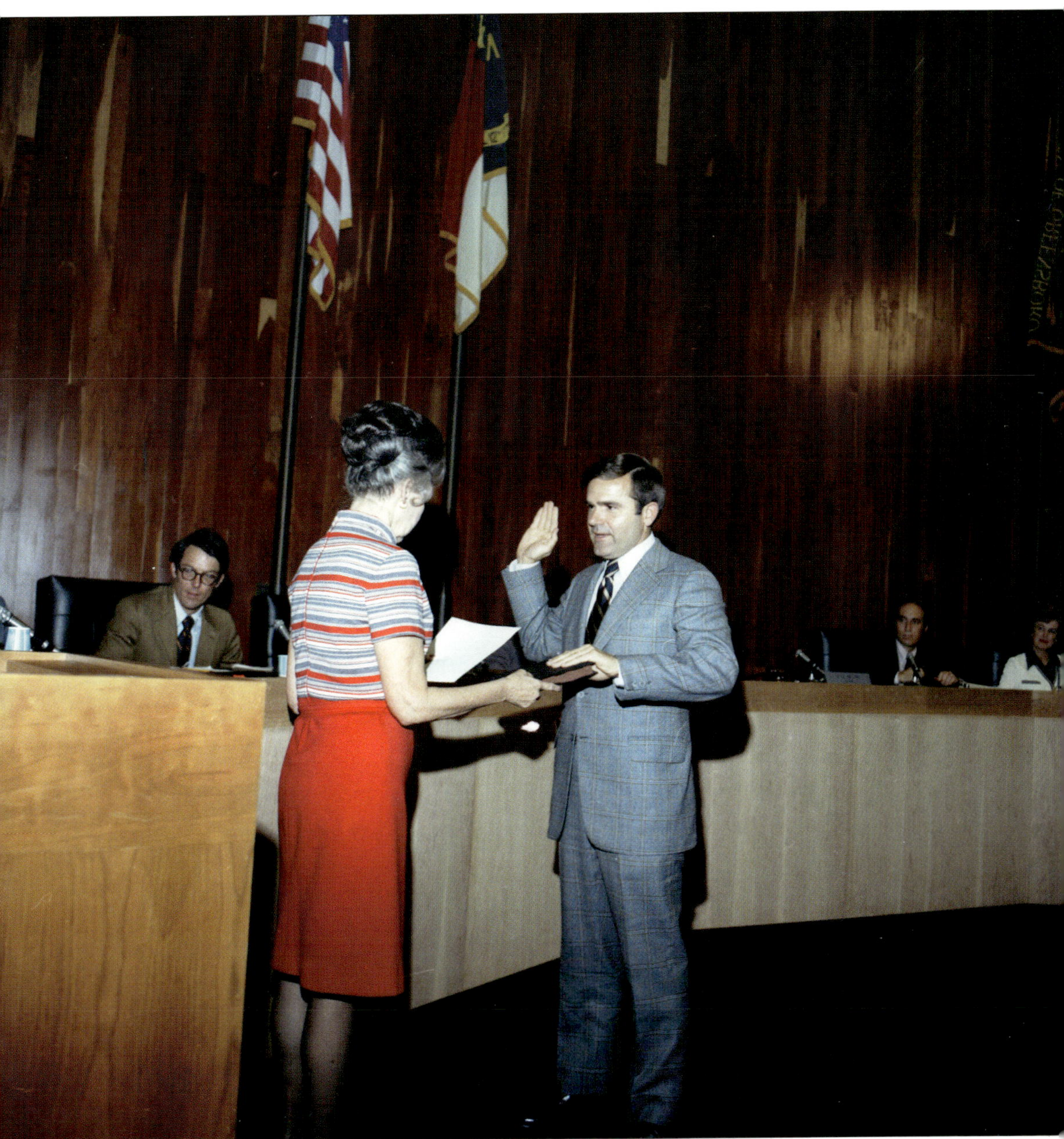

Edwin Samuel "Jim" Melvin is shown here being sworn in as mayor of Greensboro. One of his many efforts as mayor was to build a new government complex. While mayor, he left North Carolina National Bank to become president of Home Federal Savings & Loan. After retiring as Greensboro city executive of Central Carolina Bank, Melvin became president of the Joseph M. Bryan Foundation. (Courtesy of Greensboro Historical Museum.)

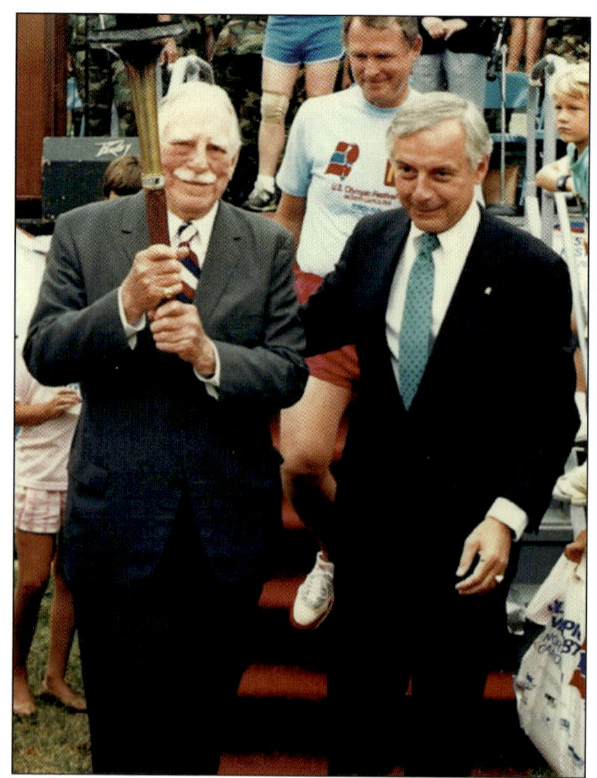

Joseph Bryan (left) was one of the most generous philanthropists in Greensboro's history. Although a member of the North Carolina Business Hall of Fame, Bryan will be best remembered for his philanthropy. Through the Bryan Family Foundation, money went to all of Greensboro's institutions of higher learning. Bryan Park was started by land he donated. John Forbis (right) succeeded Melvin as mayor. During Forbis's tenure, district representation for the Greensboro City Council election was instituted. His family owns Forbis & Dick Funeral Services. (Courtesy of Lynn Donovan.)

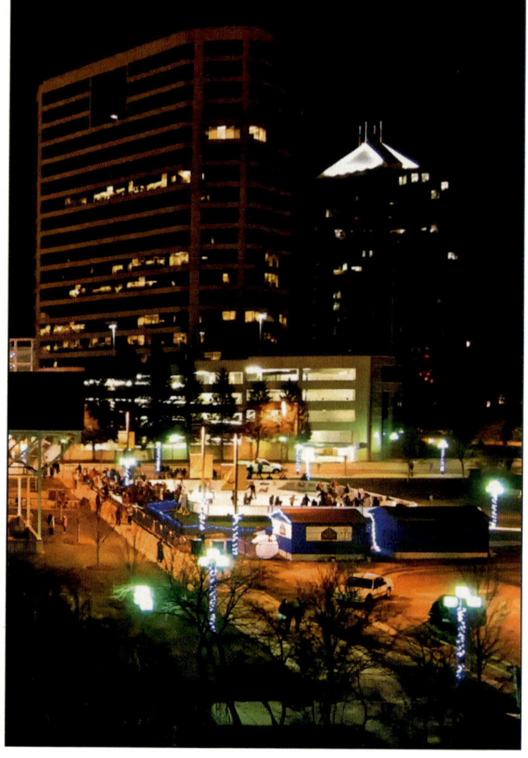

Festival Park, in the cultural arts district of downtown, becomes the city's largest outdoor ice-skating rink each winter. The Piedmont Winterfest, as it is called, began in 2010. In addition to the rink and the 120-foot ice roller, Winterfest activities include disco nights on Fridays and Saturdays and private parties. (Courtesy of Lynn Donovan.)

Lincoln Financial Group traces its roots to 1905. Its headquarters is in Radnor, Pennsylvania. In 2006, it acquired Jefferson-Pilot Corporation and the 17-story building that goes with it. Now the Lincoln Financial Building, it remains the most recognizable structure in Greensboro. Through that acquisition, Lincoln Financial picked up its group life, disability, and dental insurance divisions.

Howard Coble has represented Greensboro longer than anyone in Congress. Seen here announcing that he will not seek reelection in 2014, Coble has represented the 6th District since 1984. Other congressmen who have represented parts of Greensboro in recent years are Melvin Watt and Bradley Miller. On January, 6, 2014, Watt left office after 21 years to become head of the Federal Housing Finance Agency.

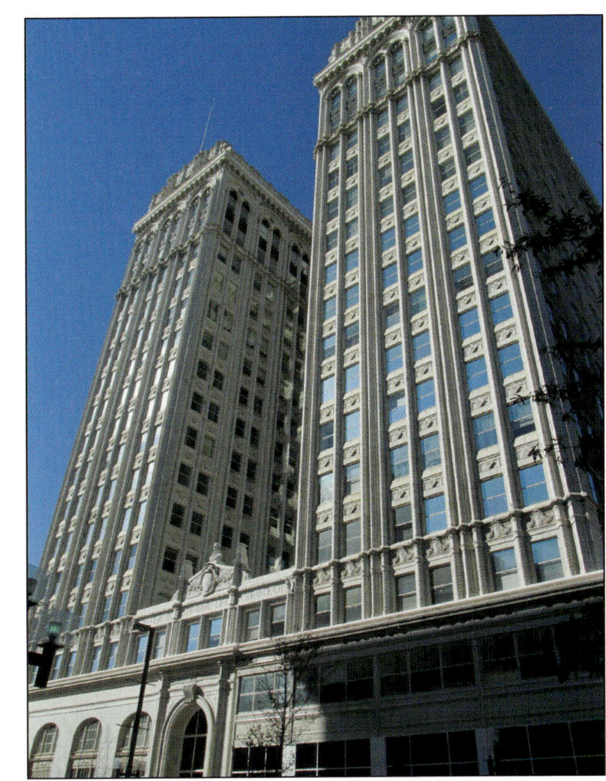

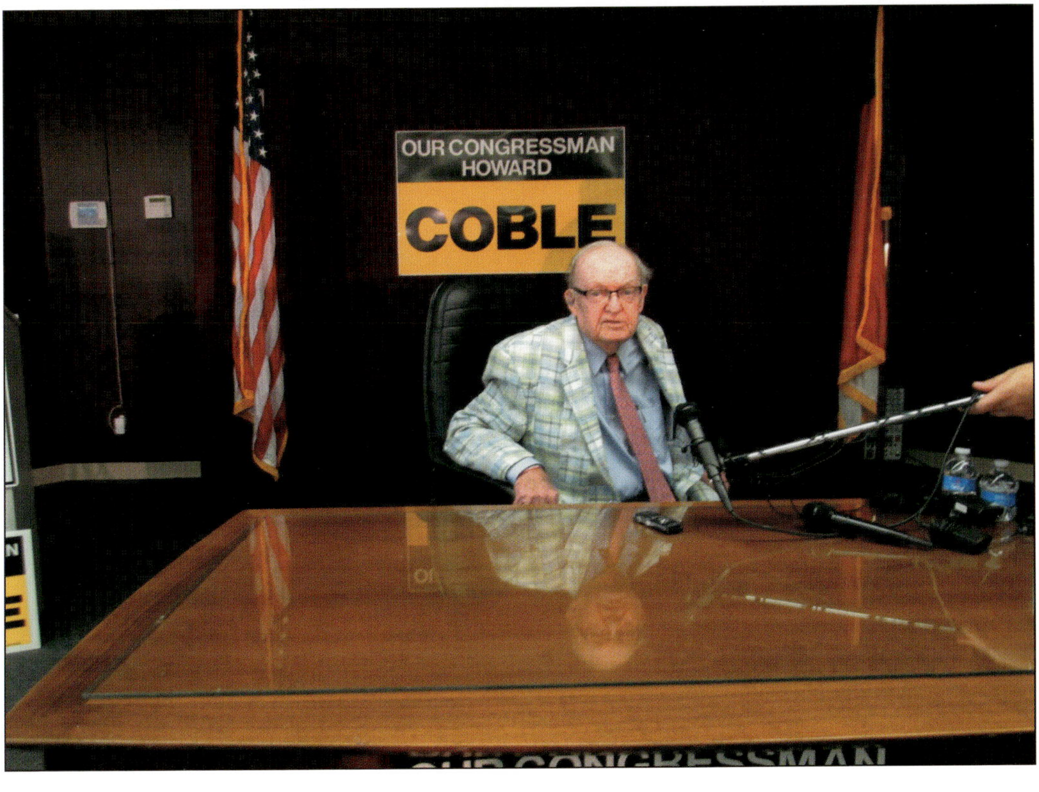

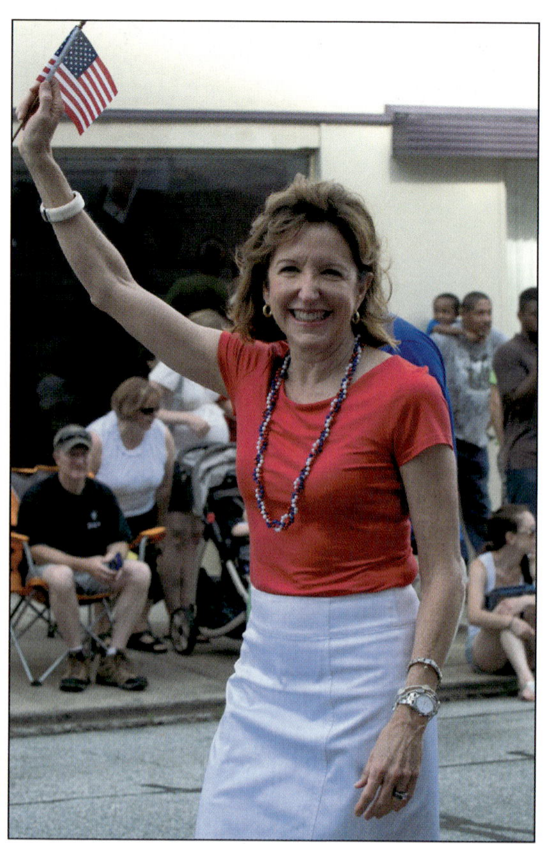

Kay Hagan, elected to the US Senate in 2008, is the only US senator in North Carolina's history to come from Greensboro. Before joining the Senate, she served 10 years in the North Carolina Senate. The Democrat, who unseated Republican incumbent Elizabeth Dole, is up for reelection in 2014. Her Republican opponent is Thom Tillis, speaker of the North Carolina House. By beating Dole, Hagan became the first woman to defeat an incumbent woman to gain election to the US Senate. (Courtesy of Lynn Donovan.)

From a distance, other than the baseball field, it is hard to distinguish the differences between this modern aerial photograph and the aerial postcard view of downtown Greensboro on page 2. There are more skyscrapers in this photograph, to be sure. From a street-level perspective, one change that may be evident is the removal of the signs over the sidewalks, following a city ordinance of the 1970s. In addition, today's downtown has more nightclubs and fewer retail establishments. (Courtesy of Joe Joseph.)

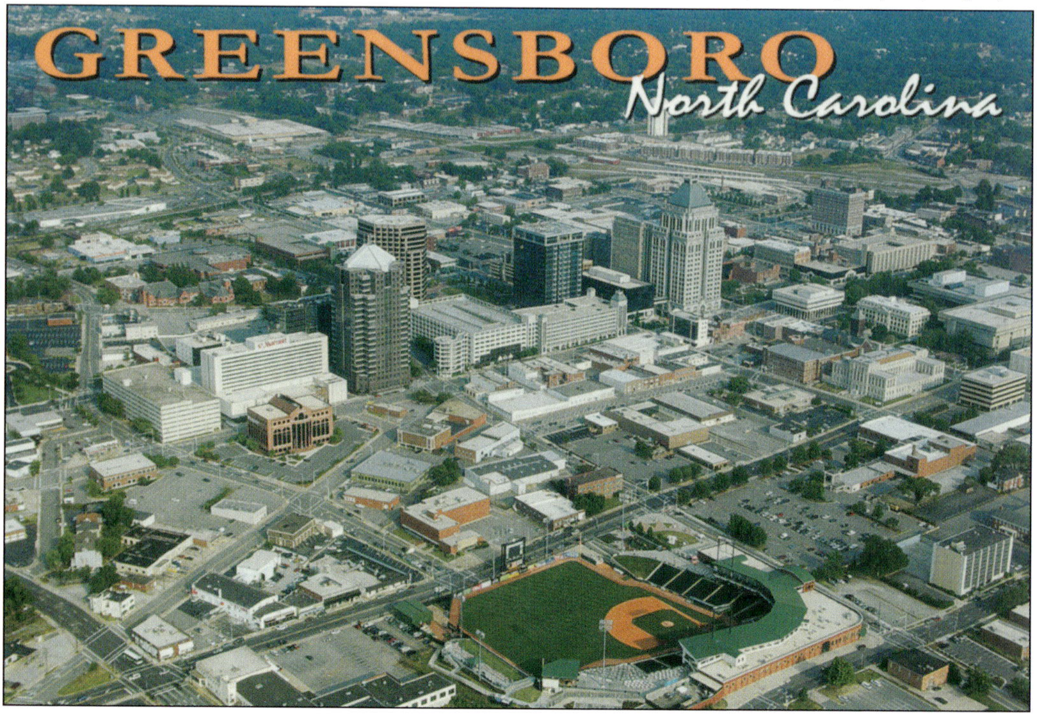

Stanley Frank came to Greensboro in 1935 and soon began running Carolina By-Products. By 1953, he was owner of the company. A national expert on the rendering business, he was a longtime chairman and member of Piedmont Triad Aviation Authority, a member of the Guilford College Board of Trustees from 1969 until 2006, and one of the largest donors in the college's history. (Courtesy of Carol Martin/Greensboro Historical Museum Collection.)

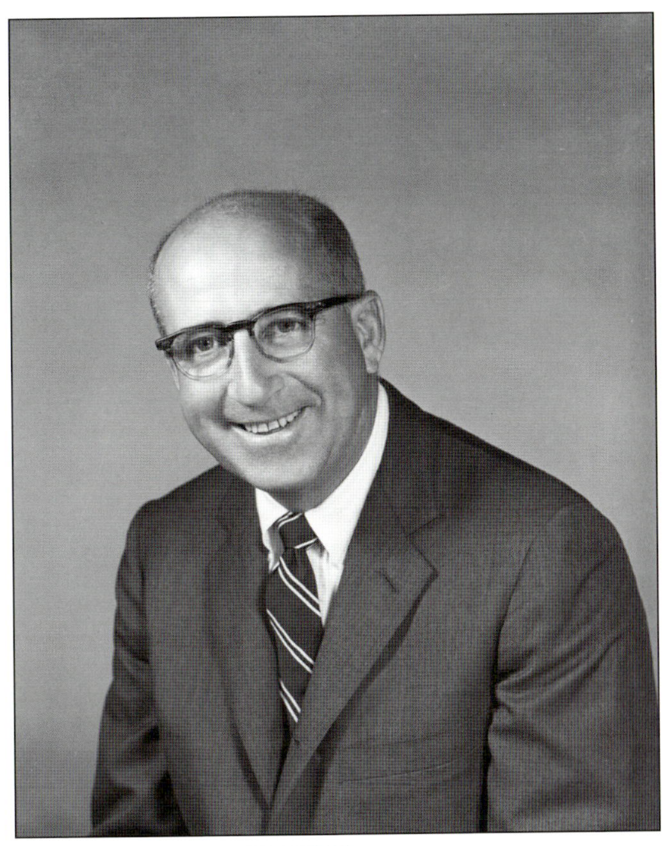

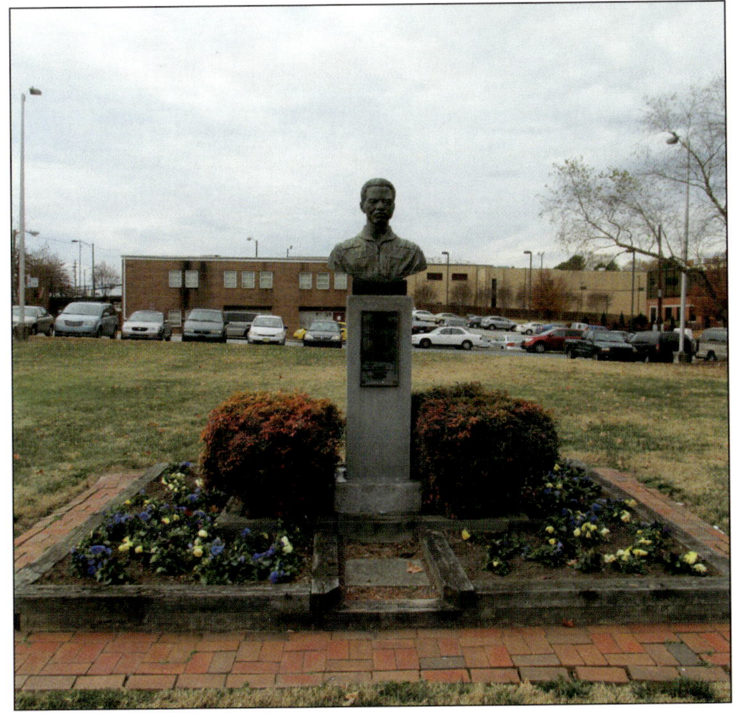

Ronald McNair graduated magna cum laude from A&T. Accepted into the NASA astronaut program, he became the second African American to fly in space. McNair was a member of the crew of the Space Shuttle *Challenger* when it exploded in 1986. Ronald McNair Elementary School in Greensboro is one of at least 16 public schools named after him. In addition, a crater on the moon, McNair, is named in his honor. This bust stands in front of the A&T engineering building named after him.

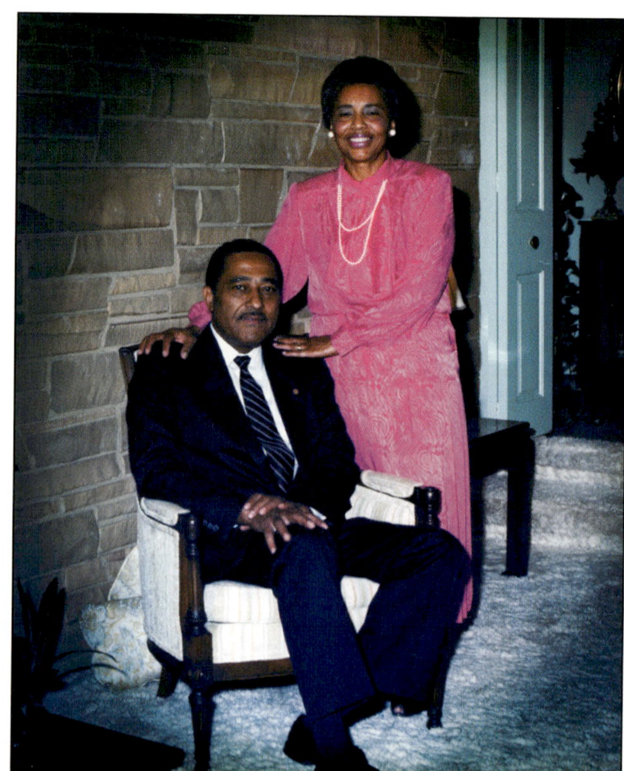

Henry Frye is the first African American chief justice of the North Carolina Supreme Court. He and his wife, Shirley, met at North Carolina A&T University, from which they both graduated. Frye was a US attorney and a North Carolina legislator in both houses before his appointment to the North Carolina Supreme Court, where he served from 1983 until 2001. Shirley has been very involved in the community, including serving as chairman of the Greensboro United Way. (Courtesy of Lynn Donovan.)

Victor M. Nussbaum Jr. founded Southern Foods in 1960 at 3500 Old Battleground Avenue, where it still operates today. He served on the Greensboro City Council and was mayor from 1987 to 1993. A tireless advocate for the less fortunate, Nussbaum also was a supporter of entrepreneurship. Upon his death, the name of the Greensboro Business Center was changed to the Nussbaum Entrepreneurial Center in his honor.

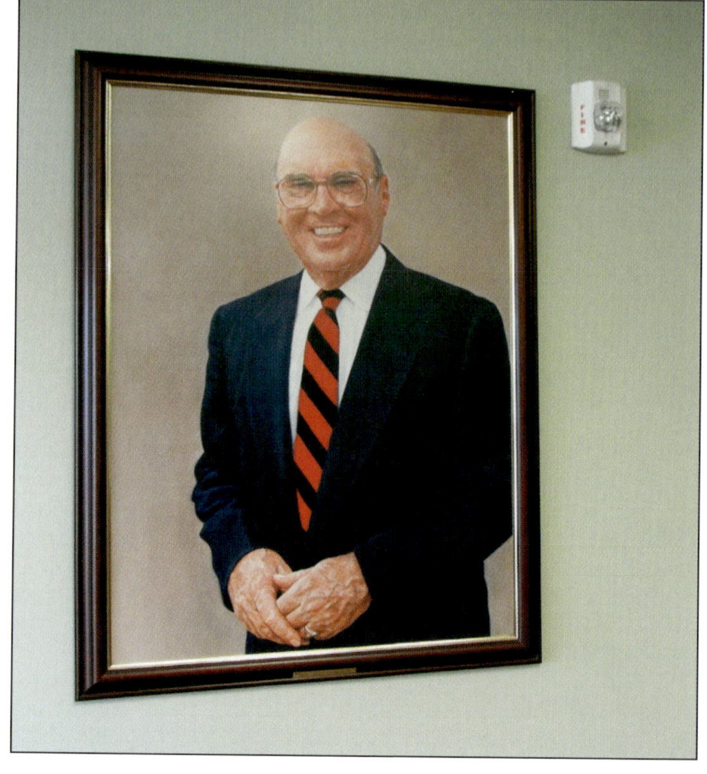

Five

LEARNING

Education is the future of Greensboro. The city had five institutions for higher learning during its sesquicentennial, and it has gained two since then. Of the colleges, two have become universities, and two of the women-only colleges have become coed institutions. The universities in particular attract a much larger enrollment than they did as colleges. Since the sesquicentennial, Greensboro has gained a community college and a law school from a university in a neighboring county.

The fact that Greensboro has such a high concentration of higher learning within its city limits is beneficial beyond just the employment at the institutions themselves. This is definitely true of Guilford Technical Community College (GTCC), which has established branches here in recent times. The college's curriculum can be altered to fit the needs of the economy. That in itself is a job creator. One strong example of this is the aviation center that GTCC has established near the airport.

One benefit to the community of the presence of a law school is that law students provide legal service to those who cannot afford it. In the years after the Civil War, Robert Dick had a law school near the location of the present one.

The entire community has access to cultural institutions as a result of these colleges and universities, such as the Weatherspoon Art Museum at UNCG. The Bryan Series, put on by Guilford College, enables Greensboro residents to attend lectures by famous people who might not otherwise come to the city. In the summer, the dorms at Guilford house students attending the Eastern Music Festival. These students, in turn, perform concerts that are open to the public.

Education has been a tradition in Greensboro ever since the first public graded school opened in the city. Its secondary schools, both public and private, are highly ranked. Bond issues for education tend to do well in Greensboro, as do those for GTCC.

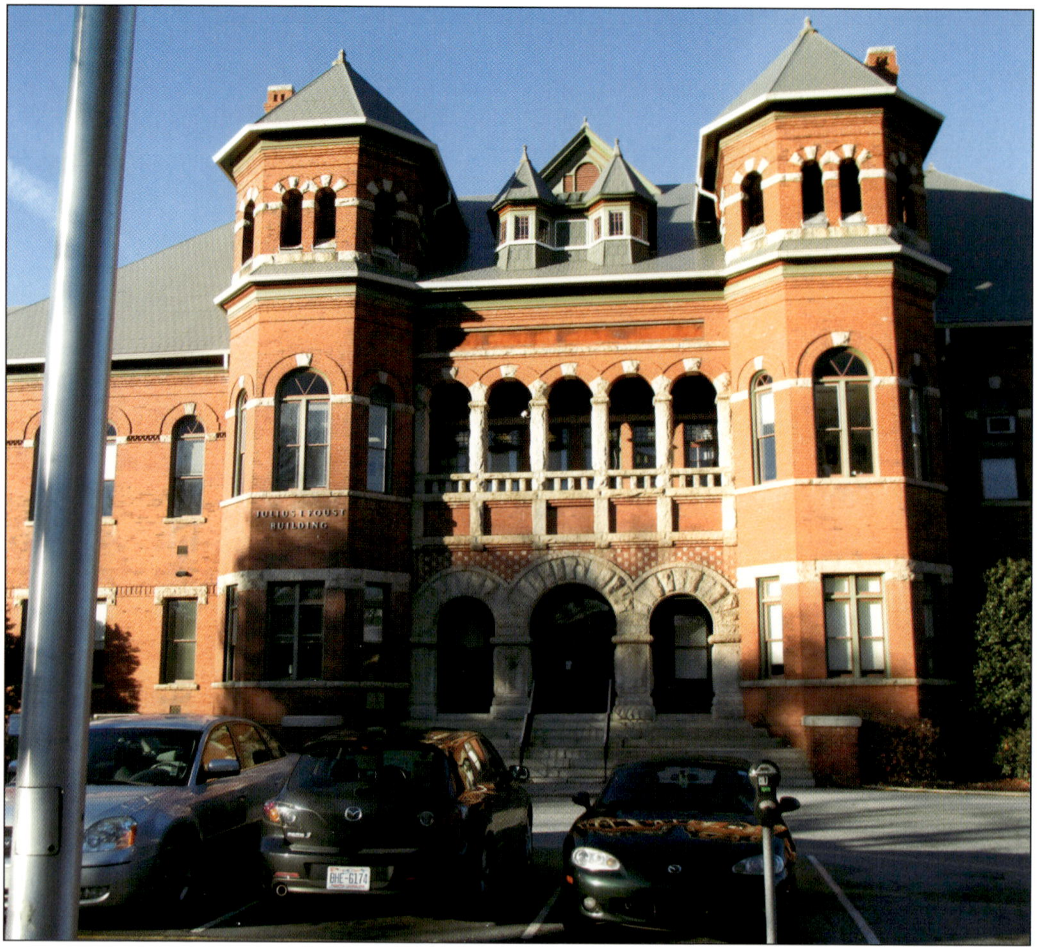

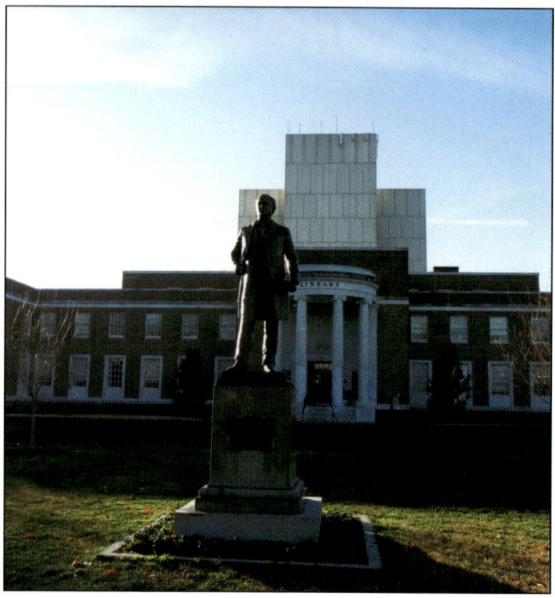

The University of North Carolina at Greensboro was chartered by the North Carolina General Assembly in 1891 as the State Normal Industrial School. It opened the next year, with 198 students and a faculty of 15. The president was Charles McIver, whose statue stands in front of the library (left). The Julius Isaac Foust Building (above), renamed in 1960 after its second president, is one of the original structures on campus. By 1932, it was called Women's College of the University of North Carolina, and it was the largest school dedicated to women in the United States. In 1963, men were admitted, and its name was changed to the current one. The Walter Clinton Jackson Library, named after its third president, added a nine-story tower. It is now the largest library in the Triad.

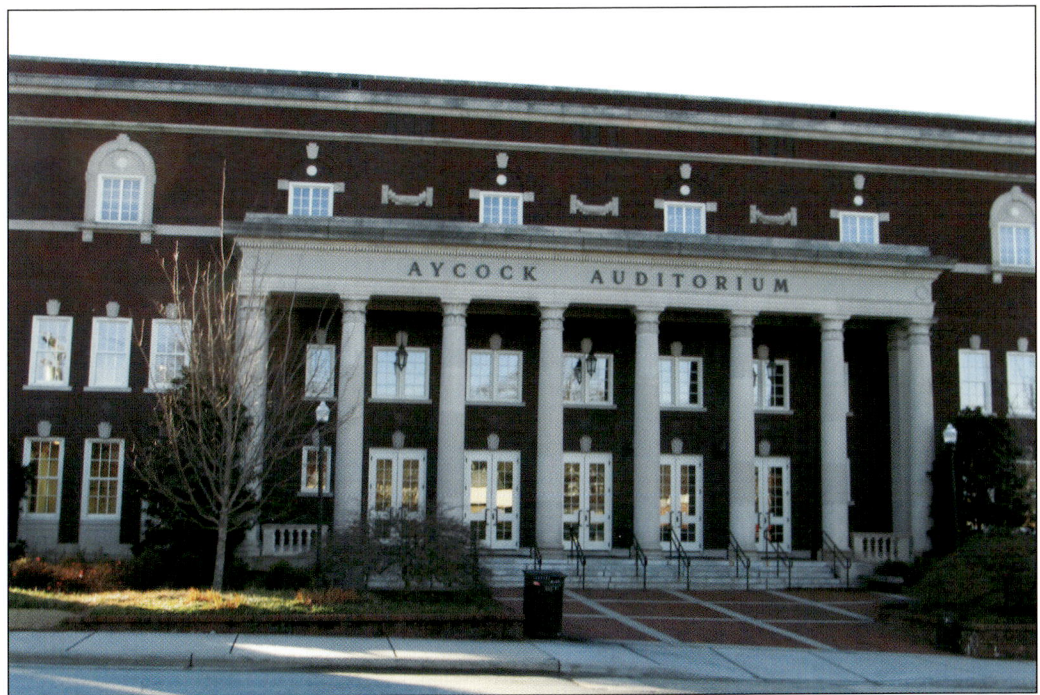

Today, UNCG has more than 18,600 students and 2,500 members on its faculty and staff. Its address is officially 1000 Spring Garden Street, but it has always stretched north to West Market Street. Aycock Auditorium, named after former North Carolina governor Charles B. Aycock, opened on Tate Street in 1927 and underwent a $19 million renovation in 2008. The university is also moving to the south, with locations on West Lee Street and in the Glenwood area. Currently, it boasts 24 residence halls and 30 academic buildings. Since admitting its first African American student in 1956, UNCG has become the most diversified of all historically white UNC campuses. The university offers 85 undergraduate majors, 61 master's programs, and 26 doctoral programs.

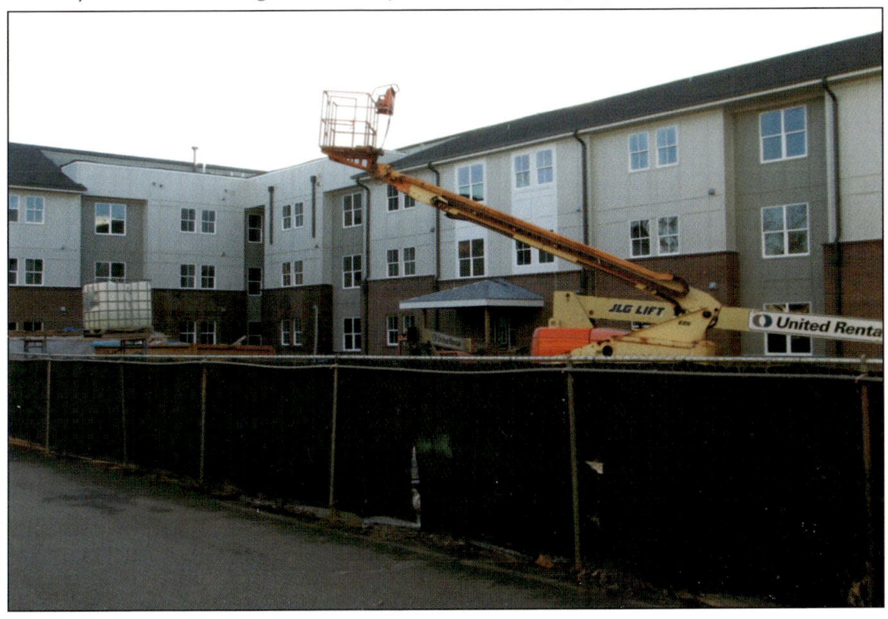

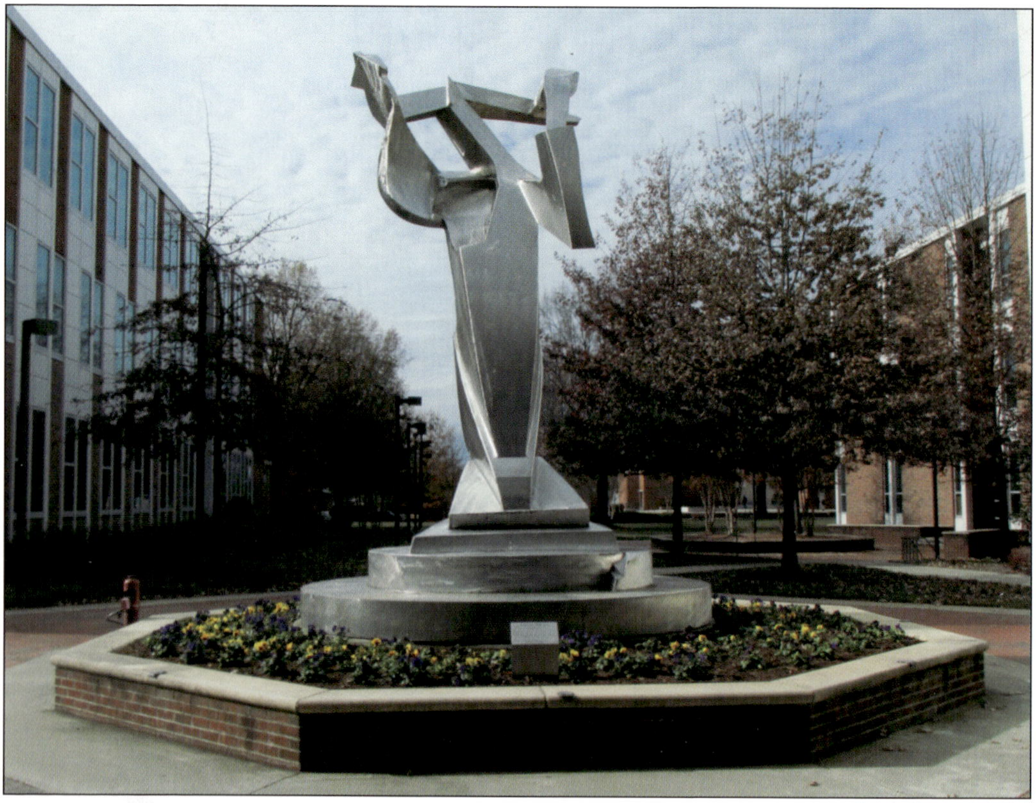

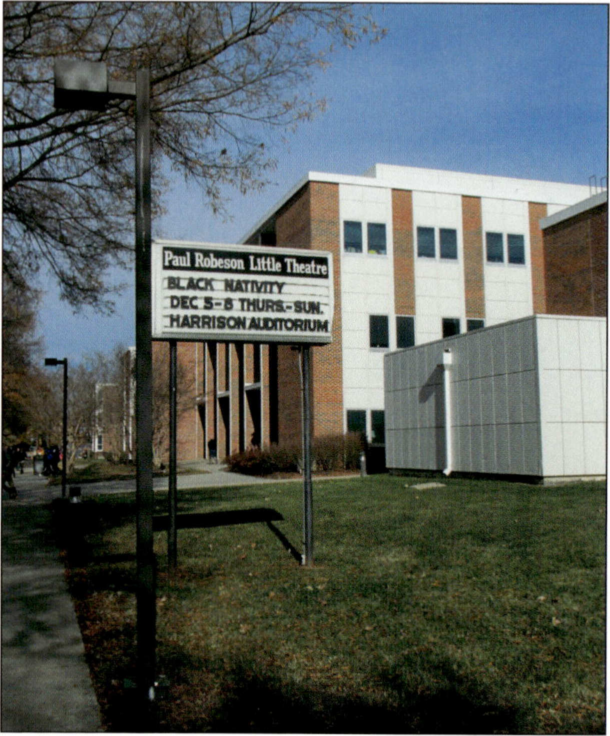

The North Carolina Agricultural and Technical State University is the largest publicly funded land-grant college in North Carolina. Founded in 1891 as the Agricultural and Mechanical College for the Colored Race, it changed its name to the Agricultural and Technical College of North Carolina in 1915 and to its current name in 1967, when it gained university status. The university has expanded to over 200 acres in and around its 1600 East Market Street address. The university offers 116 bachelor's degrees, 54 master's degrees, and doctoral studies in seven areas, most of them some form of engineering. It has a separate farm off-campus in the southeastern part of the county and is about to open a center off-campus to research Alzheimer's disease. The school's homecoming is probably the biggest in town.

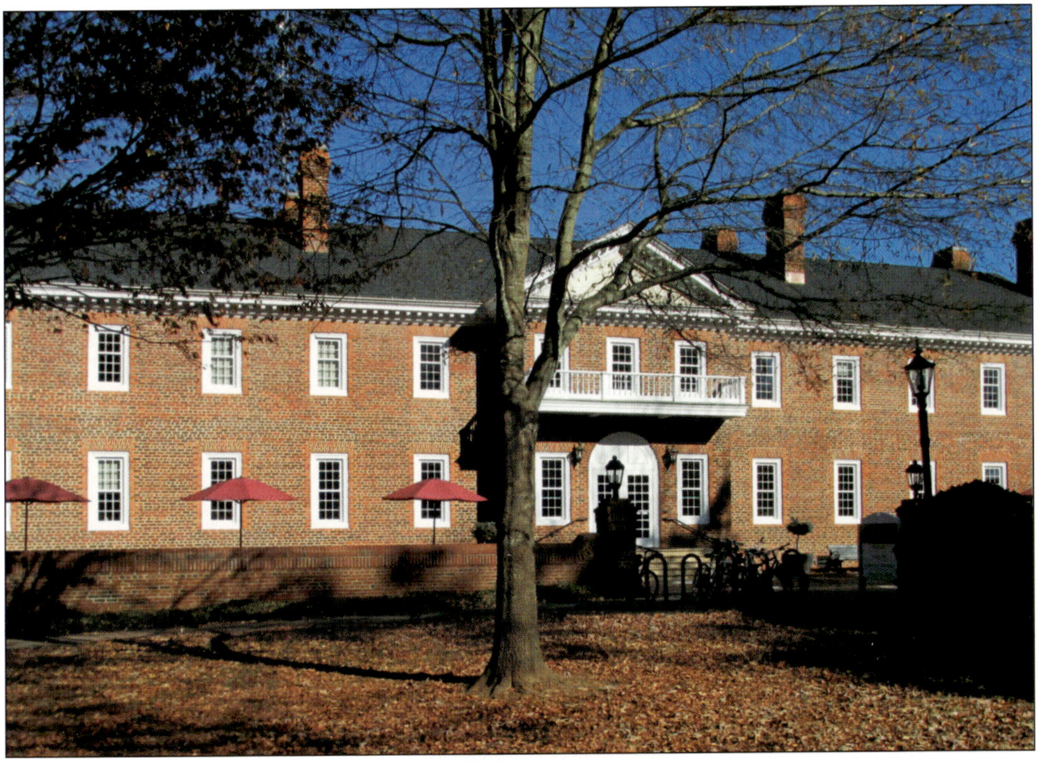

Guilford College was founded by the Quakers in 1837 as New Garden Boarding School, making it the oldest coeducational school in North Carolina. It became Guilford College in 1888. Located at 5900 West Friendly Avenue, it is the third-oldest coeducational institution in the United States and the fourth-oldest institution of higher learning in North Carolina. Shown here are Founders Hall (above) and the Frank Family Science Center (right). In addition to serving as a liberal arts college, Guilford hosts the Eastern Music Festival for five weeks each summer, providing musical entertainment for the community as well as training for musicians. It also provides the community with the Bryan Series of lectures, which has brought newsmakers like Desmond Tutu, Colin Powell, Ken Burns, Madeleine Albright, and Mikhail Gorbachev to speak to the public.

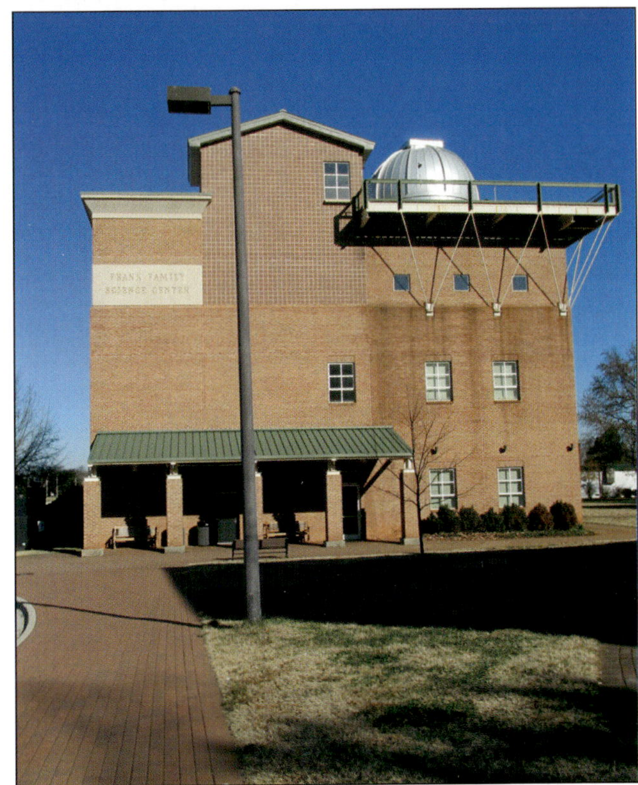

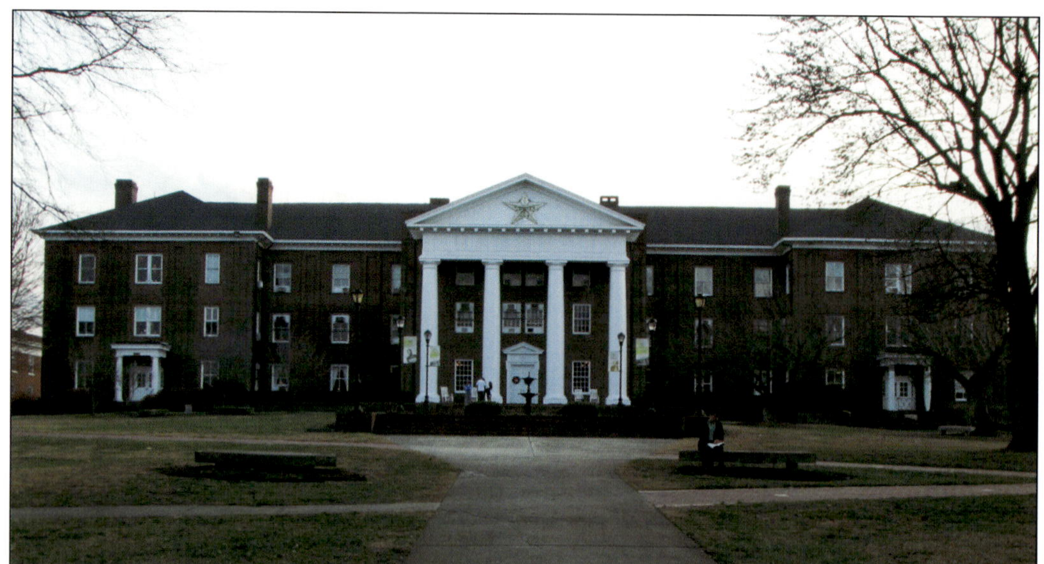

Greensboro College is one of the three institutions of higher learning in North Carolina older than Guilford College. It was founded in 1833 as Greensboro Female College, changed its name to Greensboro College early in the 20th century, and began admitting men in the late 1950s. It has a long-established relationship with the United Methodist Church. The Main Building (above), at 815 West Market Street, is the oldest building on campus. The original structures burned down in an early-1900s fire. The Odell Memorial Building (below) has been a venue for the college to showcase its music program since 1922. Its auditorium is now called Gail Brower Huggins Performance Center.

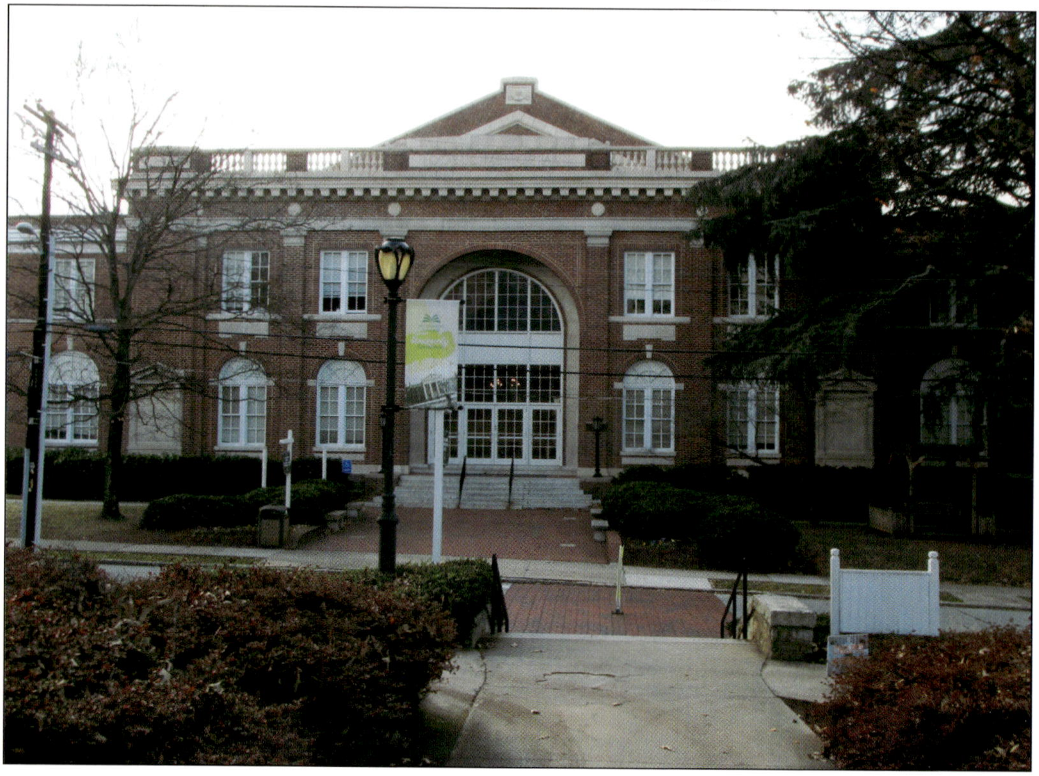

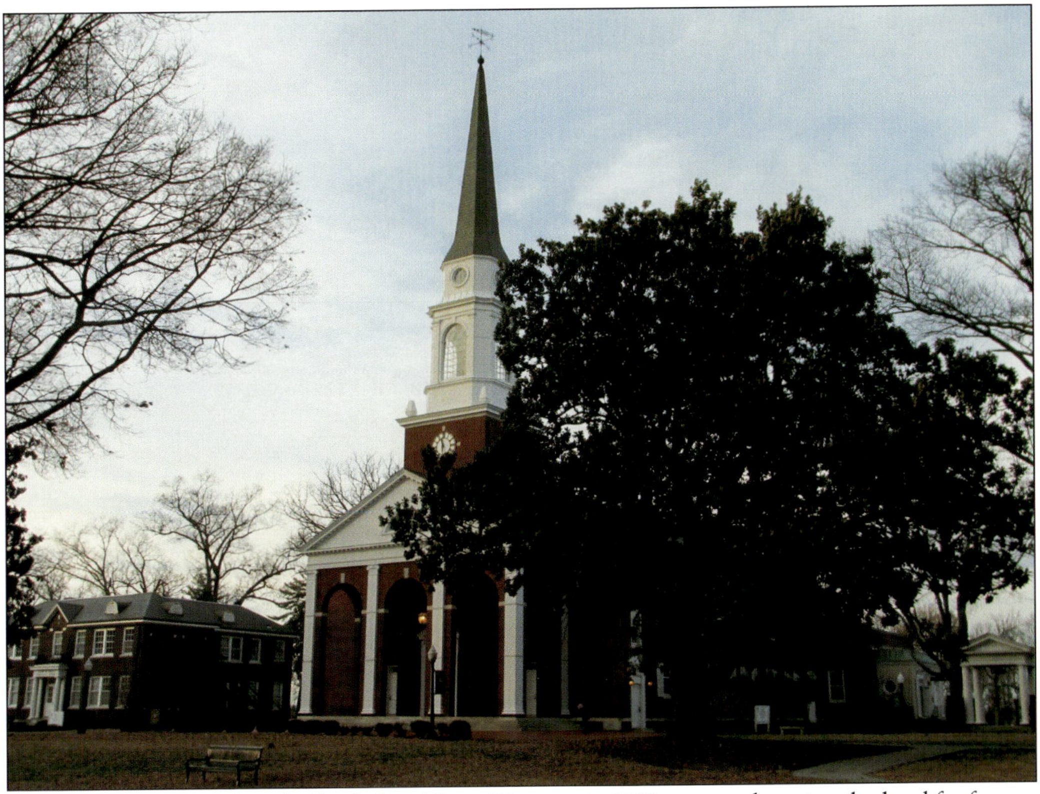

Bennett College was founded by Judge Albion Tourgee in 1873 as a coeducational school for former slaves. In 1878, Lyman Bennett, a New York businessman, heard about former slaves buying the land where the school is today (1400 East Washington Street) and gave $10,000 so that it could build its first permanent campus. The institution then took on the name Bennett Seminary. Bennett became a four-year women's college in 1926. On February 11, 1958, Dr. Willa B. Player, the first female African American president of Bennett, allowed Dr. Martin Luther King Jr. to speak in Bennett's Annie Mercer Pfeiffer Chapel, when no other place in Greensboro would do so. Affiliated with the United Methodist Church, Bennett College, which took over the library for blacks before integration, now uses the building for storage.

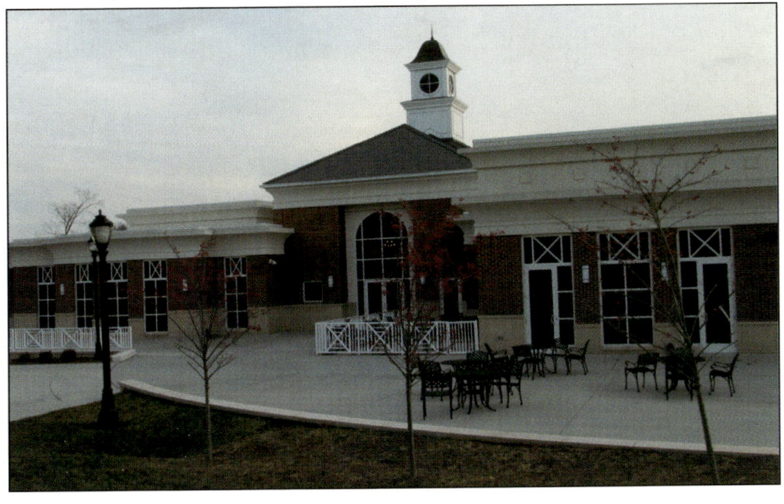

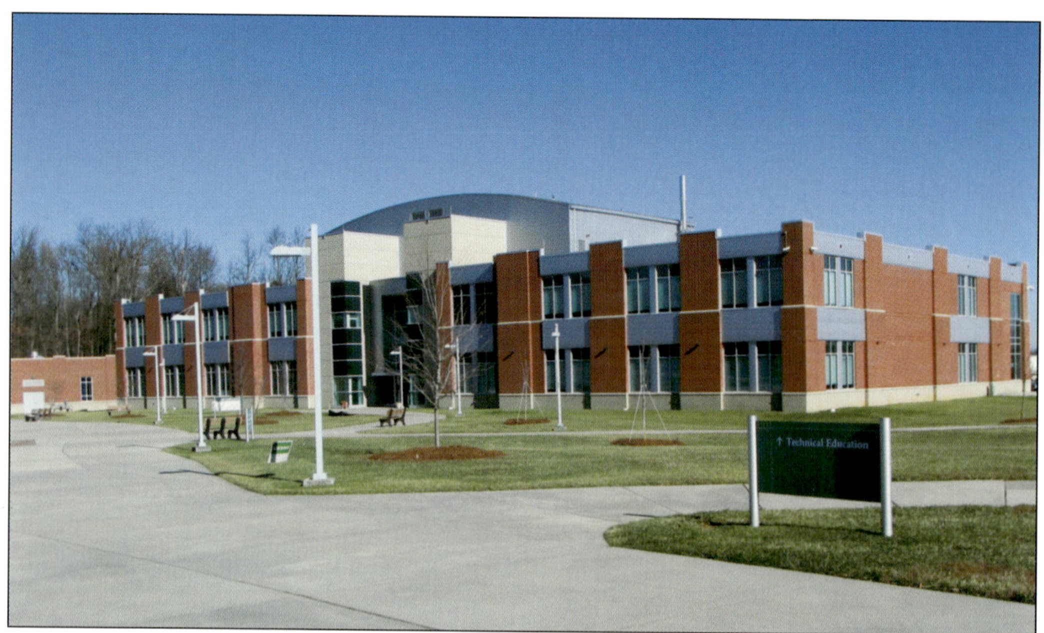

Guilford Technical Community College started as Guilford Technical Institute in 1958 at the former site of the Guilford County Tuberculosis Sanatorium in Jamestown, where the main campus remains. It opened a branch in Greensboro at West Washington Street in the 1970s, when it took the building of the former Guilford College Downtown Division. When a new state-of-the-art campus opened in 2009 at 3505 East Wendover Avenue, it replaced the Washington Street location. There is also a Small Business Center in the old Carolina Steel Building at 2726 South Elm-Eugene Street and the T.H. Davis/GTCC Aviation Center, located near the airport at 260 North Regional Road. Nearby, the Donald Cameron campus is about to open in Oak Ridge. High Point also has a campus.

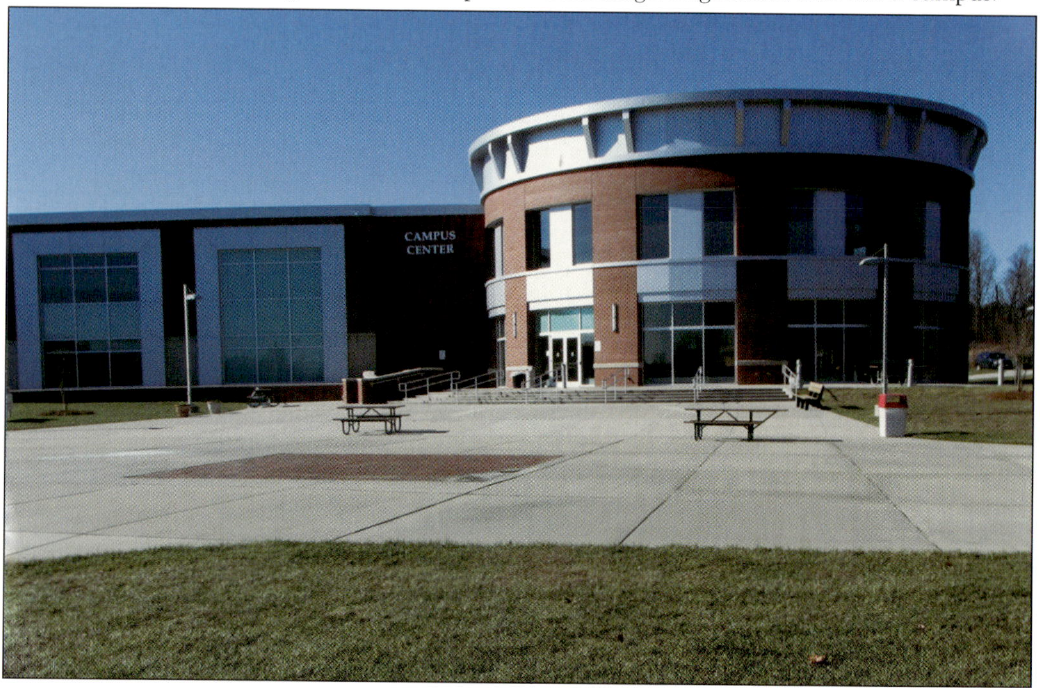

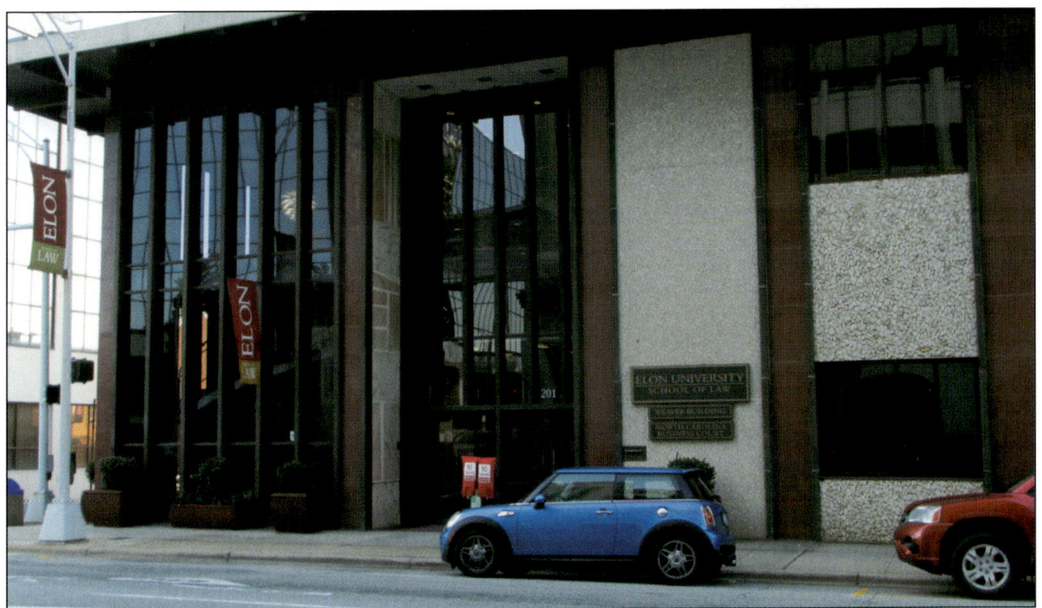

Elon University School of Law was established in the building that had held the Greensboro Central Library from 1964 until 1998. Elon College was founded in 1889 in the small Alamance County town of the same name. Although it became Elon University on June 1, 2001, it primarily operates in and around the same location. After receiving the old library as a gift from the City of Greensboro, the future law school spent about $10 million renovating the 84,000-square-foot building. On September 18, 2006, former US Supreme Court justice Sandra Day O'Connor delivered the school's dedication address. The school has since expanded to include other nearby properties. (Below, courtesy of Elon University.)

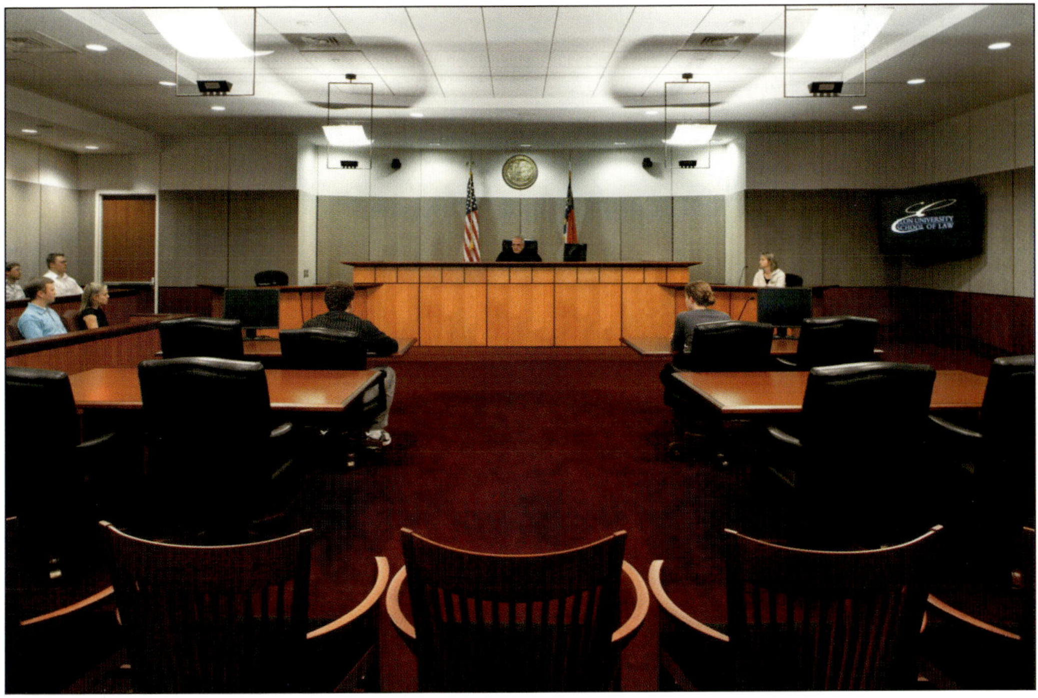

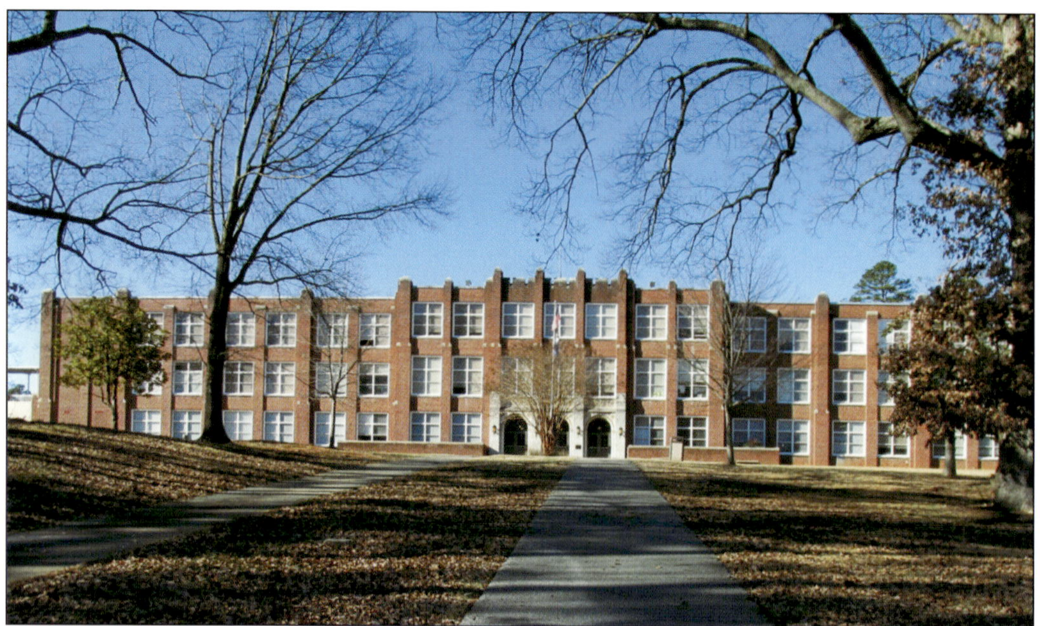

Greensboro has highly rated public schools, such as Grimsley High School (above), which started in 1900 as Greensboro High School. That school moved to Westover Terrace in 1929. Shortly thereafter, the same architect designed James B. Dudley High School (below) for African Americans, as schools were segregated at that time. Walter Hines Page High School began in 1958, and, when plans were made to open Ben L . Smith High School in 1963, the name of Greensboro High was changed to George A. Grimsley High School. Private schools appear to be growing in popularity, such as Greensboro Day School and the American Hebrew Academy. Also, colleges are offering high schools as early colleges. Guilford Early College recently obtained a No. 2 ranking in the nation.

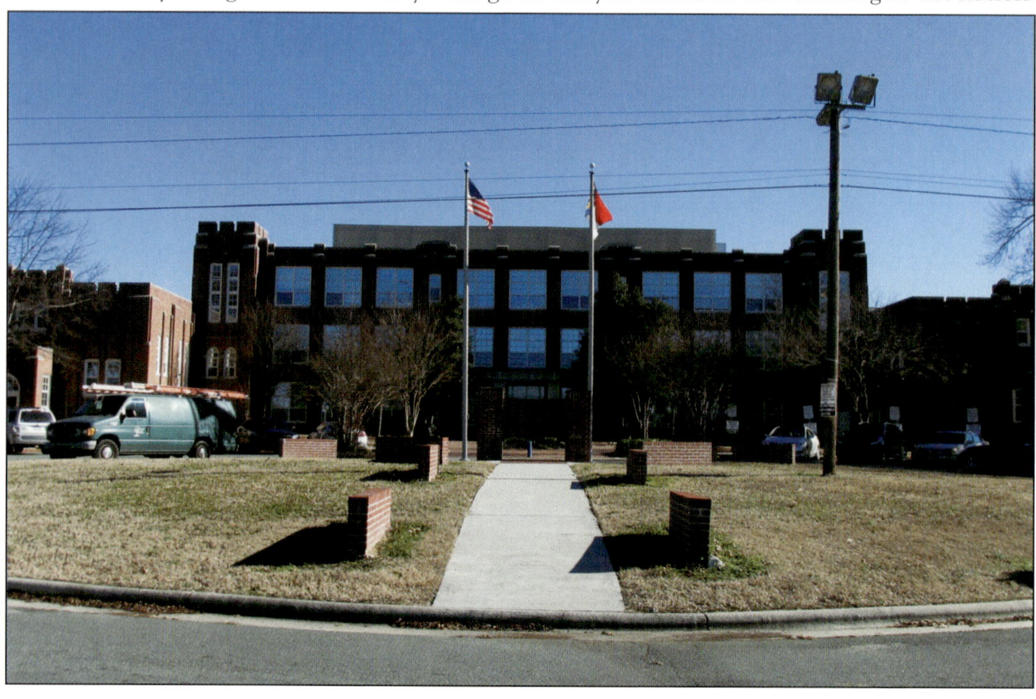

Six

CELEBRATING

Through good times and bad times, Greensboro has always come up with the ability to celebrate. A major centennial celebration was held in 1908; the sesquicentennial was celebrated in 1958; and the 2008 bicentennial built on this tradition.

One factor in Greensboro's ability to celebrate can be traced to Elizabeth "Betty" Cone, a Winston-Salem native who married into the Cone family. She is director of the Festival of Lights, a major celebration held in downtown Greensboro on an early Friday in December. She does it through Grassroots Productions Limited. Cone's organization also handles the Fun Fourth, and she has been behind a lot of activity that is mentioned in this book. It is important to note that these celebrations could not be carried out on the scale they are without volunteers. Cone is indeed one of those volunteers.

Center City Park plays host to many celebrations. This is done with full cooperation of the city, which closes streets to traffic for many occasions. Greensboro also celebrates with the arts, including the Eastern Music Festival and Greensboro Symphony. Art is also celebrated, and works are displayed for sale during these carnival-like occasions.

Although there is not enough room in this book to properly cover the subject, worshiping has always been an important characteristic of Greensboro. Before there was a city, there were churches here, and some churches are older than Greensboro itself. Since the late 19th century, Greensboro has had a large Jewish population. As Greensboro continues to diversify, houses of religions not traditional to the area, such as for Muslims and Buddhists, have begun to be established. A half century ago, there were fewer Roman Catholics than there were Methodists, Baptists, Presbyterians, and other religions. Today, though, there are more Catholics than members of any other denomination or faith in Greensboro. This can be traced to the increase in the Latin American population during the last 50 years.

Though not pictured in this book, some churches and synagogues are among the most beautiful buildings in the city.

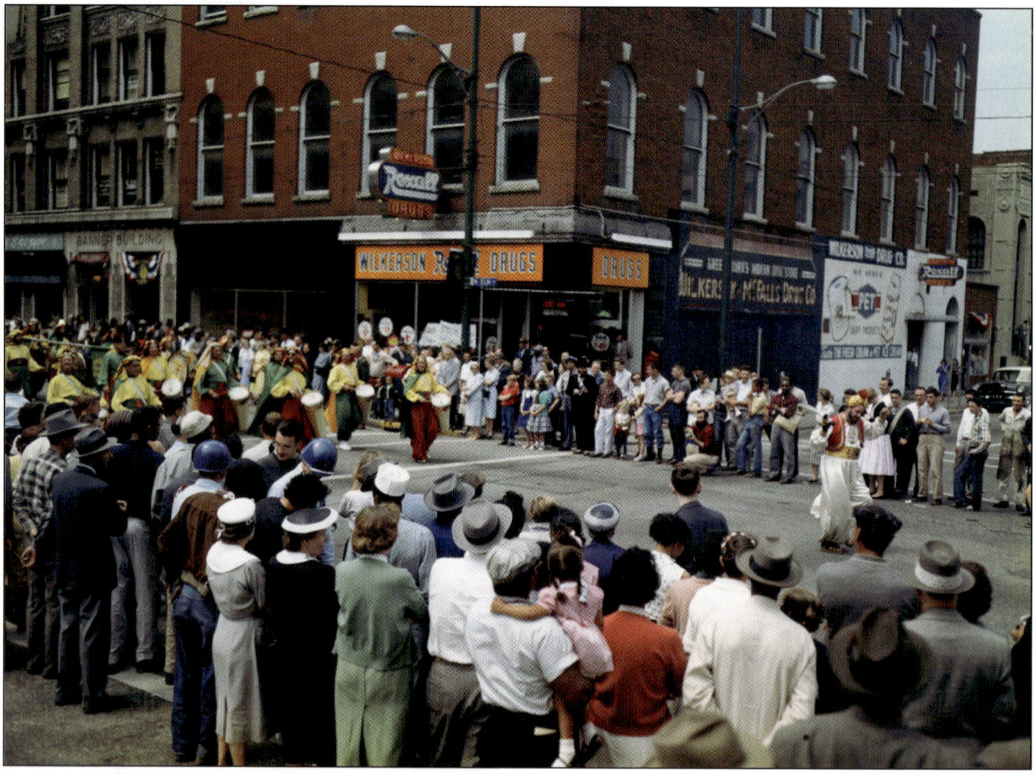

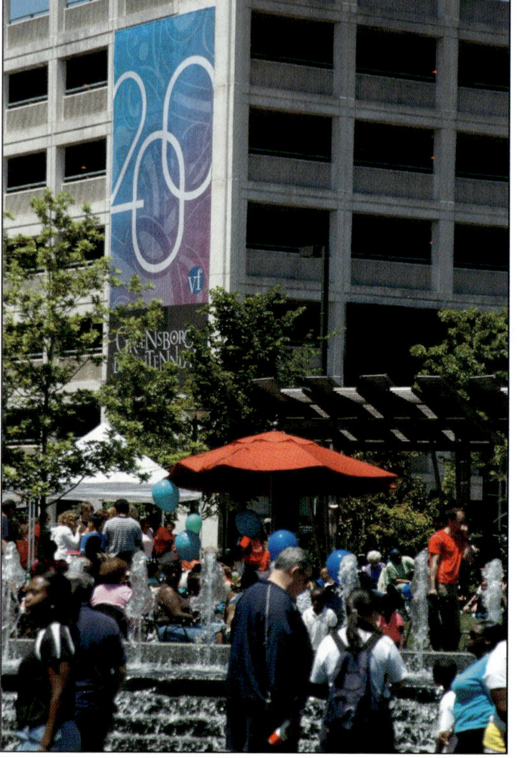

The sesquicentennial in 1958 brought programs about the city's illustrious history to the Greensboro (now Grimsley) High School stadium. Men were encouraged to grow beards to commemorate the occasion, something rather unusual in the 1950s. It was probably the biggest celebration the city had seen up to that time. (Courtesy of Carol Martin/Greensboro Historical Museum Collection.)

By the time the bicentennial arrived in 2008, beards were common enough that they didn't need to be requested. In addition to the celebration, especially downtown, permanent reminders of the historic anniversary have been constructed. The Greensboro Bicentennial Commission adopted the Downtown Greenway, 4.1 miles of walking trails enhanced by public art. The greenway is still in the process of being completed. (Courtesy of Lynn Donovan.)

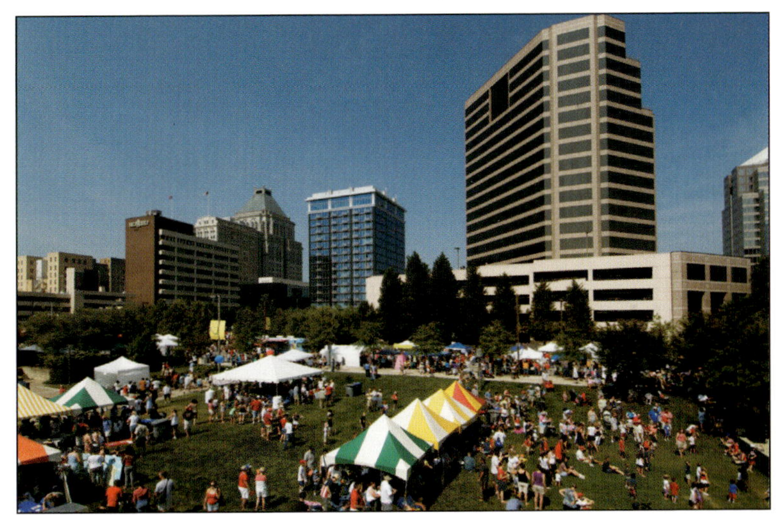

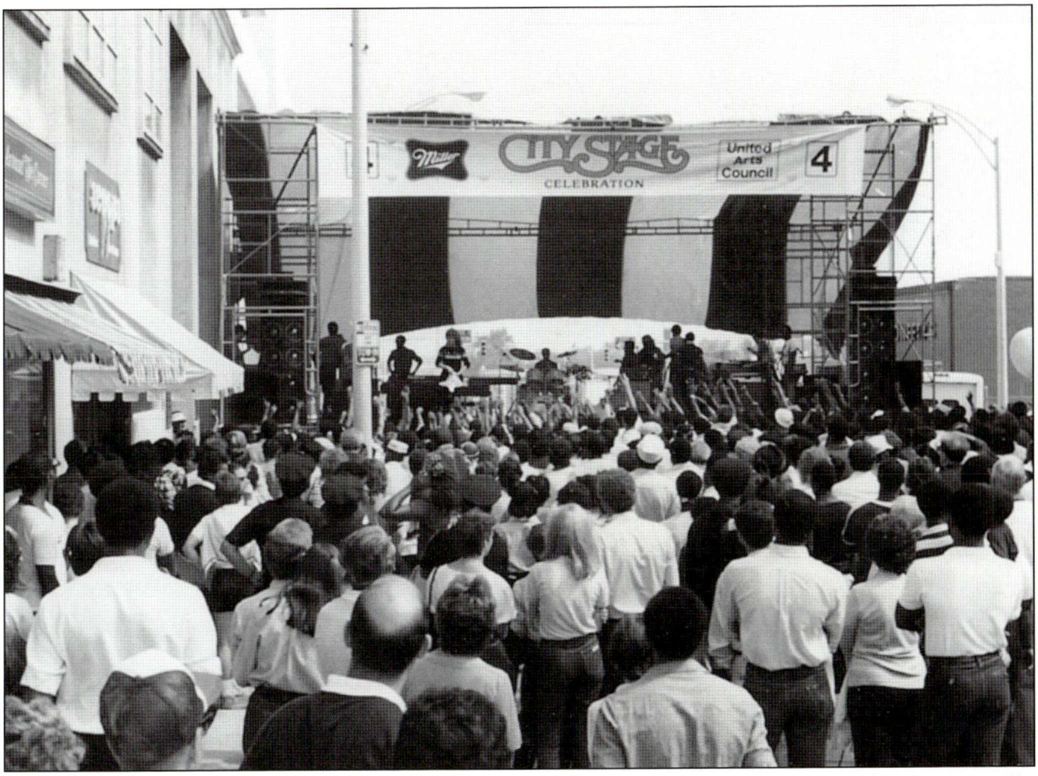

Even bigger than the Fun Fourth was City Stage, held annually from 1980 until 2001. Initially called Oktoberfest, it was always held during a weekend in October. Several stages were set up throughout the downtown area, and local as well as national acts performed. Miller Brewing Company was a leading sponsor. When Miller left Eden and the economy slowed, City Stage was discontinued. (Courtesy of Lynn Donovan.)

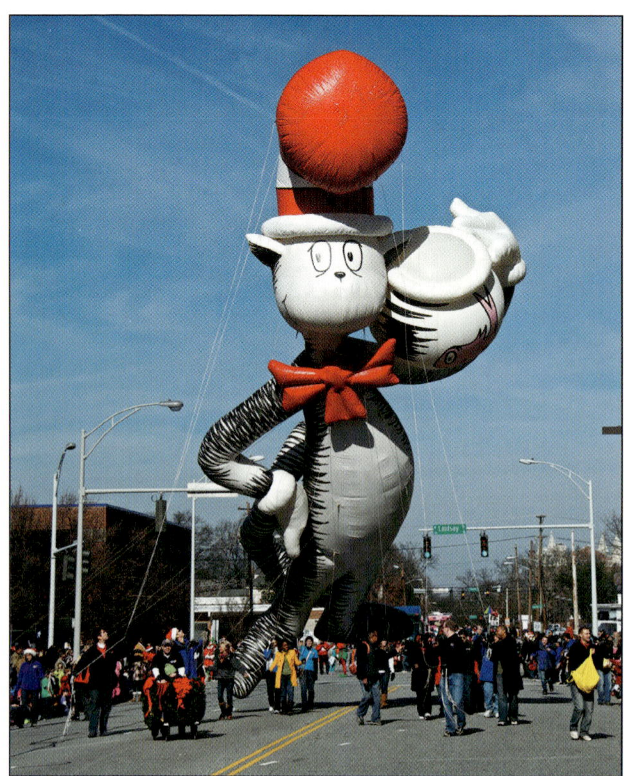

The Holiday Parade has been a part of Greensboro since 2000. Before that, downtown had a Christmas parade, but it was discontinued as the center city's popularity as a destination fell. Then, five organizations inspired the Greensboro Jaycees to continue the activity. Today, the Holiday Parade attracts as many as 100,000 people to downtown Greensboro. (Courtesy of Lynn Donovan.)

El Dia de los Ninos ("Day of the Child") is celebrated each year on April 30. It is considered a gift from the Latino community to all children. Like many communities throughout the United States, Greensboro has made efforts to embrace this and other Latin holidays. Latin Americans, particularly Mexicans, represent the largest-growing segment of Greensboro's population during the last 50 years. (Courtesy of Lynn Donovan.)

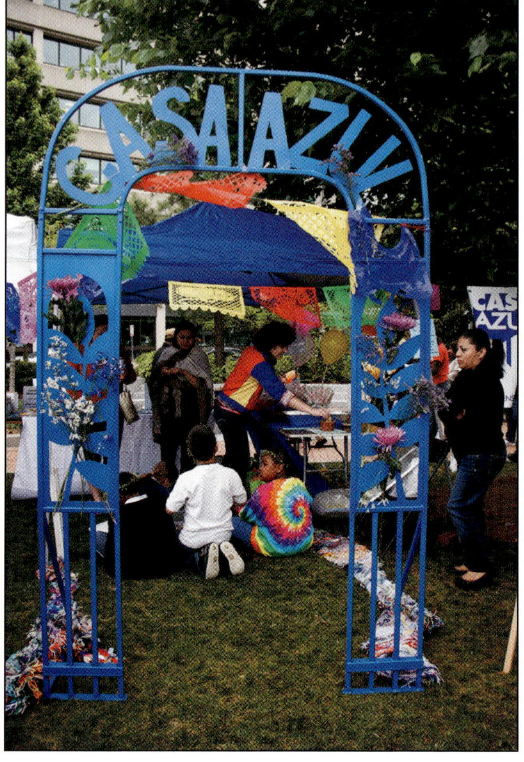

Seven

THE FUTURE

Part of Greensboro's hopes for the future comes from organizations composed of progressive thinkers who contemplate what needs to be done. How can Greensboro fit into today's economy the way it is now? What needs to be done to make it fit into such an economy? These organizations do more than just think. When they agree that an idea is worth looking into, they work to get things done.

One factor in Greensboro's favor is transportation. Credit for this is found in the mid-19th century, when former governor John Motely Morehead used his influence to get the North Carolina Railroad to travel through Greensboro rather than Asheboro. As time went on, this advantage has snowballed, to the point that the Gate City has a combination of roads, railroad tracks, and an airport with a major FedEx hub, not to mention that a seaport can be reached within the state. The highways tended to follow the tracks. Now that Greensboro has Interstates 40, 85, 73, and 74, only Atlanta and Birmingham, among Southern cities, have as many interstates passing through town. All of this indicates a great future in transportation-oriented areas for Greensboro.

Another positive factor is all of the institutions of higher learning within the city limits. With three universities and four colleges, as well as for-profit colleges, Greensboro indeed has a wealth of knowledge within its borders. Secondary education, with public and private schools, is also prevalent here. Knowledge in vast quantities, such as exists in Greensboro, means an unlimited potential.

Furthermore, there could always be an idea coming up that could lead to something big. As large as Greensboro is, there may be another Lunsford Richardson or Kermit Murphy with an idea that could lead to the employment of scores of people. Leaders in Greensboro are wise to help out entrepreneurs during the early phases of their ideas, such as is done at the Nussbaum Center.

What will work? It is too early to tell, but with the thought and cooperation going into producing a better Greensboro, there is confidence that something will.

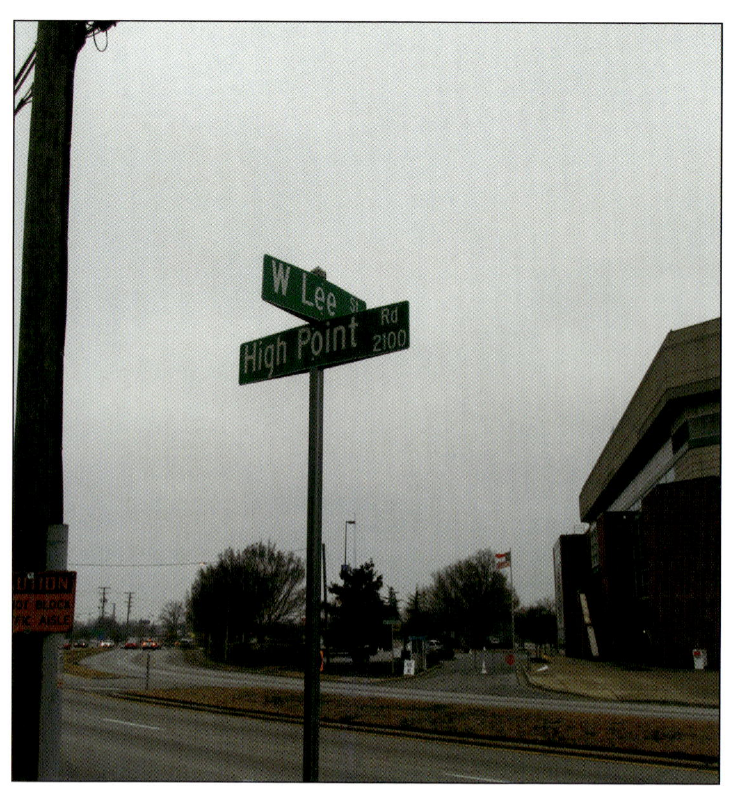

In November 2013, the outgoing Greensboro City Council voted to change the names of High Point Road and Lee Street to Gate City Boulevard in 2015. This is being done, in part, as an attempt to change the image of these two major streets. Crime on both of them has increased in recent years, and a lot of the property has deteriorated. The Greensboro Coliseum Complex is located near the intersection of these streets. High Point Road runs alongside the Koury Convention Center and the Four Seasons Town Centre. Major road and property work is planned for the area, which showcases Greensboro for those who come to visit.

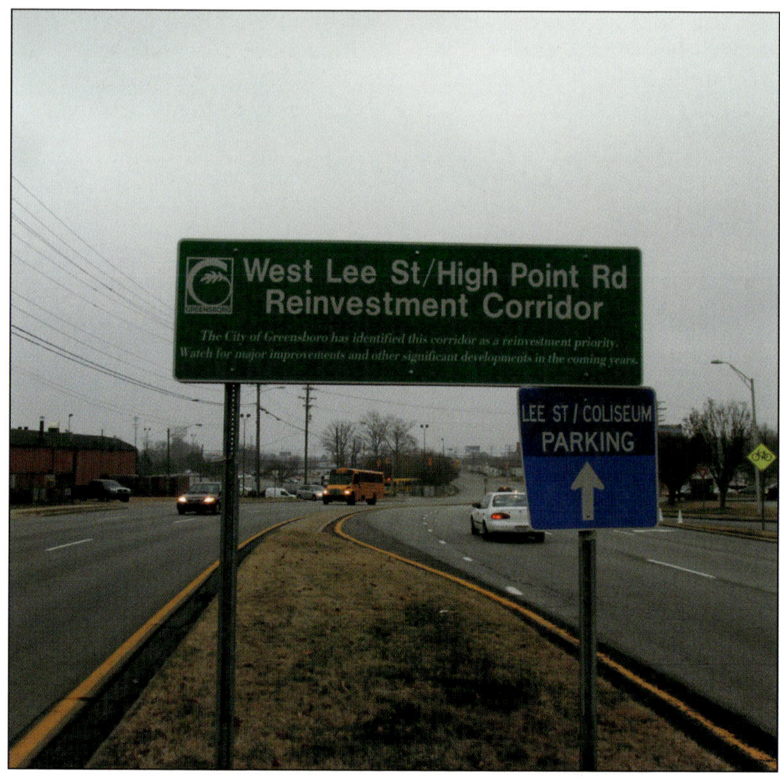

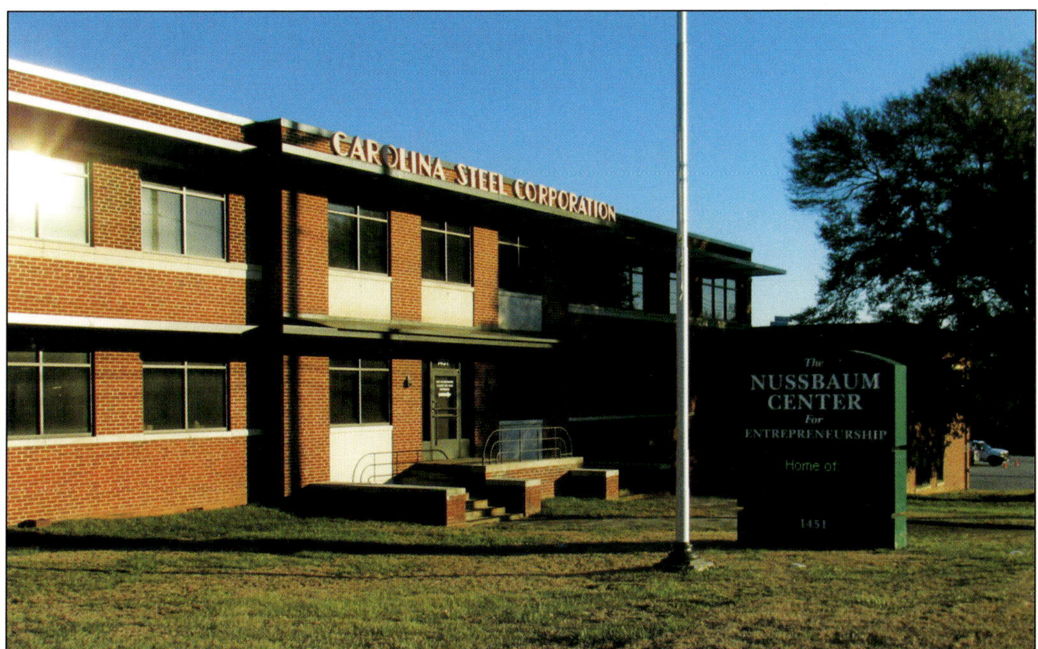

The Nussbaum Center for Entrepreneurship was founded in 1987 in Revolution Mills, at 1200 Revolution Mills Drive, after Cone Mills closed that factory building. It is a private nonprofit organization with a mission to attract, house, and advise entrepreneurs in start-up and early-stage growth. In December 2001, its name was changed to the Nussbaum Center for Entrepreneurship after the death of Victor Nussbaum, the former Greensboro mayor and president of Southern Foods. It has since moved to the old Carolina Steel location at 1451 South Elm-Eugene Street. The building has a communal receptionist, copier, fax machine, and other amenities. New businesses are the lifeblood of a city's economy, and the Nussbaum Center shows what is being done to nurture them.

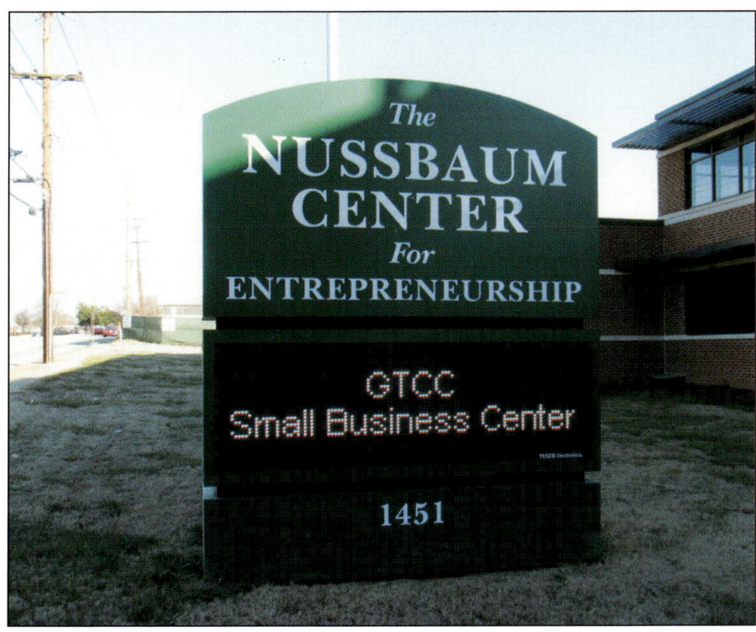

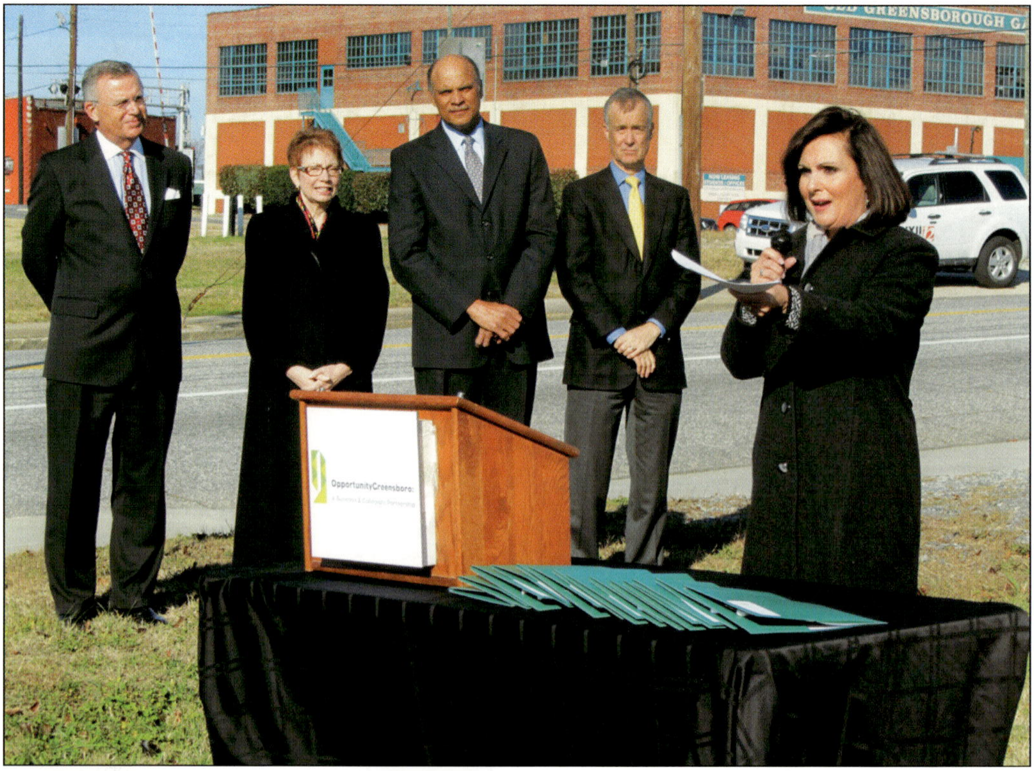

Shown here are, from left to right, Randy Parker, president of GTCC; Linda Brady, chancellor of UNCG; Harold Martin, chancellor of North Carolina A&T; Tim Rice, CEO of Cone Health; and Greensboro mayor Nancy Vaughan. The officials are gathered on November 19, 2013, at an Opportunity Greensboro press conference at 104 East Lee Street. The 2.1-acre tract had been chosen as the site to build Downtown University, a cooperative between Guilford, Greensboro, and Bennett Colleges, Elon School of Law, and the institutions represented by the officials shown here. (Courtesy of Action Greensboro.)

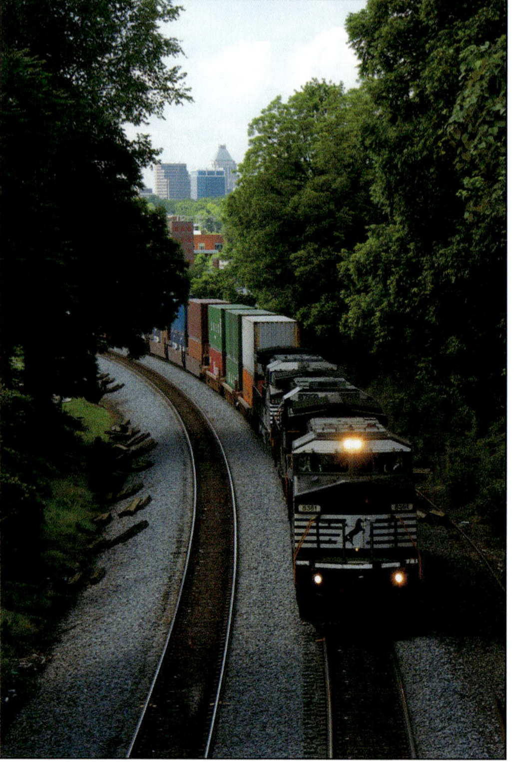

This train, seen in a recent photograph, may very well not have been making its run through Greensboro had it not been for the actions of John Motley Morehead in the mid-19th century. Now, Greensboro has four interstate highways passing through town, several other highways, a major airport, the FedEx Mid-Atlantic Hub, and other infrastructure that point to Greensboro becoming an aerotropolis. (Courtesy of Lynn Donovan.)

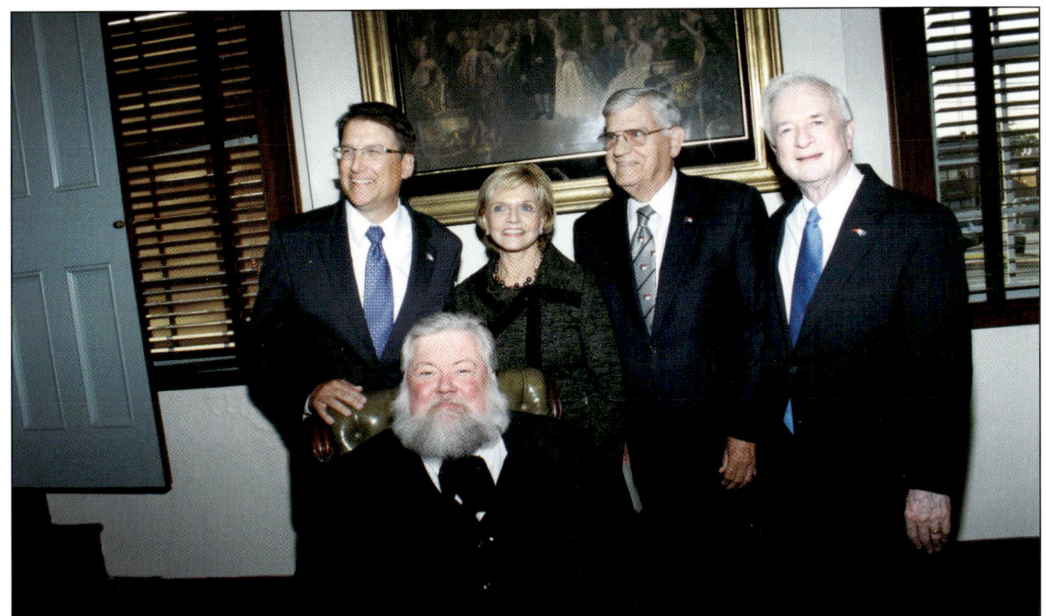

North Carolina governor Patrick McCrory (left) stands with former governors, from left to right, Beverly Perdue, James Martin, and James Hunt, as an actor portraying 19th-century governor John Motely Morehead sits in front. The governors met in Morehead's former law office at Blandwood Mansion on October 29, 2013. This event served as the kickoff for the Governor Morehead Forum. Sponsored by Preservation Greensboro, the forum will meet several times a year and discuss ideas for economic development through improvements in transportation, education, manufacturing, and historic preservation (Courtesy of the Governor Morehead Forum for Economic Development.)

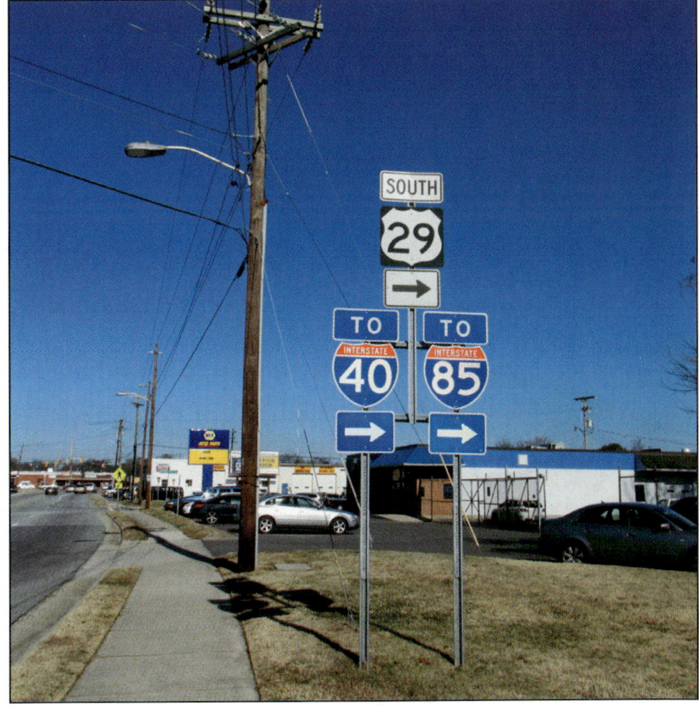

The highways indicated on this stretch of Bessemer Avenue are just some of the thoroughfares that pass through Greensboro. Other highways in town include Interstates 73 and 74, US Highways 220 and 421, and NC Highway 68. The highways tended to follow the railroad tracks, established in the mid-19th century.